NORTHERN INDEX MAP

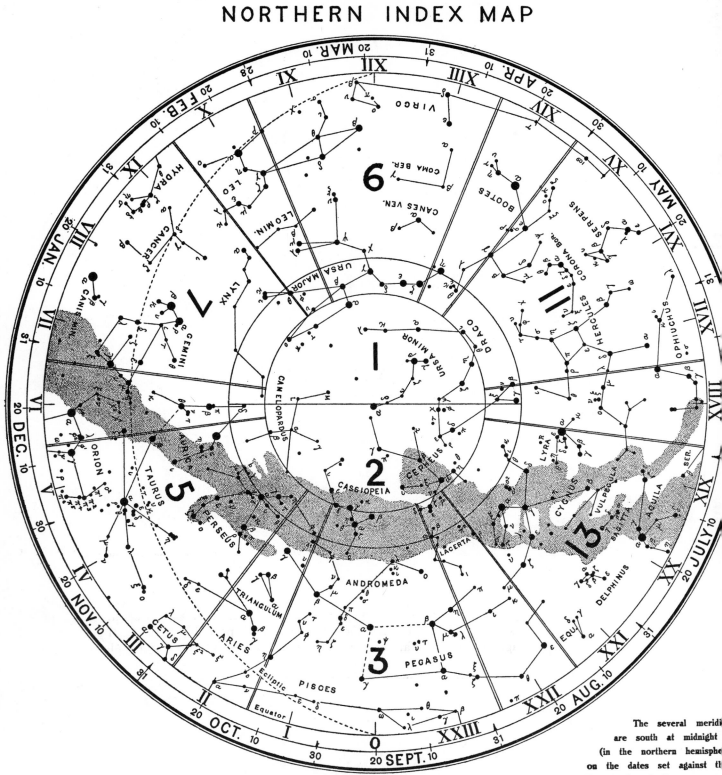

The several meridi...
are south at midnight
(in the northern hemisphe...
on the dates set against th...
in the margin of the map.

EPOCH 1950

NORTON'S STAR ATLAS

AND REFERENCE HANDBOOK

(Epoch 1950·0)   *Seventeenth Edition*

by Arthur P. Norton

THE REFERENCE HANDBOOK AND LISTS OF INTERESTING OBJECTS
REVISED AND REWRITTEN BY
CHRISTOPHER R. KITCHIN   JULIAN C. D. MARSH
HOWARD G. MILES   PATRICK MOORE   IAIN K. M. NICOLSON
& GILBERT E. SATTERTHWAITE

EDITED BY GILBERT E. SATTERTHWAITE
IN CONSULTATION WITH
PATRICK MOORE & ROBERT G. INGLIS

Longman
Scientific &
Technical

Copublished in the United States with
John Wiley & Sons, Inc., New York

Longman Scientific & Technical,
Longman Group UK Limited,
Longman House, Burnt Mill, Harlow,
Essex CM20 2JE, England
and Associated Companies throughout the world.

Copublished in the United States with
John Wiley & Sons, Inc., 605 Third Avenue, New York, NY 10158

17th edition © Robert M. Gall Inglis
This edition © Gall & Inglis Ltd. 1986

First published by Gall & Inglis Ltd. 1910

2nd edition 1919	*11th edition 1950*
3rd edition 1921	*12th edition 1954*
4th edition 1929	*13th edition 1957*
5th edition 1933	*14th edition 1959*
6th edition 1937	*15th edition 1964*
7th edition 1940	*Reprinted 1966*
8th edition 1942	*Reprinted 1969*
9th edition 1943	*16th edition 1973*
10th edition 1946	*17th edition 1978*

17th edition reprinted by Longman Group UK Ltd. 1986, 1988

British Library Cataloguing in Publication Data
Norton, Arthur P.
Norton's star atlas and reference handbook
(Epoch 1950.0).—17th ed.
1. Astronomy
I. Title   II. Kitchin, Christopher R.
III. Satterthwaite, Gilbert E.
IV. Moore, Patrick V. Inglis, Robert G.
520   QB43.2

ISBN 0-582-98898-5

ISBN 0–470–20678–0 (USA only)

Printed in Great Britain at The Bath Press, Avon

PREFACE

The First Edition of *Norton's Star Atlas* was published in 1910. It was primarily designed for those amateur observers whose telescopes were mounted on altazimuth stands or as equatorials without graduated setting circles. It was also intended to be used as a companion to Webb's *Celestial Objects for Common Telescopes* (recently reprinted in the U.S.A. as a paperback) and Smyth's *Cycle of Celestial Objects*, now out of print and unobtainable except in astronomical libraries. Almost all the objects listed in the latest editions of both works, down to and including stars of the seventh magnitude, are shown in the maps, also several fainter objects of particular interest.

The plan and arrangement of the maps, with large overlaps, enable an area of about one-fifth of the entire heavens to be seen at a single opening, and no constellation is inconveniently broken up. The distortion is slight considering the large area represented. Altogether the maps indicate the positions of over 8,400 stars and 600 nebulæ. Bright variable and red stars are indicated by 'v' and 'R' respectively. For particulars of double stars reference should be made to the lists on the backs of the maps, and to 'Webb' and 'Smyth'.

The constellation boundaries used are those prepared by Monsieur E. Delporte and adopted by the International Astronomical Union in 1930. The epoch of Delporte's boundaries was 1875, and by 1950 the change of their positions in Right Ascension and Declination, due mainly to 75 years of precession, was appreciable. With respect to the stars themselves, however, the positions of the boundaries remain unaltered. The ninth and subsequent editions of 'Norton' contain charts completely redrawn for the standard epoch 1950·0.

The Galactic Charts introduced in the fifteenth and reprinted in this edition were completely redrawn using the new system of galactic co-ordinates adopted at the Moscow general assembly of the I.A.U. in 1958. The galactic equator and poles, where they appear on the star maps, have also been plotted on the new basis. This work was undertaken by Norman G. Matthew, Director of the Observatory, Calton Hill, Edinburgh.

All the features of the original maps are retained, with certain alterations:

(*a*) Stars down to magnitude 6·35 from the *Revised Harvard Photometry* have been charted. In the original edition the star places were taken mainly from Houzeau's *Uranométrie Générale*. A careful comparison of the magnitudes of Houzeau's fainter naked-eye stars with those given in the *Harvard Photometry* and its Supplement showed that many of his stars were placed at a lower, sometimes much lower, magnitude than 6·35; such stars have generally been omitted. On the other hand, many Harvard stars not in Houzeau have been inserted, as well as several additional double stars from various sources.

(*b*) All nebulæ, except those in the Messier Catalogue and those listed in the Herschel catalogues, are designated by their N.G.C. number.

(*c*) Variable stars having a maximum brightness of magnitude 6 or 7 have been indicated on the maps by small circles.

(*d*) The Milky Way is in many places very complex in structure, with star clouds, dark spaces and dark winding lanes. No single-tone representation, as used in this work, can satisfactorily represent its real structure. The outline of R. A. Proctor is again used here, for it does at least represent the position and boundaries of the Milky Way, and gives some impression of its complexity.

(*e*) A map of the Moon, with the selenographic co-ordinates of 300 named features, is again included for the benefit of visual observers.

(*f*) For the first time a map of Mars is provided in this edition. The map reproduced is the one adopted by the I.A.U. to show the recommended nomenclature for the 128 features listed. The Editors consider this more useful to the visual observer than a detailed map of the terrain visible only on photographs obtained by space-probes.

Arthur P. Norton and James Gall Inglis, who had collaborated since 1919 in revisions of the text of the Reference Handbook, died in 1955 and 1939 respectively; later revisions were undertaken by the late proprietor, Robert M. Gall Inglis, who died in 1975. The text of the sixteenth edition of the Reference Handbook was completely rewritten and brought up to date, and the lists of telescopic objects revised and enlarged. The proprietor cannot express sufficient thanks to Patrick Moore, Gilbert Satterthwaite, Howard Miles, Iain Nicolson, Julian Marsh and Christopher Kitchin for so willingly undertaking this onerous task.

The intention of the original edition has been maintained—to provide both the amateur observer and the general reader with a reference book to which he can turn for an explanation of unfamiliar terms—especially the terminology of observational astronomy which is inadequately dealt with in many text-books. The explanations are necessarily compressed, but it is hoped that they are sufficiently complete for the purpose.

The new text has been arranged in an order differing from that of the earlier editions, in order to present the data in a coherent and logical sequence, and to avoid unnecessary duplication. In accordance with current recommendations for all scientific publications, all data have been presented in metric units in this edition; as far as possible the recommendations of the I.A.U. for astronomical publications have also been followed.

This being the first occasion on which the text of the Reference Handbook has been entirely reset, we have seized the opportunity to give it a new typographical style. Our intention has been to present the text in a more modern and spacious manner, whilst endeavouring to retain the spirit of the earlier editions. In particular we hope that the many tables retained from the previous editions will be found even more useful in their redesigned layout. The revised lists of interesting objects have also been printed in a new format.

The Editors hope that the revised edition will be found a valuable source of helpful information, especially by the observer, and that it will provide him with sufficient detail for his immediate needs. This should be amplified by consulting the many books available on most aspects of astronomy. After careful consideration the Editors decided not to include an annotated bibliography here, in view of the rate at which lists of available astronomical works go out of date, compared with the longevity enjoyed by previous editions of 'Norton' and which they hope this edition will be found useful enough to maintain.

The Editors wish to express their thanks to Peter Bate for redesigning the title page, case and jacket; to Peter Gill, for much help with the sections relating to the Sun; to Oxford Illustrators Limited for their excellent draughtsmanship; to the Comptroller of Her Majesty's Stationery Office for permission to reproduce Crown Copyright material; to the Council of the British Astronomical Association for permission to reproduce data taken from its *Handbook*, *Memoirs* and *Journal*; and to the Sky Publishing Corporation of Cambridge, Massachusetts, for permission to reproduce material from *Sky & Telescope*, and the map of the Moon.

The revision of the seventeenth edition was undertaken by Doctor R. Jakeways of Leeds University to whom we are most grateful.

CONTENTS

INDEX

viii

I. GENERAL

SOME ASTRONOMICAL TERMS

The following selection is not intended to be comprehensive, but comprises terms which have not been defined later in the text. Many similar terms are defined within the specialized sections. Reference to the Index will permit the location of any term to be readily ascertained.

Angular Diameter. Although they are at very different distances, all astronomical bodies appear to be at the same distance—hence the concept of a celestial sphere. Measurements of their relative positions are therefore made in angular measure, which is independent of their actual distances. In the same way the diameters of those bodies close enough to have them measured can be directly compared if they are expressed in angular measure, rather than actual units of length. Thus the apparent diameter of a planet at a given instant is expressed in seconds of arc; the actual diameter can be calculated from the angular diameter and the distance of the planet at the time using simple trigonometry.

Apparent/True. In astronomy the term *apparent* is used to indicate that which is seen by the observer, e.g. the apparent place of a star is its observed position at the instant of observation. Apparent is also used where an observed function is affected by other factors for which corrections must be applied to arrive at the true function: thus observed positions and movements of heavenly bodies are affected by refraction, aberration, annual parallax, light-time, diminution of brightness with distance, etc., all of which must be corrected for in order to obtain the true position or movement. In some instances 'true' = 'apparent', as in, e.g., True Time, True Equinox.

Appulse. The apparent close approach of one celestial object to another, although they may be far apart in actual distance. Thus a planet and the Moon may lie in almost the same direction in space, although at very different distances; they are said to be in appulse when closest together as seen in the sky.

Clock Star. A bright star whose position and proper motion are very accurately known and can therefore be assumed; used for the determination of the error of observatory clocks, to be applied in reducing positional observations of other stars, and for the provision of a time service.

Cusp. One of the 'horns' of the crescent phase of the Moon or an inferior planet.

Dichotomy. The instant of exact half-phase of the Moon or an inferior planet.

Earth Sciences. General term embracing all the scientific studies of the planet Earth, including geology and all its related subjects, geophysics, geodesy, physical geography, etc.

Ephemeris. A table showing the calculated positions, at regular intervals, of a celestial object. Plural *ephemerides*.

Equation. Often used in the sense of a correction to observed data to eliminate instrumental, ocular and other imperfections. These are sometimes grouped together as *systematic errors* when they recur if observations are repeated with the same instruments and under the same conditions, and as *accidental errors* when they do not repeat. The term is also used for a correction to take account of an orbital irregularity, as in *Equation of Time, Equation of Equinoxes*, etc.

The *Personal Equation* is a small error involuntarily introduced into his observations by a particular observer; its effect is usually consistent for repeated similar observations by an experienced observer, but varies quite randomly between different observers.

Exosphere. The outermost layer of the Earth's atmosphere, above the ionosphere.

Extinction. An effect of the atmosphere, which dims the light reaching us from distant objects by absorbing and dispersing it. Its effect varies with the altitude of the object above the horizon, since the closer to the horizon it appears the greater the thickness of the atmosphere its light rays will have traversed. The brightness of a star in the zenith will be reduced by only about 0·3 magnitudes, whereas the extinction at 20° altitude is about 0·9 magnitudes and at 10° altitude about 1·6 magnitudes.

Fundamental Stars. Stars whose position and proper motion are so well known that they have been adopted for use as a frame of reference for positional observations of other objects.

Geodesy. The study of the dimensions and figure of the Earth.

Geoid. The hypothetical shape of the globe of the Earth, used in geodetic calculations; the surface of the geoid is approximately the same as 'mean sea level' envisaged as extending over the entire surface of the globe.

Geology. The study of the structure, composition and history of the Earth as a planet; its techniques are now being widely applied in the study of the Moon and other planets.

Geophysics. The study of the Earth's physical state and of physical phenomena within it, such as seismology, terrestrial magnetism, etc. Its techniques are also being applied in the study of the Moon and other planets by space probes, etc.

Great Circle. A circle formed on the surface of a sphere by a plane passing through the centre of the sphere; thus the diameter of a great circle is equal to that of the sphere. The term is used in calculations based upon the concept of the celestial sphere.

Green Flash. This phenomenon, caused by the Earth's atmosphere, is seen for one or two seconds either as the last remnant of the setting Sun vanishes or just at the moment of sunrise. The general conditions required are a distant sharply defined low horizon (preferably sea). Cool weather and absence of red tints seem to favour visibility. During the last seconds of visibility, the strong red colour of the Sun suddenly changes to a vivid green. The period of visibility tends to increase in summer months with increasing latitude, i.e. as the angle of descent of the Sun decreases. In the Antarctic, it has been observed for 30 minutes. Occasionally it takes the form of a white flash followed by a deep blue one. A similar type of phenomenon, the red flash, is sometimes seen as the lower edge of the Sun is seen to emerge from a dark cloud near the horizon.

Ionosphere. Part of the Earth's atmosphere where the constituent atoms are partly ionized by ultra-violet radiation from the Sun. Its height varies, but is approximately between 80 and 400 km above the surface of the Earth.

Light Curve. A graph of the apparent magnitude of a variable star (or other variable object) plotted against an appropriate time-scale.

Light-time. The time taken for light, travelling at a velocity of 299,793 km/s, to reach the Earth from a distant object. A correction for the effect of light-time is necessary when calculating rotation periods of planets, etc. The observed times of maxima and minima of variable stars require a light-time correction depending upon the position of the Earth in its orbit at the time of observation, as periods of variation are stated for the Earth at mean distance from the star.

Limb. The apparent edge of the Sun, Moon, a planet or any body having a detectable disk. Regions adjoining a limb are termed limb regions (especially used for the Moon). The leading limb of an object as it moves due to the diurnal rotation of the Earth is termed the *preceding limb*, and the 'trailing' limb is termed the *following limb*. The other extremities are termed the north and south limbs, as appropriate.

Lunation. Term used to denote one complete cycle of phases of the Moon, occupying $29\frac{1}{2}$ days on average. It is the Moon's synodic period, also known as a *synodic month*.

Mesosphere. The upper part of the stratosphere, between about 50 and 80 km above the Earth's surface.

Metagalaxy. Term used to describe the entire cosmos, embodying all known and imagined celestial objects and the space lying between them.

Metonic Cycle. A period of 19 years, after which the phases of the Moon will recur on the same calendar date and within two hours of the same time, discovered by Meton of Athens in 432 B.C. It arises from the fact that 235 lunations equal 19 tropical years almost exactly, about $6939\frac{1}{2}$ days.

Mock Sun. Another name for *parhelion*, q.v.

North Point. The point on the celestial sphere due north of the observer, where the meridian plane intersects the horizon. The term is also used to denote the point on the hour circle through an observed object nearest to the north celestial pole, used as a zero reference for observations of position angle.

Parhelion. Sometimes termed a mock sun, this is an image of the Sun formed by refraction through ice crystals in the Earth's atmosphere; usually diffuse, and situated 22° from the real Sun. Common in polar regions, but often seen elsewhere.

Parselene. A diffuse image of the Moon formed by ice crystals in the upper atmosphere, usually seen 22° from the true Moon. Usually seen only in the polar regions.

Penumbra. The outer parts of the shadow cast by an object in a light beam from an extended source, e.g. the outer part of the Moon's shadow during a solar eclipse, falling upon part of the Earth's surface which is illuminated by only part of the Sun's disk. Also used for the outer, greyish region of a sunspot.

Planisphere. A device which can be set for the date and used to show the constellations visible from a given latitude at a given time of night. A useful aid to star recognition.

Planetology. The study of the physical nature of the planets; embraces not only their study as astronomical objects, but also the application of earth science techniques to their study, as with modern space-probe observations using geophysical techniques, the geological study of the Moon's surface, the petrological and mineralogical study of lunar rock samples, etc.

Position Angle. The position angle of a planet's axis, or of any such 'line' on the disk of a celestial object, is its inclination to the hour circle passing through the centre of the object. It is measured from the north point eastwards, from 0° to 360°.

Radius Vector. A hypothetical straight line joining an orbiting body and the focus of the orbit, e.g. the line joining a planet and the Sun. Used in dynamical calculations.

Refraction. As the Earth's atmosphere decreases in density with height above the surface, so too does its refractive index; in consequence, light from a distant object follows a curved path through the atmosphere, although the observer will believe it to have come from the direction along which it arrives at the Earth's surface. The effect of this is to cause objects to appear to have a greater altitude than they have in fact. The effect is maximal at the horizon, more than $\frac{1}{2}$°, and decreases to nil at the zenith.

Saros. A period of 18 y 11 d, after which the Sun, the Moon and the nodes of the Moon's orbit return to virtually the same relative positions. It was long believed to have been discovered by the Chaldæans more than 2500 years ago, but may date from the seventeenth century. It enables eclipses to be predicted with considerable accuracy.

Scintillation. The 'twinkling' of the stars, due to local minor variations in the refractive index of the Earth's atmosphere due to inhomogeneities and disturbances. These cause not only small variations in the brightness of a star, but also variations in its colour and small 'wanderings' about its mean observed position.

Small Circle. A circle formed on the celestial sphere by any plane through the sphere which does not pass through the centre of the sphere. The diameter of a small circle is thus less than the diameter of the sphere containing it.

Stratosphere. That part of the Earth's atmosphere at an altitude of about 11 to 80 km.

Troposphere. The lowest layer of the Earth's atmosphere, up to a height of about 11 km.

Twilight. From ancient times this has been reckoned as ending (in the evening, commencing in the morning) when 6th magnitude stars are just visible in the zenith. This coincides with the modern definition of *astronomical twilight*—when the Sun's centre is 18° below the horizon. *Nautical twilight* is defined by the instant when the Sun is 12° below the horizon, and *Civil Twilight* when it is 6° below the horizon.

Twilight lengthens with distance of the observer from the Equator, and is shortest as seen from anywhere on Earth at the equinoxes.

Twinkling. *Scintillation*, q.v.

4

Umbra. The dark part of the shadow cast by an object illuminated by an extended source, e.g. the shadow cone of the Moon within which the Sun is seen to be totally eclipsed. Also used for the dark inner portion of a sunspot.

Vertex. The point on the limb of an object farthest from the observer's horizon. The Moon's vertex is used in observations of lunar occultations. Distances from the vertex are counted eastwards from 0° to 360°.

Vertical Circle. A circle on the celestial sphere which passes through both the zenith and nadir, and is thus perpendicular to the horizon.

Some Terms Occurring in Astronomical Papers

Errors of Observation. These are of two kinds—Systematic Errors and Accidental Errors. *Systematic errors* are those which repeat (and can therefore be readily determined) when observations are repeated under similar conditions. They are often inherent in the instrument used, in which case they can be detected by the use of a different instrument. Other systematic errors may depend upon climatic conditions, and many other parameters.

Accidental errors are erratic, but can be estimated by analysis of the small discrepancies between the individual observations of a series, or between observed and calculated values; these discrepancies are known as *residuals*.

Probable Error. The probable error of a series of observations is a value derived mathematically from the residuals; it is an indication of the reliability of the figures given. It is often abbreviated to p.e., and is usually prefixed by the sign ±, indicating that it is an even chance whether a given value will be greater or smaller by the amount of the probable error. The smaller the probable error, the greater the reliability.

Mean. The mean value of a set of observations is a straight arithmetic mean or average, i.e. the sum of the individual values divided by the number of values used. If the observations are *weighted* according to their relative reliability, the individual values are first multiplied by weighting factors before they are summed and the mean taken; this is then termed a *weighted mean*.

Method of Least Squares. A method used to determine the most likely mean value derivable from a series of different observed values. It is based upon the principle that the weights of a series of observations with differing probable errors are inversely proportional to the squares of their probable errors.

Correlation. When two varying quantities are compared, the extent to which their variations appear to be inter-related is termed their correlation. It is measured by statistical methods and is usually expressed in the form of a *correlation coefficient*. This is expressed as a decimal fraction, i.e. a coefficient of 1·00 would imply perfect correlation.

Interpolation, Extrapolation. *Interpolation* is the process of finding values for dates, hours, quantities, etc., intermediate to those given in a table. For ordinary purposes, the proportional amount of the difference between the figures for the two nearest dates, quantities, etc., usually suffices, it being assumed for simplicity that the change in the interval is uniform; a more accurate result, useful when maximum or minimum occurs between the dates, is obtained by plotting on squared paper several successive dates, or figures, on each side of the one required and drawing a curve through these points.

For really accurate interpolation between the tabulated values of a complexly varying function it is necessary to apply a special formula; the one most commonly used is due to the early nineteenth-century German astronomer F. W. Bessel. Special tables of coefficients are used to facilitate the calculations.

Extrapolation, a similar process, extends a series of figures beyond the limit of the last figure actually known; there being only one limiting figure, however, it is less simple than interpolation and less accurate.

FUNDAMENTAL CONCEPTS

Celestial Sphere

A convenient means of studying the relative positions of the heavenly bodies, based upon their appearance to the observer. He seems to be at the centre of a vast hollow sphere—half of it unseen, beneath his feet—which revolves around the Earth once a day. The stars appear to be fixed on the inside surface of this sphere—i.e. at a uniform distance from the Earth—although in fact they are at vastly differing distances.

The celestial sphere may be regarded as of infinite radius, and therefore concentric with the Earth, the distance of the observers on the Earth's surface from its centre being negligible.

Positional astronomy is concerned with the relative *directions* of the heavenly bodies, and their apparent distances apart are expressed in angular measure. Most problems in positional astronomy can therefore be solved by the use of spherical trigonometry. The hypothetical concept of a celestial sphere is invaluable as the foundation upon which all fundamental considerations of the positions and motions of heavenly bodies are based.

The Geometry of the Celestial Sphere

The basic features of the celestial sphere are depicted in Figs. 1 and 2. In Fig. 1 the observer is located at O, the centre of the sphere. $NESW$ is his horizon, N, E, S and W being the north, east, south and west points. His zenith is at Z, his nadir at Z'. His meridian plane is the vertical circle $ZNZ'S$.

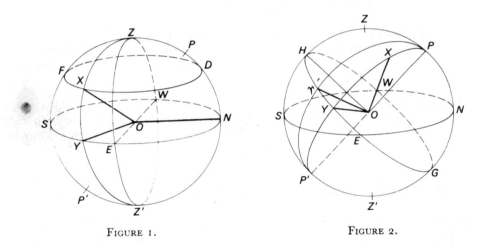

FIGURE 1. FIGURE 2.

If X represents the position of a star, its vertical is $ZXYZ'$; the small circle through the star parallel to the plane of the horizon, DXF, is termed the *almucantar* of the star.

The horizontal co-ordinates of the star are also shown in Fig. 1—the *altitude* being the angle YOX and the *azimuth* angle NOY. (Azimuth may be expressed in other ways when used by surveyors and navigators, but in modern astronomical usage is always measured eastward from the north point.)

In Fig. 2 P, P' represent the north and south celestial poles, and $NESW$ the horizon as before. PP' is thus the axis of rotation of the celestial sphere. The great circle $GEHW$ is the *celestial equator*. The *meridian* $NPZS$ is the hour circle through the zenith, and is perpendicular to both the equator and the horizon.

X again denotes the position of a star, $PXYP'$ being the *hour circle* through the star. The angle between the hour circle through the star and the meridian, $\angle HOY$, is the *hour angle* of the star. (It is usually measured westwards from the meridian, i.e. the arc $HWGEY$ or $360° - \angle HOY$.)

♈ is the *First Point of Aries*, or *Vernal Equinox*. The hour circle through ♈ ($P♈P'$) is the *equinoctial colure*. The star's Right Ascension is the angle between the equinoctial colure and the hour circle through the star, i.e. $\angle ♈OY$. The Declination of the star is $\angle XOY$, its North Polar Distance is $\angle POX$.

The Celestial Poles. These are the poles of rotation of the celestial sphere; they are directly overhead at the terrestrial poles.

The Celestial Equator (sometimes termed the *Equinoctial*) is the great circle having as its poles the celestial poles—i.e. the circle that is at all points equidistant from both of them. Every point on the celestial equator passes directly over every point on the terrestrial equator every day.

Zenith, Nadir. The *zenith* is the point immediately overhead; the *nadir* is the diametrically opposite point, i.e. immediately beneath the observer's feet. It is therefore an unobservable position, used only in a hypothetical sense.

Hour Circles. These are great circles passing through a celestial object and the celestial poles; they are therefore perpendicular to the celestial equator. They are occasionally termed declination circles, but this term is not preferred owing to the possibility of its being confused with parallels of Declination which are not necessarily great circles and are *parallel* to the equator.

It should be noted that the same terms are used, perhaps confusingly, to describe the setting circles of an equatorially mounted telescope; the circle on the polar axis is termed the 'hour circle' and is graduated in h, m and s of time; that on the declination axis is known as the 'declination circle' and is graduated in °, ′ and ″ of arc.

The Ecliptic

This is another important great circle on the star sphere, which intersects the celestial equator at an angle of $23\frac{1}{2}°$ and lies in a plane which passes through the centres of the Sun and the Earth: it represents the yearly path of the Sun's centre on the celestial sphere, as seen from the Earth, or the Earth's as seen from the Sun: it is shown in Maps 3–14. *The Ecliptic Poles*, the points on the star sphere 90° from the Ecliptic (about $23\frac{1}{2}°$ from the Terrestrial poles), are at R.A. 18 h and 6 h, and Dec. $66\frac{1}{2}°$ N and S, respectively.

The Ecliptic and its poles are 'sensibly' (i.e. for ordinary purposes) fixed on the celestial sphere, but change slightly in centuries. The former also represents (*a*) the central line of the Zodiac; (*b*) the average path of the Moon, Mercury and Venus, on the celestial sphere, but not those of the other major planets—though these are always *near* the Ecliptic, except Pluto.

Obliquity of the Ecliptic. The inclination of the Ecliptic to the celestial equator—approximately 23° 27′—which represents the maximum angular distance of the Sun north or south of the celestial equator at the solstices. The obliquity may vary from the mean value by up to 9″; the mean value was 23° 26′ 45″ on 1950 January 1 and decreases annually by 0″·47.

The Zodiac (literally 'circle of the animals'—most of the signs represent living creatures) is the belt of the sky 8–9° on each side of the Ecliptic, within which the Sun, Moon and all the planets known to the ancients are found.

Starting yearly at the First Point of Aries, it is divided into the twelve 'Signs of the Zodiac' (see symbols, p. 30)—each 30° of longitude on the Ecliptic—which, however, do *not* coincide with the constellations of the same name, although they did so some 2100 years ago when the First Point was named, precession having carried them westwards some 30°, or a whole sign.

The Equinoxes

These are the two days of the year on which, everywhere on Earth, day and night are of equal duration—hence the name. The instant when the Sun reaches its ascending node—i.e. when it crosses the celestial equator moving northwards on about March 21—is the *Vernal Equinox*. The *Autumnal Equinox* is the corresponding moment, around September 23, when the Sun reaches descending node and passes into the southern celestial hemisphere.

The Vernal Equinox, or **First Point of Aries.** This is the zero for the celestial measurements corresponding to terrestrial longitude; it is the point of intersection on the star sphere, at any moment, of the celestial equator and the ecliptic, at or near the point where the Sun crosses the former from south to north on about March 21.

This point—the *True* or *Apparent Equinox*, or *The Equinox* of any date—moves westward on the ecliptic 1/7th second of arc every day, but is nevertheless the most convenient point for the purpose, as the Sun's position in the sky, measured from it, remains practically the same on a given day of the year for thousands of years, by the leap year arrangements of the calendar, though those of the stars slowly change. 'Vernal Equinox', *when used in connection with measurements*, always means this moving True Equinox, but the *literal* Vernal Equinox is the instant when the Sun's centre actually crosses the celestial equator.

The Mean Equinox is the True Equinox corrected for the irregularity [max. $\pm 1\frac{1}{4}$ s] called *Nutation in Right Ascension*. Positions in star charts and catalogues are measured from it, at the time when the Sun's mean longitude is 280°, about Jan. 1: thus for 1950, the star positions are called 'mean places for 1950·0'. '·0' after a year always indicates the 280° start.

The position of the First Point of Aries is about nine moon-breadths west of the end of a line drawn first from α Andromedæ to γ Pegasi (which form one side of the 'Square of Pegasus'), then extended downwards for the same length.

The name originates from the time of Hipparchus, about 2100 years ago, when the vernal equinox was in the constellation Aries; due to precession it is now actually in Pisces.

The First Point of Libra. The descending node of the Sun's apparent path, or *autumnal equinox*. Due to precession the First Point of Libra is no longer situated in that constellation; at the present time it is in Virgo.

Colures. The *equinoctial colure* is the hour circle of the First Point of Aries, or vernal equinox. It also passes through the autumnal equinox, and is therefore the hour circle of R.A. 0 h and 12 h. The *solstitial colure* is the great circle which passes through the summer and winter solstices, i.e. the hour circle of R.A. 6 h and 18 h.

The Solstices

These are the two days in the year when the Sun is at its greatest angular distance from the equator, i.e. the occasion of the longest day and shortest night in one hemisphere of the Earth, and vice versa in the other. The longest day in the northern hemisphere occurs on about June 21—the *summer solstice*—and the shortest on about December 22, the *winter solstice*. These dates mark the winter solstice and summer solstice respectively in the southern hemisphere. The Sun's positions when it is momentarily stationary on these occasions are termed the *solstitial points*.

Diurnal Rotation

The apparent rotation of the celestial sphere, due to the axial rotation of the Earth. It is the motion which gives rise to the daily rising and setting of the Sun, the stars and all other heavenly bodies.

Culmination, or *Southing*. A celestial object *culminates* when it reaches its highest point above the observer's horizon. In the northern terrestrial hemisphere, *souths* is used in the same sense, as culmination is always at the instant when the object is due south of the observer; in the southern hemisphere, objects culminate when due north of the south pole.

Rising and Setting of Stars. At the terrestrial equator, the celestial poles lie on the horizon; all the stars remain above the horizon for half a day, and their rising and setting are at right angles to the horizon. At the terrestrial poles, on the other hand, the celestial equator coincides with the horizon, parallel with which the stars move in circles, neither rising nor setting, the other half of the star sphere being never seen.

In intermediate latitudes there is every variety between these extremes, but always some stars never set (and a corresponding area round the opposite pole, never rise); also the paths in the sky cut the horizon obliquely—all in proportion to the observer's distance from the terrestrial pole or equator.

The stars which rise and set always do so at the same points on the horizon—unlike the Sun, Moon and planets, which rise and set at different points on successive days. In temperate latitudes, especially, those nearest the celestial pole rise far north (in the southern hemisphere, *south*), and are above the horizon most of the twenty-four hours; at increasing distances from the celestial pole they rise further and further south (or *north*) and their time above the horizon diminishes until, for the stars furthest south (or *north*), they set again a very short time after rising. Stars on the celestial equator rise due east and set due west, and are above the horizon for twelve hours as seen from all over the Earth—except at the poles.

Stars rise, 'south' or 'north', and set, at a given hour *only once a year*, always on or about the same date, for they culminate nearly four minutes earlier each day, and make $366\frac{1}{4}$ revolutions in $365\frac{1}{4}$ solar days.

On one day in the year 'southing', etc., occurs *twice*, for when a star souths at 12.01 a.m. it will south again at 11.57 p.m. the same day. This occurs with the superior planets also—Mars, and the asteroids in general, about each second year—their mean daily motions being less than the Earth's. Mars and Venus, however, may not south at all on one day in the year.

Circumpolar Stars (stars that never set or rise). Stars never set when their distance from the celestial pole is less than the observer's latitude on Earth; i.e. stars with Declinations greater than the observer's co-latitude never set—those in the corresponding area around the opposite celestial pole never rise.

The Meridian

An observer's meridian is the great circle of the celestial sphere which passes through both celestial poles and the zenith; it always meets the horizon in the north and south points. The term *meridian plane* is also used. 'On the meridian', 'meridian passage', etc., have the same meaning as *culmination*, or *transit*, q.v.

Prime Meridian. The meridian adopted as the zero of longitude measurement on the surface of a planet. In the case of the Earth, the Prime Meridian adopted by international agreement in 1894 is that of the Airy Transit Circle at the Royal Observatory, Greenwich, England.

Transit. A celestial object *transits* when it crosses a particular meridian. The term is also used for a meridian or surface marking crossing the *central meridian* of the disk of a rotating planet.

Upper Transit, or *Upper Culmination*, is used to describe the meridian passage from east to west of an object 'above the pole'—i.e. between the north pole and the south point on the horizon for an observer in the northern hemisphere.

Lower Transit, or *Lower Culmination*, of a circumpolar star is the meridian passage from west to east—'below pole'—which takes place twelve sidereal hours after upper transit. For an observer in the northern hemisphere this is when the star is between the north pole and the north point on the horizon, and is the instant of closest approach of the star to the horizon.

The term transit is also used to denote the passage of an inferior planet across the Sun's disk, or the passage of a planet's satellite or its shadow across the disk of the primary.

Epoch

A fixed point in time. Thus the instant at which a particular observation is made is known as the *epoch of observation*. Observations of the same object made at various times are usually referred to a single epoch—either the beginning of the year (e.g. the epoch 1972·0) or to the *standard* or *fundamental epoch*.

Standard Epoch. This is an epoch used as the basis for comparison of observations, especially positional observations, over a long period of time—half a century or so. The fundamental epoch at present used is 1950·0; it will remain in use until the new epoch 2000·0 is adopted by international agreement.

POSITION

Celestial Co-ordinate Systems

Astronomical positions are normally measured on the celestial sphere, using one of three systems of spherical co-ordinates, each of which has a different reference plane.

Horizontal Co-ordinates. These are referred to the plane of the observer's horizon. The co-ordinates used are the *altitude* (the angular distance of the body above the horizon) and the *azimuth* (the angle between the vertical plane through the object and the observer's meridian plane). Altitude is measured as the object's vertical angular distance above the horizon, azimuth as the angular distance eastwards around the horizon from the north point.

Equatorial Co-ordinates. These are referred to the plane of the celestial equator. The co-ordinates used are the Right Ascension or Hour Angle, and the Declination or Polar Distance.

Right Ascension is the angle between the hour circle through the object and the First Point of Aries;

it is usually abbreviated to R.A. or α. It is measured eastwards along the celestial equator from the True Equinox, sometimes in arc (0° to 360°) but usually in sidereal time (h, m, s). One hour is equivalent to 15°, one degree to 4 m. The R.A. is the interval in sidereal time between the transit of the True Equinox and that of the body concerned. An alternative sometimes used is the *Hour Angle*—the angle between the hour circle through the object and the observer's meridian. It is the difference between the R.A. of the object and the R.A. circle on the meridian at the time of observation, and is measured westwards from the meridian.

The *Declination* is the angular distance of the object north or south of the celestial equator, reckoned positive when north and negative when south of the equator. It is usually abbreviated to Dec. or δ. In some calculations where it is desirable to avoid the use of negative values, the polar distance is used, i.e. the angular distance from the north celestial pole—the North Polar Distance (N.P.D.) or from the south celestial pole—the South Polar Distance (S.P.D.). The polar distance is, of course, equivalent to 90° − Dec.

Ecliptic Co-ordinates. These are referred to the plane of the ecliptic. The co-ordinates used are *celestial latitude* (the perpendicular distance of the object from the ecliptic in angular measure) and *celestial longitude* (the angular distance along the ecliptic between the plane through the object and the First Point of Aries). These co-ordinates are strictly *geocentric* latitude and longitude—i.e. as observed from the Earth's centre. Observations are of course *topocentric*—observed from a point on the surface of the Earth—but geocentric co-ordinates are usually tabulated as they are universally applicable, whereas the slight corrections required to convert them to topocentric values for a given location can be simply made.

Heliocentric Co-ordinates are also used—these too are referred to the plane of the ecliptic but indicate the position of an object as seen from the centre of the Sun. They are particularly used in calculations of the relative positions of the planets and other bodies of the solar system. The Earth's heliocentric longitude at a given instant is equal to the Sun's geocentric longitude plus 180°.

Alternative Planes of Reference

The celestial equator, though most convenient for finding or recording positions on the celestial sphere, by means of the R.A. and Dec., is a less suitable plane of reference for many purposes and other planes and great circles are used instead. Briefly, the position of an object is indicated, with respect to the:

Celestial Equator . .	. by its Declination, and Right Ascension, from the Vernal Equinox.
Ecliptic,	
(a) from the Earth's centre	. by its Geocentric Latitude, and Longitude, from the Vernal Equinox.
(b) from the Sun's centre .	. by its Heliocentric Latitude, and Longitude, from the Vernal Equinox.
Horizon of the observer .	. by its Altitude, and Azimuth, from the North Point.
Meridian	. by its Hour Angle from the meridian, and Declination from the Celestial Equator.
Hour Circle or Declination Circle	by its Position Angle, from the North Point.
Galactic Plane, or Milky Way	. by its Galactic Latitude, and Longitude, from the direction of the presumed centre of the Galaxy.
Sun's Equator . . .	. by its Heliographic Latitiude, and Longitude, from arbitrary zero.
Planet's or Moon's Equator	. by its Planetographic Latitude, and Longitude.
Limb of the Sun, Moon, or Planet	by its Distance (a) from the North Point; (b) from the Vertex.

The Invariable Plane of the Solar System, passing through the System's centre of gravity, forms an unvarying reference plane, since it does not change its position in space due to planetary perturbations, as the ecliptic does. Inclined 1° 35′ to the ecliptic plane, 7° to Sun's equator; longitude of ascending node 106° 35′ (epoch 1850).

The Fundamental Plane, used in occultations and eclipses, is the plane passing through the centre of the Earth perpendicular to a line drawn from the star, or the centre of the Sun, through the centre of the Moon.

Galactic Co-ordinates

Studies of the distribution of stars, nebulæ and clusters within the Galaxy require their positions to be measured in a special co-ordinate system referred to the plane of the Galaxy. The co-ordinates used are Galactic Latitude and Longitude. The poles of the Galactic Plane and the zero of Galactic Longitude were redefined by the International Astronomical Union in 1959. The north galactic pole is at R.A. 12 h 49 m, Dec. +27° 24′ (epoch 1950·0). The zero of galactic longitude is the direction of the presumed centre of the Galaxy, R.A. 17 h 42·4 m, Dec. −28° 55′ (epoch 1950·0).

Galactic Latitude is the angular distance of the object perpendicularly from the Galactic Plane. *Galactic Longitude* is measured in arc around the galactic equator from the defined zero point, from 0° to 360°.

Star Places

The positions of the 'fixed' stars are usually given in Right Ascension and Declination, i.e. referred to the equator and equinox. Due to precession, the positions of the equator and equinox on the celestial sphere are constantly changing, and it is therefore necessary for accurate star positions to be referred to the equator and equinox at a given date or epoch.

Three forms of star place are used, the true place, apparent place and mean place.

The True Place is given by the heliocentric co-ordinates of the star on the celestial sphere at the instant of observation, i.e. referred to the true equator and equinox of that instant.

The Apparent Place is the geocentric position of the star on the celestial sphere as observed from the Earth. It differs from the True Place by small quantities due to annual parallax and aberration.

The Mean Place is the heliocentric position of the star on the celestial sphere, reduced to the mean equator and equinox for the beginning of the year of the observation (see below).

Reduction of Star Places

In order to facilitate the analysis and comparison of observations made during a given year it is usual to reduce the observed place of the star to a mean place—i.e. to the mean equator and equinox for the beginning of the year. This requires corrections to the observed co-ordinates for the effects of precession, nutation, aberration, annual parallax and proper motion during the interval elapsed between the beginning of the year and the moment of observation.

Fundamental Epoch. When observations made over a period of some years are to be compared it is necessary for them all to be reduced to a common epoch; to facilitate intercomparison of observations a fundamental epoch is adopted to which all appropriate observations are reduced. Star places are also listed in catalogues reduced to the fundamental epoch. It is usual for a fundamental epoch to be used for half a century or so; thus the fundamental epoch currently in use is 1950·0, which is unlikely to be superseded until 2000·0 is universally adopted.

Precession. The precession of the equinoxes is a westward movement of the nodes of the ecliptic (the equinoxes), relative to the background stars, of 50″·2 per annum. It is caused by the gravitational attraction of the Sun and Moon on the Earth's equatorial bulge. The Earth's axis (inclined at 23½° to the plane of its orbit) completes a whole rotation in 25,800 years. The pole of the heavens therefore traces out a circle 23½° in radius in that period. As a result of this *Polaris* is only temporarily the closest bright star to the north celestial pole. About 4500 years ago it was *Thuban* (α Draconis); 8000 years hence it will be *Deneb* (α Cygni) and in 12,000 years time *Vega* (α Lyræ).

The apparent movement of the pole is undetectable to the naked eye in a lifetime; its effects on the accurate measurement of star positions are however considerable. All positional observations are made relative to the celestial poles at the time of observation, but are usually reduced to a standard epoch (see *Mean Place*, above); corrections for the effects of precession have therefore to be made when reducing the star's observed R.A. and Dec. to the standard epoch.

Due to precession every star—except those less than 23½° from the ecliptic poles—passes through every hour of Right Ascension from 0 h to 24 h once every 25,800 years; also the Declinations swing through 47° (23½° × 2) every 12,900 years; as a result the stars visible from a given place or at a given season are greatly changed during that time.

In star catalogues the values for precession in R.A. and Dec. represent the co-ordinates of the total annual linear precessional motion of each star along the ecliptic. Near the celestial poles the values seem very great, but this is misleading. Close to the poles, where the hour circles of R.A. are converging, a movement of many seconds in R.A., as measured along the very small declination parallels, is equivalent to only a few seconds in equatorial great-circle measure.

Nutation. The precessional path traced out on the celestial sphere by the celestial pole is a wavy line varying slightly from a true circle. This irregularity is called nutation, being a regular 'nodding' of the celestial poles to and from the ecliptic poles; it perceptibly modifies the precessional displacement in R.A. and Dec. The Earth's axis passes the mean position about 2800 times in the 25,800 year precessional period. Nutation is a slight variation in the obliquity of the ecliptic, and should be known in precise terms as the *nutation in obliquity*. Its component measured along the celestial equator is the *nutation in R.A.* and that measured along the ecliptic is termed the *nutation in longitude* or *equation of the equinoxes*.

Nutation is due to the varying distances and relative directions of the Sun and the Moon; their gravitational attraction on the Earth therefore varies in both strength and direction. The total effect is a combination of three components; these are the *lunar nutation*, which causes the pole to wander from its mean position by $\pm 9''$ in a period of 18·6 y, the *solar nutation* ($\pm 1''\cdot 2$ in 0·5 y) and the *fortnightly nutation* ($\pm 0''\cdot 1$ in 15 days).

Aberration. The velocity of light is not infinite compared with the Earth's orbital velocity, and the two velocities combined result in a small displacement of celestial objects from their true positions. The rotation of the Earth causes a lesser aberration. After an entire sidereal year the object returns to its original place, however, so far as aberration is concerned.

The maximum displacement of an object due to this phenomenon, properly termed the *aberration of light*, is $20''\cdot 47$.

Annual Parallax. Positional observations of a distant object made from the surface of the Earth are, of course, being made from a moving object; if the positional observations are being made to sufficient precision an annual variation in the apparent position of the object will be revealed, which is in fact a reflection of the Earth's annual motion around the Sun. To permit intercomparison of observations made throughout a year it is necessary to calculate and remove the effect of this variation in apparent position, known as the *annual parallax*. It is defined as the angle subtended at the object by the semi-major axis of the Earth's orbit. The largest parallax known for an object outside the solar system is that of the nearest star *Proxima Centauri*, $0''\cdot 762$; most stellar parallaxes are very much smaller than this however, only some 700 or so having parallaxes greater than $0''\cdot 05$ and only about 4000 greater than $0''\cdot 01$ (equivalent to a distance of 100 parsecs). [1 parsec = 3·26 light years—see p. 28.]

Proper Motion. In general all stars, including the sun, are in motion relative to one another. Stars sufficiently close to the sun are thus seen to move against the background of very remote stars and galaxies. The steady progression of an individual star across that distant background, once the parallactic apparent motion arising from the sun's motion and the earth's orbital motion have been subtracted, is known as the star's proper motion.

Latitude Variation. The measured Declinations of stars show minute, irregular cyclic changes, up to a maximum value of $0''\cdot 04$, due to the poles of rotation of the Earth wandering around a mean position in a counter-clockwise direction. The variation consists of two components. The principal component is due to the fact that the Earth's axis of rotation is slightly inclined to its axis of symmetry; this causes a polar wandering of maximum amplitude $0''\cdot 36$ (equivalent to about ± 30 feet on the ground) in a period of 432 days. The second component is due to seasonal movements of air masses, and has an amplitude of $\pm 0''\cdot 18$ (± 15 feet) in a period of one year.

The Measurement of Position on the Surface of a Body

There are two systems in which the positions of features on the surface of a near-spherical body such as a planet or satellite may be recorded—the *planetocentric* and *planetographic* co-ordinates. In addition to these general terms specific designations are also used, thus: *heliocentric* and *heliographic* co-ordinates for the Sun; *selenocentric* and *selenographic* for the Moon; *geocentric* and *geographic* for the Earth; *areocentric* and *areographic* for Mars; *zenocentric* and *zenographic* for Jupiter; *saturnicentric* and *saturnigraphic* for Saturn; etc.

Planetocentric Co-ordinates. These are referred to the equatorial plane of the body concerned, and are much used in the calculations of celestial mechanics. *Planetocentric longitude* is measured around the equator of the body from a prime meridian defined and adopted by international agreement. (The prime meridian may be referred to a visible feature in the case of a solid-surfaced body such as Mars, but in the case of a gaseous planet such as Jupiter it is a purely hypothetical concept.) *Planetocentric latitude* is measured in arc above or below the equator of the object in the usual way.

Planetographic Co-ordinates. These are used for observations of the surface features of those planets whose figures are not truly spherical, but oblate. They are referred to the mean surface of the planet, and are the co-ordinates actually determined by observation. They can readily be converted to planetocentric co-ordinates if required. As the oblate planets are symmetrical about their axes of rotation, there is little difference in practice between planetocentric and planetographic longitudes; the differences between planetocentric and planetographic latitudes are quite significant for very oblate bodies such as Jupiter and Saturn.

TIME

The Earth

The Sidereal Year is the time taken by the Earth to make one complete circuit round the star sphere *as seen from the Sun*. It can also be considered as the time taken by the Sun to make one complete circuit round the star field as seen from the centre of the Earth.

The Anomalistic Year is the time interval between successive passages of the Earth through perihelion (or aphelion).

The Tropical Year is the time interval between successive vernal equinoxes, or the time taken by the Sun to complete one revolution relative to the *First Point of Aries*. If the First Point of Aries were a fixed point amongst the stars, the sidereal and tropical years would be identical, but as it has an annual retrograde motion of $50.26''$ relative to the stars, the tropical year is somewhat shorter than the sidereal. Relative to the stars, the Sun describes:

In the Sidereal Year, $360°$
In the Tropical Year, $360° - 50''·26$
In the Anomalistic Year, $360° + 11''·25$

The length of the years are:

Sidereal Year $= 365·25636$ days
Tropical Year $= 365·24219$ days
Anomalistic Year $= 365·25964$ days

The Civil Year, of necessity an exact number of days, is normally 365 days, but is modified according to the following rules:

If the year is exactly divisible by 4, then the year consists of 366 days, unless the year is a multiple of 100. In these cases, if the number of the century is divisible by 4, then the year has 366 days, otherwise it has only 365 days.

The Julian Calendar, based on a year of exactly $365\frac{1}{4}$ days, was instituted in 45 B.C., but the 'century' modifications were introduced by Pope Gregory XIII in 1582. This *Gregorian Calendar* still leaves an error of about 1 d 4 h 55 m in 4000 years.

The Eclipse Year, $346·6203$ days, is the interval between successive returns of the Sun to the same node of the Moon's orbit. This period is responsible for the regular recurrence of both solar and lunar eclipses, which can only take place when these bodies are within a small distance of the node. Nineteen eclipse years are $6585·78$ days, almost exactly the same as the ancient 'Saros' cycle of $6585·32$ days, the period which separates eclipses in a given series.

The Day

The True Sidereal Day is the time interval between two successive upper transits of a 'fixed' star from a fixed point on the Earth's surface. It is equal to 23 h 56 m 04 s · 098904.

The Equinoctial Sidereal Day is the time interval between two successive transits of the First Point of Aries. This unit is used in preference to the True Sidereal Day and is the one normally referred to as simply the *Sidereal Day*. It is equal to 23 h 56 m 04 s · 09054.

The Solar Day (or Apparent Solar Day) is the time interval between two consecutive upper transits of the Sun. This varies with time of year and so it is necessary to define the *Mean Solar Day* as the average solar day. The variations in the length of the day are due to two causes:

(i) the Sun does not move along the ecliptic at a uniform rate, due to varying distance of the Earth from Sun during the year;

(ii) the Sun moves in the ecliptic and not along the celestial equator. The celestial longitude is in general different from its Right Ascension (R.A.).

The Dynamic Mean Sun is defined to be a point which coincides with the true Sun at perigee and which moves round the ecliptic in the same period as the Sun (1 year) but at a uniform rate.

The Astronomical Mean Sun is defined to be a point which moves round the celestial equator in such a way that its R.A. is always equal to the longitude of the Dynamic Mean Sun. The Astronomical Mean Sun (usually called simply the Mean Sun) is the moving point chosen in defining mean solar time.

The Equation of Time is the name given to the amount which must be added to the mean (or clock) time to obtain the apparent (or sundial) time:

$$\text{Clock Time} + \text{Equation of Time} = \text{Apparent Time}.$$

In Table 1, Mean Time plus the tabulated value of the Equation of Time gives the apparent or 'sundial' time (take account of sign: − indicates clock fast on Sun, + indicates clock slow on Sun).

TABLE 1. VALUES OF THE EQUATION OF TIME

Date	Eqn. m	Date	Eqn. m	Date	Eqn. m	Date	Eqn. m	Date	Eqn. m	Date	Eqn. m	Date	Eqn. m
Jan. 1	−3	Feb. 20	−14	Apr. 8	−2	Jun. 19	−1	Aug. 29	−1	Oct. 7	+12	Dec. 7	+9
3	−4	24	−13½	12	−1	24	−2	Sept. 2	0	11	+13	9	+8
5	−5	27	−13	16	0	29	−3	5	+1	15	+14	11	+7
7	−6	Mar. 4	−12	20	+1	July 4	−4	8	+2	20	+15	13	+6
9	−7	8	−11	25	+2	10	−5	11	+3	27	+16	16	+5
12	−8	12	−10	May 2	+3	14	−5½	14	+4	Nov. 4	+16½	18	+4
15	−9	16	−9	7	+3½	19	−6	17	+5	11	+16	20	+3
18	−10	20	−8	15	+3¾	27	−6½	19	+6	18	+15	22	+2
21	−11	23	−7	23	+3½	Aug. 5	−6	22	+7	22	+14	24	+1
24	−12	26	−6	28	+3	13	−5	25	+8	26	+13	26	0
29	−13	29	−5	Jun. 4	+2	18	−4	28	+9	29	+12	28	−1
Feb. 4	−14	Apr. 2	−4	10	+1	22	−3	Oct. 1	+10	Dec. 1	+11	30	−2
12	−14⅓	5	−3	15	0	26	−2	4	+11	4	+10		

Lunar Months

The Synodic Month or *Lunation* (mean, 29·53059 days) is the period between successive New Moons. The actual value varies between 29¼ and 29¾ days.

The Anomalistic Month (mean, 27·55455 days) is the period between successive perigees.

The Sidereal Month (mean, 27·32166 days) is the period taken by the Moon to make one complete circuit round the star sphere, as seen from the centre of the Earth.

The Tropical Month (mean, 27·32158 days) is the period between successive conjunctions with the First Point of Aries.

The Draconic Month (mean, 27·21222 days) is the period between successive passages through ascending nodes.

Astronomical Time

The measurement of astronomical time is based on the 24 hour clock, with zero at midnight. Prior to 1925 Jan. 1, the astronomical day ran from noon to noon with the last twelve hours in the following civil day.

The Julian Period is used to calculate the exact interval between dates at long intervals apart. It started on Jan. 1, 4713 B.C. at noon. The Julian Date (J.D.) is the number of days that have elapsed since the beginning of the Julian Period. The Julian Day is given in decimal form, and not in hours and minutes. It is reckoned from Greenwich noon. Thus, 1971 Jan. 1, 9 p.m. is J.D. 2440953.375. Any astronomical time less than 12 hours (0.5 day) still belongs to the Julian Day *preceding* the civil date.

The Modified Julian Date is found by subtracting 2,400,000.5 from the Julian Day numbers.

e.g. 1964 Dec. 31 midnight is J.D.   2438395.5

M.J.D.   38395.0

The Measurement of Time

Sidereal Time, used for measuring R.A., is the interval in sidereal hours, minutes and seconds since the preceding meridian passage at a given place of the First Point of Aries. The sidereal day is 3 m 55.91 s shorter than the mean solar day.

To calculate the sidereal time an almanac must be consulted for the year in question: *The Astronomical Ephemeris* and the *Handbook of the British Astronomical Association* publish tables of the Sidereal Time at Greenwich at regular intervals throughout the year, for instance. The nearest value prior to the time of observation is taken from the almanac, and is converted to the sidereal time at the precise instant by adding a correction of 3.9 m for each completed day since the tabulated instant plus a further correction for the part day from the following critical table:

h	m	m	h	m	m	h	m	m	h	m	m
0	00.0		5	46.9		11	52.2		17	57.4	
		0.0			1.0			2.0			3.0
0	18.2		6	23.5		12	28.7		18	33.9	
		0.1			1.1			2.1			3.1
0	54.7		7	00.0		13	05.2		19	10.5	
		0.2			1.2			2.2			3.2
1	31.3		7	36.5		13	41.7		19	47.0	
		0.3			1.3			2.3			3.3
2	07.8		8	13.0		14	18.3		20	23.5	
		0.4			1.4			2.4			3.4
2	44.3		8	49.6		14	54.8		21	00.0	
		0.5			1.5			2.5			3.5
3	20.8		9	26.1		15	31.3		21	36.6	
		0.6			1.6			2.6			3.6
3	57.4		10	02.6		16	07.8		22	31.1	
		0.7			1.7			2.7			3.7
4	33.9		10	39.1		16	44.4		22	49.6	
		0.8			1.8			2.8			3.8
5	10.4		11	15.6		17	20.9		23	26.1	
		0.9			1.9			2.9			3.9
5	46.9		11	52.2		17	57.4		24	02.7	
		1.0			2.0			3.0			4.0
6	23.5		12	28.7		18	33.9		24	39.2	

(In critical cases ascend.)

To obtain local sidereal time a further correction must be added for the longitude difference between Greenwich and the observing station—1 hour being added to the time for every 15° longitude east of Greenwich, or subtracted for every 15° west.

Mean Time is the time shown by ordinary clocks and is the time interval since the preceding 'mean midnight'.

Local Mean Time is the correct *mean* time of the meridian of a place. It is found by adding 4 minutes for each degree longitude the place is east of the reference meridian. (Subtract 4 minutes per degree if place is west of the reference meridian.)

Universal Time (U.T.) denotes Mean Time for the Greenwich Meridian beginning at midnight.

Standard Zone Times are used by international agreement. This enables local noon to occur at about 12.00 hours local time. These zone times differ normally from Greenwich Mean Time by exact multiples of one hour but in some cases by exact multiples of half an hour. For the various standard times see almanacs.

Ephemeris Time (E.T.)

This is a uniform time system which is used only in computing. In this system, Newcomb's tables of the Sun agree with observation. E.T. is not subject to the fluctuation due to the variable rotation of the Earth, so that it is ahead of U.T. by a small amount ΔT which must be determined by

$$E.T. = U.T. + \Delta T.$$

In 1971, ΔT was about 41 seconds.

SPECTROSCOPY

In 1825 the French philospher, Auguste Comte, writing in his *Philosophie Positive*, quoted the chemical composition of the stars as an indisputable example of knowledge that would remain permanently unknown to mankind. At that time, however, work was in progress which was soon to confound this assertion; work which laid the basis of the scientific discipline of spectroscopy which is now regarded as a fundamental aspect of astronomical research.

The chromatic nature of light was first demonstrated by Newton in 1666. He found that white light from the Sun when passed through a glass prism emerged as a rainbow band of colour, or spectrum, ranging from red to blue, and further showed that not only were no new colours produced when this light was passed through a further prism, but that the colours could be recombined to form white light again by passage through a prism oriented in the opposite sense to the first.

As early as 1802 Wollaston showed, by passing sunlight through a narrow slit followed by a prism, that the rainbow band of colour was interrupted by several dark lines. Although Wollaston regarded these lines simply as the divisions between the colours, in the years subsequent to 1814 Fraunhofer was able to observe several hundred dark lines in the solar spectrum; and in 1859 Kirchhoff was able to demonstrate that the wavelengths of the dark lines in the solar spectrum coincided with bright emission lines produced in the laboratory from low density, high temperature gas. He conclusively demonstrated that each element displays its own characteristic spectrum of lines and laid down three basic laws.

1. An incandescent solid, liquid or gas under high pressure will produce a *continuous spectrum*, i.e. a rainbow band of colours.

2. A luminous gas under low pressure will produce a spectrum consisting of a series of bright isolated lines, known as an *emission* or *bright-line spectrum*.

3. If a continuous spectrum is passed through an element in gaseous state then light is absorbed by the gas at precisely the same wavelengths as the gas would emit under the conditions of 2 above. Such lines are called *absorption lines* and such a spectrum an *absorption spectrum*.

The work of Kirchhoff was fundamental to understanding stellar spectra. We shall now consider the mechanisms responsible for the production of spectra of the various types.

The Continuous Spectrum

When a solid body is heated to incandescence it emits radiation distributed over the entire electro-magnetic spectrum and if the body is an ideal radiator, or *black body*, then the amount of radiation emitted over the range of wavelengths of the electromagnetic spectrum will be distributed in a Planck curve as shown in Fig. 3 below. The wavelength at which maximum energy is emitted, λ_{max}, decreases as the

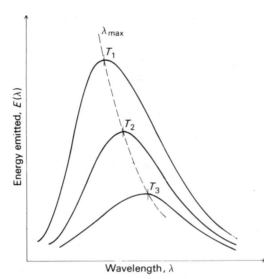

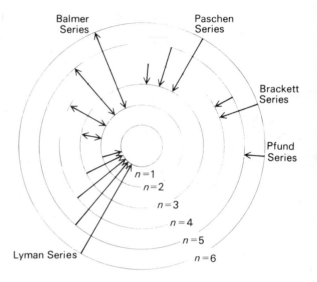

FIGURE 3. Planck curves corresponding to bodies at temperatures T_1, T_2, T_3 where T_1 is greater than T_2 and T_2 is greater than T_3

FIGURE 4. Line series in the hydrogen atom

temperature increases, and the value of this wavelength, is given classically by the *Wien Displacement Law*, $\lambda_{max} = C/T$, where C is a constant, and T is the absolute temperature of the body.

The total amount of radiation emitted by a black body, i.e. its *luminosity L*, depends only on its absolute temperature and is given by $L = 4\pi r^2 \sigma T^4$ where r is the radius of the body (if spherical), and σ is a constant known as *Stefan's Constant*. Thus as the temperature of a body is increased, the proportion of short-wave radiation is increased and the total amount of radiation is also increased. The form of the distribution curve is derived from the assumption, due to Max Planck, that radiation is emitted in discrete units or quanta as described in the next section.

Line Spectra

In 1885 Balmer showed the wavelengths of the bright lines in the series due to the element hydrogen could be repre nted by a simple empirical formula,

$$\frac{1}{\lambda} = \bar{\nu} = R\left(\frac{1}{2^2} - \frac{1}{n^2}\right)$$

where, λ is the wavelength of each line, $\bar{\nu}$ is known as *wave number*, R is a constant known as the *Rydberg Constant* and n is an integer having values 3, 4, 5, ..., etc.

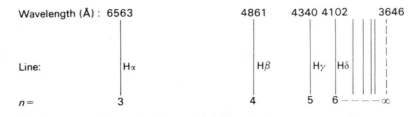

FIGURE 5. The Balmer series of hydrogen lines

The series of lines in the visible region of the spectrum described by this formula, and known as the *Balmer Series*, is illustrated above in Fig. 5. The series converged to a limit (the *Balmer Limit*) at a wavelength of 3646 Å which corresponded to $n = \infty$ in the formula.

Later work in the ultra-violet by Lyman uncovered a further series, and Paschen showed the existence of a series in the infra-red. In general it seemed that all series could be described by formulæ of the form

$$\frac{1}{\lambda} = \bar{\nu} = R\left(\frac{1}{n_1^2} - \frac{1}{n_2^2}\right)$$

where $n_1 = 1, 2, 3, \ldots$ and $n_2 = n_1 + 1, n_1 + 2$, etc. The value of R is taken to be 109,678 cm^{-1}.

These series may be interpreted in terms of the structure of the atom on the basis of the work of Bohr in 1913. The *Bohr model* of the hydrogen atom consists of a relatively massive, positively charged nucleus, i.e. a *proton*, around which moves—in a circular orbit—a much less massive particle of negative charge, the *electron* (the mass ratio proton : electron is approximately 1840 : 1). The electron is constrained to move only in orbits of particular radii such that angular momentum $= nh/2\pi$ where $n = 1, 2, 3, \ldots$ and h is a constant known as *Planck's constant*. The greater the radius of the orbit the greater the potential energy of the electron in that state. When an electron is in a particular orbit no energy is emitted, but when an electron moves from a high energy orbit E_1 to a lower energy level E_2 then the energy lost in this *transition* is emitted in the form of a packet, or *quantum* of radiation. The frequency, and hence wavelength, of the emitted radiation is given by $E_1 - E_2 = h\nu = hc/\lambda$ where c is the velocity of light.

Furthermore, if an electron in a low energy state absorbs a quantum of radiation of the appropriate energy corresponding to a jump from E_1 to a higher energy level E_2, then it will make that transition. A high energy level is known as an *excited* state.

Bright-line spectra are thus produced by downward transitions from excited states, whereas dark absorption spectra are produced by absorption from continuum radiation of selected wavelengths corresponding to transitions from low energy levels to high energy levels.

The atom can be visualized as a series of discrete orbits corresponding to various energy states, $n = 1, 2, 3, \ldots$, etc. in which the electron may exist. As can be seen in Fig. 4 the various spectral series correspond to transitions between high levels and various base levels. The lowest energy level is known as the *ground state*. The energy levels and transition values are often measured in units of *electron volts* (eV) where 1 eV is the energy acquired by an electron on being accelerated through a potential difference of 1 volt. A common multiple of this is the MeV (one million eV) where 1 MeV $= 1.6 \times 10^{-13}$ joules. The series limit corresponds to the transition between the highest possible energy level and the ground state. If excess energy is supplied to the electron it will be removed from the atom, and the atom is then said to be *ionized*. The atom is then no longer electrically neutral but is positively charged due to the loss of the negatively charged electron.

Ionization Potential. This is a term used to describe the minimum amount of energy required to remove an electron completely from an atom or an ion which is in its lowest energy state. It is given in *volts* and the *energy* is equal to the same number of electron volts. Ionization may be caused by (*a*) absorption of a sufficiently energetic quantum or (*b*) collision with another atom or electron. The latter process is important at the high temperatures of stellar atmospheres where the random velocities of atoms and electrons are very great.

Neutral, i.e. un-ionized, atoms are denoted by the element symbol followed by the Roman numeral I (neutral hydrogen could thus be H I, neutral oxygen O I); singly ionized atoms—i.e., those which have lost one electron—are denoted H II, O II, etc.; doubly ionized (having lost two electrons) are denoted H III, O III, and so on.

Excitation Potential is a measure of the energy required to excite the electron (or electrons in the case of heavier elements) from the ground state to an excited state. If undisturbed an excited atom returns to the ground state with the emission of radiation in about 10^{-8} seconds—possibly in several stages. Certain transitions are, however, *metastable* in which case the atom may remain in an excited state for the order of a few seconds.

Although the Bohr model allows a fairly full description of the hydrogen spectrum, the situation for heavier elements with more electrons is more complex. Nonetheless, the line spectra for all the elements can be explained in terms of transitions between energy levels.

A heavy atom is visualized as consisting of a nucleus surrounded by shells in which electrons can exist. The number of electrons contained in each shell—the shells being denoted in order of distance from the nucleus by the letters K, L, M, . . .—is restricted to a maximum of 2 for the K shell, 8 (L shell), 18 (M shell), etc., by the *Pauli Exclusion Principle*. The chemical and spectroscopic properties of elements are largely determined by the electrons in the outermost shell—the *valence* electrons. These are also the most readily removed electrons.

Although in the hydrogen atom lines can be observed corresponding to transitions between all possible energy states, the lines which are observed in more complex atoms are restricted by *selection rules*. Under the extreme conditions found in stellar atmospheres certain transitions can occur which are normally not permitted under laboratory conditions, the lines due to these transitions being known as *forbidden lines*. The existence of forbidden lines provides information on the conditions in stellar atmospheres. In complicated atoms, *doublets* and *multiplets*—groups of closely spaced lines due to transitions between sub-levels of particular energy levels which differ slightly in energy—are found and are usually easier to recognize than series.

The spectra of stars consist of a bright continuum of radiation on which are superimposed series of absorption lines, and under certain conditions emission lines, corresponding to conditions existing in the stellar atmospheres. The continuous spectrum is emitted from the 'surface' of the star (the *photosphere* in the case of the Sun) and the dark lines produced by absorption in the stellar atmosphere. The principal criterion for the production of particular lines is temperature.

The lines seen in stellar spectra are not generally perfectly sharp but have width and may shade off into the continuum (when they are said to have *wings*). The intensity contour of a line is known as the *line profile*, the deep part of the profile is the *core*. An ideal rectangular-shaped line can be constructed which subtracts the same area from the continuum radiation as the real line—the width of this rectangle being known as the *equivalent width* of the line. The profiles of spectral lines are due to several causes, notably (*a*) instrumental effects due to the finite resolution of the spectroscope, and (*b*) broadening of the line in the stellar atmosphere itself. The intensity of a line is due to the number of atoms in that state, the width of a line is due to a number of causes, some of which are listed below.

Natural Broadening. The width of an energy level increases the quicker the atom can return to a lower state from an excited state by a transition. Consequently, the higher energy levels tend to have a finite width, the effect of which is to smear out the energy difference corresponding to a transition, so that the line due to the transition is spread out around a central mean value of wavelength.

Doppler Broadening. Due to the Doppler effect (see below) the random velocities of the atoms in a stellar atmosphere will cause a small displacement in the wavelength of a given spectral line about a mean position. Since the observed spectra are due to the cumulative effect of the atoms in the stellar atmosphere the result of this effect is to broaden the spectral lines. This effect increases with temperature. Turbulence in stellar atmospheres and rapid rotation produce line broadening also due to the Doppler Effect.

Stark Effect. Strong local electric fields can split energy levels, so that averaged out over the surface of a star the resultant splitting of lines is smeared into a line-broadening effect. It is generally only noted for hydrogen and helium lines.

Zeeman Effect. A broadening of spectral lines can similarly occur in the presence of magnetic fields.

In addition to broadened lines a spectrum may show relatively broad *bands* due to the superposition of large numbers of lines. Such bands are due to the presence of molecules (which have highly complex spectra). Bands are found in the spectra of cool stars only, as high temperatures break down molecular structure.

As well as intrinsic lines produced in the stellar atmosphere, the spectrum of a star may be complicated by the superposition of *telluric lines* due to absorption in the Earth's atmosphere, and *interstellar lines* and bands due to absorption caused by passage through interstellar matter.

Doppler Effect. The measured wavelength of a spectral line compared to the laboratory wavelength of that line varies according to the velocity of the light source relative to the observer. If the source is receding, the wavelength of a spectral line is increased (i.e., displaced towards the red end of the visible spectrum, giving rise to the term *red shift*), while if the source is approaching, the wavelength is decreased (*blue shift*). This effect is of great importance since it allows the velocity of a light source to be determined. If the velocity v of the source is small compared to the velocity of light c, then the change in wavelength

$\varDelta\lambda$ resulting, compared with the wavelength in the stationary case, λ, is given by:

red shift $z = \varDelta\lambda/\lambda = v/c$. As the speed of the source approaches that of light then the relativistic form must be adopted, viz. $z = \varDelta\lambda/\lambda = \sqrt{(c+v)/(c-v)} - 1$.

Spectroscopes

Spectroscopes are instruments which break up light into a spectrum. The detailed design of these instruments is highly complex, and they have many different forms. Basically, however, the majority of spectroscopes have the following main components:

(i) A *light-dispersing element* to split white light into a spectrum. This may either be a *prism* or a *diffraction grating*. The prism splits light because the different wavelengths have different refractive indices. The diffraction grating (which may be either a transmission, or a reflection grating) uses a large number of closely spaced, parallel lines to cause differential interference of the light waves which results in the light being split into its component colours.

(ii) A *collimating system* which provides a parallel beam of white light. Usually, this consists of a slit to cut down stray light and to reduce the image size, behind which a telescope works in reverse to produce parallel light.

(iii) A *focusing system* to produce a sharp image of the spectrum.

(iv) A *recording system*—this may just simply be the eye, or it may be a photographic plate, or it may be a photo-electric recording system.

The principal components of a spectroscope, mentioned above, are drawn schematically in Fig. 6 to show the principle of operation of the instrument.

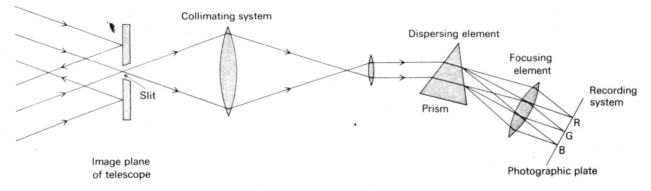

FIGURE 6. The spectroscope

Two specialized forms of the spectroscope are the *objective-prism spectroscope* and the *spectrohelioscope*. The former allows low dispersion spectra of a large number of stars to be photographed simultaneously. It consists of a large, low-dispersion prism or grating placed before the objective of the telescope. Thus on a direct photograph, the star's images are in the form of short spectra. The spectrohelioscope is a device which allows a picture of the Sun to be built up in the light of a single spectrum line only.

INVISIBLE ASTRONOMY

Radio Astronomy

The study of radio emission of astronomical objects has rapidly established itself as an important branch of astronomy. In fact much of the progress made in understanding the universe as a whole and the near-Earth region in particular has been due to the discoveries made by studying the radiation beyond the infra-red portion of the spectrum. It started in 1932, when Karl Jansky, in his investigations to find the causes of the crackling sounds heard in short-wave radio transmissions, discovered that the hissing noise was a maximum when the aerial pointed to a region in the sky in the constellation of

Sagittarius. Grote Reber, ten years later, located further radio sources in Cassiopeia and Cygnus, and also found that the Sun itself was a source of radio waves. After the 1939–45 war many countries, principally England, the United States, Australia and the Soviet Union, built observatories solely for study at radio wavelengths. Some of these have become as well known and as famous as the large optical observatories.

In radio astronomy, the signals are very weak and it is therefore necessary to use large collecting surfaces. These may take many forms, ranging from large arrays of dipoles covering several acres, such as that installed at the Mullard Radio Astronomy Observatory at Cambridge, to the steerable dish such as the 250 ft diameter Mark I dish at Jodrell Bank.

As with optical telescopes, the resolution depends on the wavelength used and the diameter of the dish, but since radio wavelengths are over 1000 times greater, it is impossible to construct dishes of a size capable of giving a resolution comparable with the large optical telescopes. Interferometric techniques have however been developed which have gone a long way to closing the gap.

Radio astronomy has been used to study all regions from the Moon to the most distant objects. Lunar investigations have been concerned with radiation from the surface at wavelengths around 8 mm. The planets have been studied at various wavelengths and, as in the case of Venus, it has been shown that this provides a capability of studying layers quite different from those seen in the optical telescope.

The Sun is a strong source of radio radiation. Some of this is thermal but some is not. The areas from which the radiation originates depends on the wavelength used. At centimetre wavelengths the area of the radio Sun is similar to that of the visible Sun, but radiation at metre wavelengths show a much larger body. The intensity of the radiation is linked closely to the sunspot cycle. Some non-thermal emission is linked with flare activity.

The radio emission from stars is normally too weak to be identified, but the interstellar hydrogen gas clouds have provided much information, enabling astronomers to plot the positions of these clouds and also their movements. Other molecules, such as those of hydroxyl (OH), water (H_2O), ammonia (NH_3) and formaldehyde (HCOH) have also been detected.

Other sources, such as remnants of supernovæ explosions (e.g. the Crab Nebula), the splitting apart of 2 galaxies (Cygnus A), extragalactic nebulæ and quasars, are sufficient to illustrate the range of objects being studied by the radio astronomer. For details, reference should be made to books devoted to radio astronomy.

The following are the strongest radio sources:

Taurus A	Crab Nebula
Puppis A	Peculiar nebulosity
Virgo A	Elliptical Galaxy M87
Centaurus A	Double Galaxy NGC 5128
Sagittarius A	Galactic Centre
Cygnus A	Double Galaxy
Cassiopeia A	Peculiar Galaxy

Radar Astronomy has so far been confined to objects relatively near to the Earth. The technique involves the transmitting of radio pulses and the recording of the signal which has been reflected from some distant object. Originally radar techniques were applied to the study of meteors. As a meteor rushes through the upper regions of the atmosphere, it leaves behind a trail of ionized gas which behaves as a very good reflector for short-wave radio signals. The studies of meteors by radar techniques have shown that, prior to Earth encounter, they were permanent members of the solar system.

With improved techniques, it has been possible to make radar contact with the Moon, Venus, Mercury, Mars and the solar corona. Radar studies of Venus have shown it to have a rotation period of 243 days retrograde, and have shown it to have a solid but very irregular surface.

Infra-Red Astronomy

The region attributed normally to infra-red radiation lies between wavelengths of 1 micron and 1 mm. Because of absorption by gases such as water vapour, carbon dioxide and ozone, it is not possible to study incoming radiation at all wavelengths within the above range from ground-based observatories. Use is therefore made of balloons, rockets and satellites. Certain wavelengths in the near infra-red, however, can be studied from stations situated in dry areas.

Infra-red studies of the Moon have shown localized hot spots, areas where the temperature is higher than the surrounding regions. In some cases these areas coincide with rayed craters such as Copernicus and Tycho. On Venus, it has been possible to detect small amounts of carbon monoxide and hydrogen chloride in a predominantly carbon dioxide atmosphere. The atmospheres of Mars and Jupiter have also been studied. Infra-red observations in the region 5–25 microns show that Jupiter and Saturn are both radiating more total energy than they receive from the Sun.

Outside the solar system, an infra-red source has been located in Orion, but no optical object has yet been associated directly with it. In other cases, infra-red sources have been linked with very faint stars. The centre of the galaxy has also been shown to be a source of such radiation. Other galaxies, especially the Seyfert galaxies, have been identified as IR sources.

Ultra-Violet Wave Astronomy

It is not possible to give precise ranges for the various types of radiation, but as a general guide the range 3400–500 Å is usually referred to as the UV range and the 40–500 Å range as the extreme ultra-violet (abbreviated to XUV). Note here that there is some overlap with the X-ray range.

In the UV range, concentration has been made on spectroscopic studies, using gratings and photographic plates in the case of rockets but for satellites use has been made of the grating spectrophotometer. In this instrument, the lens is often made of quartz. In the XUV region no lenses are used, just a pinhole, since the problems associated with diffraction are reduced considerably at such short wavelengths.

Recently, discrete sources emitting UV radiation have been identified. For details of these readers should refer to standard textbooks and scientific journals.

X-Ray Astronomy

Studies in this region of the spectrum (1–140 Å) have to be made from rockets and satellites. These are carried out either by counters such as Geiger–Muller counters or by specially designed telescopes. X-ray stars have been found in many parts of the sky, e.g. sources in the constellations of Scorpio and Cygnus, known as SCO X-1 and CYG X-1, both of which have been identified visually as faint blue stars. Another strong source is the Crab Nebula.

Extra-galactic sources include the radio source Cygnus A, the radio galaxy Virgo A (M87) and the quasar 3C 273. There is, in addition, evidence of a weak background emission, which has important implications in cosmology.

HINTS ON VISUAL OBSERVING

Notes on the observation of specific objects are included in the relevant sections of the text; this section deals only with a few topics pertaining to observation generally.

Direction in an Inverting Telescope

In the inverted view of an object, as seen in astronomical telescopes, to observers in the northern hemisphere the upper part of the field of view is south, while the lower part is north; east is on the right hand of the object, and west on its left side.

To observers south of the Equator the reverse is the case: the upper part of the field is north, and the lower south; east is on the left hand of the object, west, on its right.

For circumpolar stars, however (i.e. those a less number of degrees from the Pole than the latitude of the observer) the rule does not hold, as the observer is facing the other way, and objects on opposite sides of the Pole are moving in opposite directions.

North Preceding, etc. To overcome these difficulties in describing how to find a celestial object in the field of view, the phrases 'north (or south) preceding' or 'north (or south) following' a certain star are commonly used. *North* (or *south*) indicates that the object is nearer the north (or south) celestial pole than the star referred to; *preceding* that its Right Ascension is *less* than that of the reference star, and *following*, that its R.A. is *greater*, thus indicating the direction in which to find the required object. Figure 7 indicates how the hour circle—which coincides with the line SN in the diagram—lies with respect to the horizon in an inverting telescope in different positions, and how a position angle in consequence occupies varying positions in the field of view.

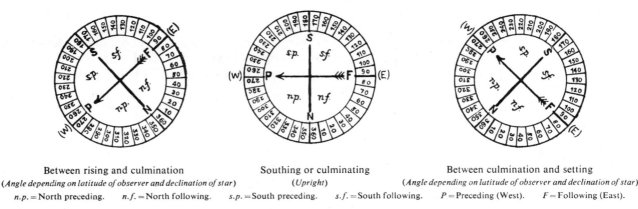

Between rising and culmination	Southing or culminating	Between culmination and setting
(Angle depending on latitude of observer and declination of star)	*(Upright)*	*(Angle depending on latitude of observer and declination of star)*

n.p. = North preceding.   *n.f.* = North following.   *s.p.* = South preceding.   *s.f.* = South following.   *P* = Preceding (West).   *F* = Following (East).

FIGURE 7.

In Fig. 7 the arrow denotes the apparent path of a star with reference to the horizon as it crosses the field of view of a fixed inverting telescope in the northern hemisphere. This path will be horizontal only when the object is on the meridian, but the relative positions remain unchanged.

Angular Distances on the Star Sphere. The following approximations are convenient for rough estimates; others can easily be made up from the star charts. The degrees are those of a great circle, as of Declination, or the celestial equator.

$\frac{1}{2}°$ = the angular diameter of the Moon

$1\frac{1}{4}°$ = δ to ε Orionis; or β to λ Crucis

$2°$ = α to γ Aquilæ; or α to σ Scorpii

$2\frac{1}{2}°$ = α to β Aquilæ; or α to δ Reticuli

$4°$ = α to β Canis Minoris; or α to β Crucis

$5°$ = α to β Ursæ Majoris; or α to β Centauri

The Star Sphere contains 41,253 square degrees.

Observing Faint Objects

'Dark adaptation' is very important, as the eye becomes much more sensitive to very faint impressions when it has been kept in the dark for some time. Once exposed to bright light the adaptation will be lost until a further period has been spent in darkness. Very faint objects can often best be detected by the use of *averted vision*: the eye is directed slightly to one side, while the observer's attention is concentrated on the spot where he believes the object to be. A slight change of focus is often restful to a tired eye.

Atmospheric Conditions

To get the best results, objects should be viewed when they are as far as possible above the horizon, i.e. when near culmination. Satisfactory observations cannot be made of objects at low altitudes, owing to the increased intervening thickness of the atmosphere, and the haze and mist which so often obscure the horizon. The nights when the sky is darkest, and the stars most brilliant, are not always the best for observations. Faint and ill-defined objects, such as some nebulæ, may, however, often be seen to advantage on such nights. If the stars twinkle much, it indicates that the air is unsteady and not very satisfactory for observation. During a slight haze, the air is often very steady, and splendid views of bright objects may then be obtained.

Seeing

The term *seeing* is used to indicate the quality of the observing conditions at the time of observation; it is an attempt by the observer to evaluate the effects of atmospheric turbulence and impurities on the results of his observing. An indication of the seeing is invaluable in comparing observations with others made on other occasions. The effects of poor seeing upon visual observation are, principally, small and erratic movements of the object and diffusion of its image (i.e. a star will have a point image in good seeing, with the diffraction pattern of the telescope if it is a bright star, but will dissolve into a large fuzzy blob in moments of poor seeing). In the case of a bright object having a visible disk, such as the Sun, poor seeing results in the limbs appearing to 'boil'; they appear really steady only in the most perfect conditions.

The observer should record the seeing by the use of carefully chosen phrases, in the light of his experience of good and bad seeing in the past—e.g. 'images unsteady and rather diffuse', 'limbs boiling', etc. As an additional record of the conditions it is useful in many types of observation, especially planetary work, to use a numerical scale. Numerous such scales have been devised over many years, but they are rather subjective and unreliable in use; it is therefore recommended that observers use the simplest—the well-tried scale devised by the great planetary observer E. M. Antoniadi. Most organized groups of planetary observers have adopted the Antoniadi Scale.

Antoniadi Scale. The observer indicates with a roman numeral the quality of the seeing according to the following scale:

I—Perfect seeing, without a quiver;
II—Slight undulations, with moments of calm lasting several seconds;
III—Moderate seeing, with larger air tremors;
IV—Poor seeing, with constant troublesome undulations;
V—Very bad seeing, scarcely allowing the making of a rough sketch.

Recording Observations

All observations should be written down at the time when they are made. The notes should be clearly worded, and should have entered on them the year, month, day, hour and minute (U.T.) of the observation, together with the aperture and power of the telescope, and the seeing conditions.

Observational records should be kept in a permanent observing book; many observers keep a specific book for each type of observation. Rough drawings made at the telescope should be worked up or copied as finished drawings as soon as possible after the observation is made, while it is fresh in the observer's mind.

Illumination of the work-book at the telescope, and of maps, charts, etc., is best provided by a small pocket torch or, ideally, a shaded, clip-on lamp, powered by a battery and with a switch. The illumination should be the faintest possible that will permit the work to be done, in order to minimize loss of dark adaptation. A bright light can be reduced by partially masking its aperture, or by substituting a bulb of higher voltage. Many observers prefer to use a red light, as it has very much less effect upon the eye's adaptation to faint light.

The Timing of Observations

The provision of reasonably accurate time at the telescope is important: many kinds of observation are enhanced in value if the U.T. at which the observation was made is recorded. Accurate setting of the observer's watch against a time signal may be sufficient for many purposes, but where the telescope is housed in some kind of permanent observatory building a clock fixed therein is a considerable advantage.

For many kinds of observational work it will be found very useful to have a clock or watch regulated to keep *sidereal time*; a normal watch set to gain 4 minutes a day will do for most purposes.

The Provision of Accurate Time at the telescope is often a difficult problem for the amateur observer. A fully equipped observatory should have clocks capable of maintaining both mean and sidereal time accurately over long periods, and some means of checking them—e.g. a suitable radio receiver to pick up broadcast time signals. Observers who lack these facilities but wish to make timed observations (e.g. lunar occultations, timing of central-meridian transits on Jupiter, etc.) should use a reliable meantime watch, and discover its gaining or losing rate by regular comparison with broadcast time signals or the Post Office speaking clock. Such comparisons should be made immediately before and after (and if necessary during) the observing session.

Accurate Timings can be made very effectively by the additional use of a *stop-watch* (the split-action type is especially recommended) or *chronograph*. There are various forms of the latter instrument, which provide for the comparison of clock and observation signals, or of clock and time signals (to determine the clock error) to considerable accuracy.

ASTRONOMICAL PHOTOGRAPHY

Photography has become widely used to record all types of astronomical objects, and there are a number of excellent books and articles on astronomical photography available, e.g. the Presidential Address to the B.A.A. by Dr G. Merton (*J. Brit. Astr. Ass.*, **63** (7), 1952). Many articles have appeared in the B.A.A. Journal in the 20 years since Merton's paper appeared.

The Camera

Any camera will do, though it will be appreciated that for the best results a degree of sophistication is required. The requirement is that the film or photographic plate should be held flat and rigid and aligned so that the astronomical image which falls upon it is perfectly in focus. A shutter mechanism is useful but not absolutely essential; many exposures have been made using a piece of cardboard or even an old hat as a shutter; simply being used to cut off the image-forming light rays from the film, removing for a short time and then replacing. In fact the normal camera mechanism can cause trouble by introducing excessive vibration, which of course causes blurring. The camera may be used with the lens in place (in which case it should be focused at infinity) or without a lens, using the eyepiece to project the image on to the film. (This is called eyepiece projection.) The film or plate can be mounted in the focal plane of the telescope, in which case only a plateholder or camera back is required—no lens or eyepiece.

The Film (or Plate)

For 35 mm work on the Moon and planets in black and white, it is recommended that a low- to medium-speed fine-grain emulsion is used. Where plenty of light is available, as in the case of the Moon, a film such as Ilford FP4 or Kodak Plus X is suitable, but any equivalent film can be employed. The effective speed of these films is nominally 125 ASA, but it may be increased by suitable development techniques. These techniques allow maximum contrast to be obtained without too much deterioration of the image due to increased grain-size. Typical developers are *Promicrol* or *Acutol*, diluted according to the manufacturer's instructions. Photographic positive can be obtained from the ordinary black and white films mentioned by using a proprietary 'reversal kit' at a very reasonable cost. These positives are most suitable for projection. If a plate camera is employed, then the choice of plate will depend on the subject to be photographed. Both Ilford and Kodak make scientific plates and will be pleased to advise the user on exposures, etc. A good plate for stellar work is the fast blue-sensitive Ilford SRO plate, which has a small reciprocity failure.

Colour Photography

The choice of which 35 mm colour-transparency film to use is something of a matter of taste. Typically Agfa CT-18, rated at about 50 ASA, gives reasonably balanced results although High Speed Ektachrome is a shade faster. CT-18 appears marginally red sensitive and is fast enough to record 11th magnitude stars using a 7·5 cm (3 in.) aperture, $f/5\cdot5$, 400 mm telephoto lens with an exposure of about ten minutes. At a focal ratio of $f/5\cdot5$ sky fogging should not be troublesome in exposures of less than half an hour.

Magnification. It is debatable whether it is better to photograph a small image at the telescope and enlarge in the darkroom under optimum conditions, or use the excellent telescope optics to produce a large image at the telescope and photograph directly. The merits of the first method are a bright image, short exposure time, less effect of atmospheric turbulence or drive imperfections, and enlargement under controlled conditions in the darkroom. The demerits are a very small primary image—which means high enlargement, necessitating excellent enlarging equipment and a very fine-grain film (and this means a very slow film). This in turn means a longer exposure and the difficulties that this entails. Whichever method is employed the use of a reflex viewing system will make possible accurate focusing and allow the fleeting moments of good seeing to be utilized.

Effective Focal Ratio. When eyepiece projection is used the effective focal ratio, or f number, of the optical system differs from the focal ratio of the objective on its own and exposure times should be adjusted accordingly.

A useful *approximate* formula is

$$\mathrm{EFR} = Fa/fD$$

where F = focal length of objective (or equivalent focal length of a Cassegrain system)
   f = focal length of eyepiece
   a = distance from the eye lens of the eyepiece to the film plane (which should be several times f)
   D = diameter of objective

The f number is in fact increased by the degree of image magnification given by the projecting eyepiece and photographic exposures of extended objects will need to be increased by the square of this quantity.

For example suppose $F=48$ in., $D=6$ in., $f=\frac{1}{2}$ in., and $a=3$ in. The EFR is approximately equal to $48 \times 3/6 \times \frac{1}{2}=48$ compared with the f number of the objective of 8. Exposure times would need to be increased by a factor of 36 in this case.

Photographing the Sun

As always when dealing with the Sun, care is essential. An extremely bright image is available and very high shutter speeds are a necessity even with a neutral density filter interposed. It is equally easy to photograph a projected solar image. One advantage of the bright image is that tracking becomes significantly less important. Sunspot photography can be carried out using eyepiece projection, and filters can often be used to enhance the image.

Photographing the Moon

The Moon is a comparatively bright object, but nevertheless care is essential if a good photograph is to be obtained. For all practical purposes the Moon moves at the same rate in R.A. as the stars, i.e. 15 seconds of arc in 1 second of real time. Assuming a telescope of 11 cm ($4\frac{1}{2}$ in.) aperture the resolution (detail seen) may be calculated from $4.52/D$, where D is the diameter of the mirror in inches, so that in this case the theoretical resolution is about 1 second of arc which is about 1 mile on the Moon. Therefore to 'stop' the Moon and achieve detail of one mile the exposure should be less than 1/15 second. This means that to avoid under-exposure a small lunar image should be employed, probably at the focal plane of the telescope. For a larger image (and hence a fainter one), a longer exposure is required and a telescope drive in Right Ascension is essential.

At certain times during a lunation the Declination of the Moon changes quite rapidly, up to 7° per day or 1 second of arc in three seconds of real time. Hence if the exposure time exceeds three seconds, a Declination drive is necessary.

Planetary Photography

Here a telescope is essential if any detail is to be recorded. Eyepiece projection is commonly used and exposures depend on the usual parameters—aperture of telescope, brightness of planet, chosen EFR, speed of film, and so on. Atmospheric conditions also play a large part and in all cases a rigid mounting and accurate and steady drive is essential. Typically the exposure for Saturn when it is near opposition (magnitude 0·7) with an EFR of 80 on a 20 cm aperture telescope on fine grain (125 ASA) film, is about three seconds.

Photographing the Stars

Star trails may be obtained by pointing the camera in the region of *Polaris* and leaving the shutter open for some time, e.g. one hour. To photograph stars and stellar clusters, however, requires a quite different technique from either lunar or planetary photography.

Stars may be regarded as point sources at an infinite distance. It is required to record stellar images in the presence of the background illumination of the night sky (sky fog). Assuming a homogeneous night-sky background, the number of photons captured is proportional to the diameter of the lens (or mirror), as in the case of a star, but the area of sky from which they are collected depends on the field of view of the lens/mirror which in turn depends on the focal length. Generally the larger the diameter of the lens/mirror the better. Since the intensity of the stellar image is independent of F, however, and the intensity of the night sky is proportional to $1/F^2$, it is apparent that for stellar photography the longest focal length should be used for the longest possible exposure. In practice, of course, other points must be considered. These are:

(*a*) Stars are not true point sources (due to the effects of the Earth's atmosphere and imperfections in the telescope) and do not give point images on the film.

(*b*) All films exhibit reciprocity failure, and there is no point in continuing the exposure when the rate of collecting information tends to zero.

(*c*) The longer the focal length, the narrower the field of view and the higher the magnification. The telescope drive assumes paramount importance and guiding is essential.

(*d*) The field of view must be sufficiently wide to include all stars required. Thus in the special case of stellar photography the more conventional rules do not apply, e.g. the 'speed' or *f*-number of a lens is no guide to its usefulness. A 35 mm lens (typically 48 mm, $f/3.5$) is inferior to a '$2\frac{1}{4}$ in. square' camera having a lens $f/6.3$ if such things as definition, colour correction and flat film plane are ignored. Also, for a given focal length, increasing the lens diameter will reduce the exposure time required to reach a given fog level, and will not significantly increase the number of fainter stars recorded. Finally, for a given lens diameter increasing the focal length will give a gain in reaching fainter stars since fogging will be reduced, and it becomes possible to use a longer exposure. Of course attendant difficulties of tracking and guiding for the longer period with a high magnification must now be appreciated and compensated for. If the tracking is not accurate faint star images will be spread over the emulsion and will not be recorded.

Extended Objects

For apparently diffuse objects normal photographic techniques apply, i.e. a faster lens is better than a slow lens. A comet, nebula or galaxy may be likened generally to a region of sky where the background brightness is locally enhanced. Since no improvement can be obtained by using a long focal length lens the shortest possible exposure should be used, i.e. employ the fastest lens available compatible with scale size. *Note*: For most of these objects the standard 35 mm lens has too short a focal length to show any detail. Generally it is necessary to use the focal plane of the telescope. Here, of course, a guide telescope is vital. The focal length of the guide system should be as great as possible and certainly not less than ten times the focal length of the photographic system.

UNITS, SYMBOLS AND ABBREVIATIONS

Units—General

In astronomy, as in all the physical sciences, the metric system of measurement has long been preferred; the usual c.g.s. (centimetre–gram–second) system of units for physical quantities were, however, supplemented by a number of units created especially for various astronomical requirements. In recent years almost all nations have begun to adopt the metric system for most civil purposes, and the *SI system* of units (Système International d'Unités) has become the accepted standard. In common with all scientific disciplines, astronomy will in future use SI units also, although certain of the special astronomical units are likely to remain in use also for many years to come. Those units most commonly used in astronomy are set out below.

27

Metric Units

Basic units	length	metre, m
	volume	litre, l
	mass	gram, g

Special units 1 micron $(\mu) = 10^{-6}$ metres $\Big\}$ used in wavelengths
1 Ångström $(Å) = 10^{-10}$ metres

Other units met in astronomical literature

tonne (or metric ton, t) = megagram (Mg)   hertz (Hz) = cycles per second
   or 1000 kg   megahertz (MHz) = 10^{6} Hz
newton (N) = 1 kg m s^{-2} electronvolt (eV) = $1 \cdot 6021 \times 10^{-19}$ J
joule (J) = 1 newton metre (Nm) = 1 kg m^{2}s^{-2} kiloelectronvolt (keV) = 10^{3} eV
watt (W) = joule per second (J s^{-1})
hectare (ha) = 10^{4} square metres

Unit conversion factors

1 cm = $0 \cdot 3937$ in.	1 in. = $25 \cdot 4$ mm
1 m = $1 \cdot 0936$ yd	1 ft = $0 \cdot 3048$ m
1 km = $0 \cdot 6214$ mile	1 yd = $0 \cdot 9144$ m
	1 mile = $1 \cdot 6093$ km
	1 nautical mile (n.m.) = $1 \cdot 8532$ km
1 sq km = $0 \cdot 3861$ sq mile	1 sq mile = $259 \cdot 0$ ha
1 kg = $2 \cdot 2046$ lb	1 lb = $0 \cdot 4536$ kg
1 tonne = $0 \cdot 9842$ ton	1 ton = $1 \cdot 016$ tonnes

Notation. Large numbers, such as are encountered in astronomy, are expressed in the metric system using contracted notation; this employs the factor 10, with superscript indices. The index figure may be taken as indicating the number of ciphers to be added after the 10. A minus sign before the superscript index figure indicates a fractional number, i.e. 1 divided by that number; thus $10^{-6} = 1/1,000,000$th, or $\cdot 000001$, from which it will be noted that negative index figures show the position, after the decimal point, of the first significant figure of the decimal fraction, the number of ciphers before the first significant figure being one less than the index number. The following are examples of the use of decimal factors:

$$1 \cdot 23 \times 10^{6} = 1 \cdot 23 \times 1,000,000 = 1,230,000.$$

$$1 \cdot 23 \times 10^{-6} = 1 \cdot 23 \times \cdot 000001 = \cdot 00000123.$$

Note that if the index of 10 is chosen such that the figure before the decimal in the other factor is in the range 1 to 9, the index of 10 (both $+$ and $-$) will be the characteristic of the logarithm of the number. In the SI system it is recommended that prefixes adopted should be limited to the form $10^{\pm 3n}$, however, thus: 10^{3}, 10^{6}, etc., by using two- or three-digit numbers before the decimal point in the first factor, i.e. $123 \cdot 4 \times 10^{3}$ is preferred to $1 \cdot 234 \times 10^{5}$. The factors 10^{2}, 10^{-1} and 10^{-2} are, however, frequently used in practice.

Prefixes for multiples and sub-multiples:

10^{12}	tera	T		10^{-2}	centi	c
10^{9}	giga	G		10^{-3}	milli	m
10^{6}	mega	M		10^{-6}	micro	μ
10^{3}	kilo	k		10^{-9}	nano	n
10^{2}	hecto	h		10^{-12}	pico	p
10	deka	da		10^{-15}	femto	f
10^{-1}	deci	d		10^{-18}	atto	a

The words *billion* and *billionth* should be avoided whenever possible because of the ambiguity of meaning.

1 billion (British) = 10^{12}	1 billionth (British) = 10^{-12}	1 dex = power of 10,
1 billion (American) = 10^{9}	1 billionth (American) = 10^{-9}	e.g. 1 million = 10^{6} = 6 dex

Measurement of Length and Distance

Angular Measure. The distances used in positional astronomy are usually measured 'in the celestial sphere' in angular measure, with the usual units:

degrees (°), minutes (') and seconds (") of arc.

Ångström Unit. The unit most commonly used for the measurement of wavelengths in astronomical spectroscopy, named after the nineteenth-century pioneer spectroscopist, A. J. Ångström.

One ångström unit equals one ten-millionth of a millimetre, or 1×10^{-10} m.

Astronomical Unit. The unit used for distance measurement within the solar system; also the base-line for measurements of stellar parallax. It is very nearly the mean distance of the Earth from the Sun, 149,600,000 km (92,957,130 miles). It is usually abbreviated A.U.

Solar Parallax. The mean equatorial horizontal parallax of the Sun is one of the fundamental measured dimensions in astronomy; it is the angle subtended by the Earth's mean equatorial radius at the mean distance of the Sun. Accurate determinations of the solar parallax, made from observations of the motion of, e.g., minor planets passing close to the Earth, provide the means of evaluating the mean Earth–Sun distance, or one A.U. The adopted value of the solar parallax is 8"·79405, based upon the above value for the Astronomical Unit.

Unit Distance. The angular diameter of a planet 'at unit distance', used when comparing the diameters of planets, is that which the planet would have, as seen from the centre of the Sun, from a distance of exactly one A.U.

Light Year. A unit of distance, still much used in descriptive astronomy; usually abbreviated to l.y. It is equivalent to the distance travelled in one year by a particle travelling at the velocity of light (299,792 km/s), i.e. $94,607 \times 10^8$ km or 63,240 A.U.

Parsec. A unit used to express large distances in astronomy. It is the distance at which an object would have a parallax of one second of arc, taking the mean Earth–Sun distance (1 A.U.) as baseline. One parsec (abbreviated pc) is equivalent to 3·2616 l.y. or 206,265 A.U. (about $30,857 \times 10^9$ km). Extra-galactic distances are measured in *kiloparsecs* (kpc, = 1000 pc) or *megaparsecs* (Mpc, = 1,000,000 pc).

Distance Units	= Parsecs	= a Parallax of	= Astronomical Units	= Light Years	= Kilometres	= Miles
Light year	0·3066	3·2616"	63,240	1	$94,607 \times 10^8$	5879×10^9
Parsec	1	1·000"	206,265	3·2616	$30,857 \times 10^9$	$19,174 \times 10^9$

Measurement of Time

It is usual practice in astronomy to combine the date and time of an observation and to express it in the usual time units but arranged in descending order of size, thus:

1973 February 11 d 21 h 41 m 45·005 s.

The recommended abbreviations are:

a (or y)	year	msec	millisecond
d	day	m.y.	million years
h (or hr*)	hour		(used in geological texts)
m (or min*)	minute		
s (or sec*)	second		* May be used when necessary to avoid ambiguity.

Symbols and Abbreviations—General

There is no unique system of symbols, abbreviations and contractions for use in astronomical literature, but as in most disciplines considerable efforts have been made to create a standard usage which will, if universally adopted, greatly facilitate the international exchange of information. The most important contribution to a standard notation is the extensive list of recommended symbols published by the International Astronomical Union in 1938 (*Trans. Int. Astr. Un.* **6**, 345–55). Most of the recommended notation has remained in use ever since, with a few additions necessitated by recent developments. A selection of the most commonly encountered letter symbols are listed in Table 2, and some special symbols widely used in astronomical publications in Table 3.

TABLE 2. LETTER SYMBOLS USED IN ASTRONOMY

SPHERICAL AND POSITIONAL ASTRONOMY

A (or Az)	Azimuth	$\mathbb{C}$	Mean longitude of the Moon
h	Altitude	l	Heliocentric longitude
z	Zenith distance	b	Heliocentric latitude
ϕ (or φ)	Altitude of north pole	g	Acceleration due to gravity
H (or t)	Hour angle	P_0	Equatorial horizontal parallax
α	Right ascension	p	General precession in longitude in one tropical year
δ	Declination		
θ	Sidereal time	p_1	Luni-solar precession in one tropical year
θ_0	Sidereal time at mean midnight	p_2	Planetary precession in one tropical year
E	Equation of time (true solar time minus mean solar time)	p_a	Annual precession in right ascension
		p_δ	Annual precession in declination
L	Geographical longitude	T	Observed clock time of transit
ϕ (or φ)	Geographical latitude	ΔT	Clock correction (+ve if clock slow)
ϵ	Obliquity of the ecliptic	p (or P.A.)	Position angle (measured eastwards from north point)
λ	Geocentric longitude		
β	Geocentric latitude	d	Angular distance

CELESTIAL MECHANICS

Elements of planetary orbit		ϕ (or φ)	Angle of eccentricity (from $e = \sin \phi$)
a	Semi-major axis	q	Perihelion distance
e	Eccentricity	P	Orbital period
i	Inclination	M	Mean anomaly
Ω	Longitude of ascending node	M_0	Mean anomaly at epoch
ϖ	Longitude of perihelion	E	Eccentric anomaly
T	Time of epoch	v	True anomaly
n	Mean angular motion per solar day	r	Radius vector from centre of Sun
$\mho$	Longitude of descending node	R	Distance between centres of Sun and Earth
G	Gravitational constant	L (or $\odot$)	Sun's geocentric longitude with reference to ecliptic
k	Gaussian gravitational constant		
m	Planetary mass (in units of solar mass)	B	Sun's geocentric latitude with reference to ecliptic
t	Time of observation		
T	Time of perihelion	Δ	Geocentric distance of object

ASTROPHYSICS

I	Intensity	V	Radial velocity
m	Apparent magnitude	T	Tangential velocity
m_v	Apparent visual magnitude	W	Spatial velocity
m_{pg}	Apparent photographic magnitude	π	Parallax in seconds of arc
m_{pv}	Apparent photovisual magnitude	r	Distance in parsecs
m_{rad}	Apparent radiometric magnitude	l	Galactic (i.e. galactocentric) longitude
m_{bol}	Apparent bolometric magnitude	b	Galactic latitude
m_{pe}	Apparent photoelectric magnitude		[N.B. l^{I}, b^{I}: galactic co-ordinates according to pre-1959 system; l^{II}, b^{II}: system adopted by I.A.U. in 1959]
M	Absolute magnitude (corresponding to standard distance of 10 parsecs); subscripts as for m		
		μ	Total proper motion, in seconds of arc per year
E	Colour excess		
λ	Wavelength	μ_a	Proper motion in right ascension, in seconds of time per year
λ_e	Effective wavelength		
v	Frequency	μ_δ	Proper motion in declination, in seconds of arc per year
T	Temperature		
T_e	Effective temperature	a	Absorption coefficient, in interstellar space, in magnitudes per 1000 parsecs
T_c	Colour temperature		

MISCELLANEOUS

$\mathscr{L}$	Luminosity	c	Velocity of light
$\mathscr{V}$	Volume	p.e.	Probable error
$\mathscr{R}$	Radius	s.d.	Standard deviation
$\mathscr{M}$	Mass	s.e.	Standard error
ρ	Mean density		

TABLE 3. SPECIAL SYMBOLS USED IN ASTRONOMY

○	Sun	○	Full Moon	♈ or	Aries
⊕ or ♁	Earth	●	New Moon	♉ or	Taurus
☿	Mercury	◔ or ◑	Gibbous Moon	♊ or	Gemini
♀	Venus	◐ or ☽	First Quarter Moon	♋ or	Cancer
♂	Mars	◑ or ☾	Last Quarter Moon	♌ or	Leo
♃	Jupiter	☆ or ★	Star	♍ or	Virgo
♄	Saturn	☍	Opposition	♎ or	Libra
♅ or ♅	Uranus	☌	Conjunction	♏ or	Scorpio
♆ or ♆	Neptune	□	Quadrature	♐ or	Sagittarius
♇	Pluto	☊	Ascending node	♑ or	Capricornus
⑭	Minor planet	☋	Descending node	♒ or	Aquarius
☄	Comet	♈	First Point of Aries	♓ or	Pisces
☾	Moon	♎	First Point of Libra		

Contractions and Abbreviations. The contractions and abbreviations found in astronomical literature are many and varied; those used for the names of notable publications, organizations and catalogues are listed elsewhere in this volume. A few of the others most frequently encountered are detailed in Table 4. They occur both with and without full points, e.g. UV and U.V.

TABLE 4. CONTRACTIONS AND ABBREVIATIONS USED IN ASTRONOMY

C.I.	Colour index	H.R. [diagram]	Hertzsprung–Russell diagram	P.A.	Position angle
C.M.	Central meridian			P.M.	Proper motion
Dec.	Declination	I.R.	Infra-red	P.Z.T.	Photographic zenith tube
E.T.	Ephemeris Time	J.D.	Julian Day	R.A.	Right ascension
G.E.	Greatest elongation	J.P.	Julian Period	S.D.	Semi-diameter
G.C.T.	Greenwich Civil Time	L.H.A.	Local hour angle	T.C.	Transit circle
G.H.A.	Greenwich hour angle	L.S.T.	Local sidereal time	U.T.	Universal Time
G.M.A.T.	Greenwich Mean Astronomical Time	Mag.	Magnitude	U.V.	Ultra-violet
		N.P.D.	North polar distance	X.U.V.	X-ray and extreme UV region
G.M.T.	Greenwich Mean Time	N.P.S.	North polar sequence		
H.I.	Heat index	O – C	Observed minus computed (residuals)	Z.D.	Zenith distance
H.P.	Horizontal parallax				

Significance of Plus and Minus

For Direction, + indicates (*a*) northwards, (*b*) 'direct' or 'positive' motion—i.e. to the left, or eastwards, when looking south; − indicates (*a*) southwards, (*b*) 'retrograde' or 'negative' motion—i.e. to the right, or westwards, when looking south.

For Variable Stars, + indicates that the maximum or minimum is later than the predicted date, − that it is earlier.

For Comets, + indicates later than ephemeris prediction, − indicates earlier.

For the Planetographic Declination of the Earth, + indicates that the planet's north pole is tilted towards the Earth, and − the south pole.

Declination
+ = north of celestial equator
− = south of celestial equator

Latitude
+ = north of equator
− = south of equator

Longitude
+ = west of prime meridian
− = east of prime meridian

Libration
(in latitude):
+ = mean centre displaced to south
− = mean centre displaced to north

Libration (in longitude)
+ = mean centre displaced to east
− = mean centre displaced to west

Light-time
+ = later
− = earlier

Magnitude
+ = fainter than mag. 0·0
− = brighter than mag. 0·0

Position Angle of Sun's Axis
+ = north pole east of the hour circle
− = north pole west of the hour circle

Proper Motion and Precession
(in Declination):
+ = northwards
− = southwards

Proper Motion and Precession
(in Right Ascension):
+ = direct
− = retrograde

Radial Velocity
+ = receding from Sun
− = approaching Sun

Saturn's Rings
+ = Earth north of ring-plane
− = Earth south of ring-plane

Sun's Equator
+ = south of disk centre
− = north of disk centre

II. USEFUL TABLES

TABLE 5. KILOMETRES CONVERTED INTO MILES

Multiples by 10, 100, 1000, shift decimal point one, two, three places to the right.

km	miles	km	miles	km	miles	km	miles	km	miles	km	miles	km	miles	km	miles
1	0·621	6	3·728	11	6·835	16	9·942	21	13·049	30	18·641	55	34·176	80	49·710
2	1·243	7	4·350	12	7·456	17	10·563	22	13·670	35	21·748	60	37·282	85	52·817
3	1·864	8	4·971	13	8·078	18	11·185	23	14·292	40	24·855	65	40·389	90	55·923
4	2·485	9	5·592	14	8·699	19	11·806	24	14·913	45	27·962	70	43·496	95	59·030
5	3·107	10	6·214	15	9·321	20	12·427	25	15·534	50	31·069	75	46·603	100	62·137

TABLE 6. MILES CONVERTED INTO KILOMETRES

mi	km	mi	km	mi	km	mi	km	mi	km	mi	km	mi	km	mi	km
1	1·61	6	9·66	11	17·70	16	25·75	21	33·80	30	48·28	55	88·51	80	128·74
2	3·22	7	11·27	12	19·31	17	27·36	22	35·41	35	56·33	60	96·56	85	136·79
3	4·83	8	12·87	13	20·92	18	28·97	23	37·02	40	64·37	65	104·61	90	144·84
4	6·44	9	14·48	14	22·53	19	30·58	24	38·63	45	72·42	70	112·65	95	152·89
5	8·05	10	16·09	15	24·14	20	32·19	25	40·24	50	80·47	75	120·70	100	160·93

TABLE 7. RATIO OF BRIGHTNESS

Ratio of brightness, fainter or brighter, for a difference in magnitude ('Diff.').

Diff.	Ratio	Diff.	Ratio	Diff.	Ratio	Diff.	Ratio	Diff.	Ratio	Diff.	Ratio
0·1	1·10	0·9	2·29	1·75	5·01	5·5	158·49	10·5	15,849		
0·2	1·20	1·0	2·51	1·8	5·25	6·0	251·19	11·0	25,119		
0·25	1·26	1·1	2·75	1·9	5·75	6·5	398·11	11·5	39,811		
0·3	1·32	1·2	3·02	2·0	6·31	7·0	630·96	12·0	63,096		
0·4	1·45	1·25	3·16	2·5	10·00	7·5	1000·00	12·5	100,000		
0·5	1·58	1·3	3·31	3·0	15·85	8·0	1584·9	13·0	158,490		
0·6	1·74	1·4	3·63	3·5	25·12	8·5	2511·9	13·5	251,190		
0·7	1·91	1·5	3·98	4·0	39·81	9·0	3981·1	14·0	398,110		
0·75	2·00	1·6	4·37	4·5	63·10	9·5	6309·6	14·5	630,960		
0·8	2·09	1·7	4·79	5·0	100·00	10·0	10,000·0	15·0	1,000,000		

TABLE 8. DISTANCE AND MAGNITUDE

Increase of distance ('Dist.') for a difference ('Diff.') of 1 to 20 magnitudes. Thus a Mag. 5 star placed 100 times farther away would be 10 magnitudes fainter, or Mag. 15. (Mag. diff. × 0·2 = logarithm of distance increase.)

Diff.	Dist.	Diff.	Dist.	Diff.	Dist.	Diff.	Dist.	Diff.	Dist.	Diff.	Dist.	Diff.	Dist.	Diff.	Dist.
½	1·26	3	3·98	6	15·85	9	63·10	12	251·2	15	1000	18	3981	19½	7943
1	1·59	4	6·31	7	25·12	10	100·0	13	398·1	16	1585	18½	5012	20	10,000
2	2·51	5	10·00	8	39·81	11	158·5	14	631·0	17	2512	19	6310		

TABLE 9. LIGHT YEARS EQUIVALENT TO PARSECS

Multiples by 10, 100, shift point one, two, places to right: pc, parsecs; l.y., light years.

pc	l.y.	pc	l.y.	pc	l.y.	pc	l.y.	pc	l.y.	pc	l.y.	pc	l.y.	pc	l.y.	pc	l.y.	pc	l.y.	pc	l.y.
1	3·262	6	19·57	11	35·90	16	52·18	21	68·49	26	84·80	31	101·1	36	117·4	41	133·7	46	150·0	60	195·7
2	6·523	7	22·83	12	39·14	17	55·45	22	71·75	27	88·06	32	104·4	37	120·7	42	137·0	47	153·3	70	228·3
3	9·785	8	26·09	13	42·40	18	58·71	23	75·02	28	91·32	33	107·6	38	123·9	43	140·2	48	156·5	80	260·9
4	13·05	9	29·35	14	45·66	19	61·97	24	78·28	29	94·59	34	110·9	39	127·2	44	143·5	49	159·8	90	293·5
5	16·31	10	32·62	15	48·92	20	65·23	25	81·54	30	97·85	35	114·2	40	130·5	45	146·8	50	163·1	100	326·2

TABLE 10. PARSECS AND LIGHT YEARS EQUIVALENT TO ANY PARALLAX (π)

For ·0001, ·0002, etc., move parsec or light year decimal one place to right.

$\pi('')$	pc	l.y.	$\pi('')$	pc	l.y.	$\pi('')$	pc	l.y.	$\pi('')$	pc	l.y.	$\pi('')$	pc	l.y.	$\pi('')$	pc	l.y.
·001	1000	3262·0	·021	47·62	155·3	·041	24·39	79·55	·061	16·39	53·47	·081	12·35	40·27	·12	8·33	27·18
·002	500·0	1631·0	·022	45·45	148·2	·042	23·81	77·66	·062	16·13	52·61	·082	12·20	39·77	·14	7·14	23·30
·003	333·3	1087·0	·023	43·48	141·8	·043	23·26	75·85	·063	15·87	51·77	·083	12·05	39·30	·16	6·25	20·38
·004	250·0	815·4	·024	41·67	135·9	·044	22·73	74·13	·064	15·63	50·96	·084	11·90	38·83	·18	5·56	18·12
·005	200·0	652·3	·025	40·00	130·5	·045	22·22	72·48	·065	15·38	50·18	·085	11·76	38·37	·20	5·00	16·31
·006	166·7	543·6	·026	38·46	125·4	·046	21·74	70·90	·066	15·15	49·42	·086	11·63	37·92	·22	4·55	14·82
·007	142·9	465·9	·027	37·04	120·8	·047	21·28	69·40	·067	14·93	48·68	·087	11·49	37·49	·24	4·17	13·59
·008	125·0	407·7	·028	35·71	116·5	·048	20·83	67·95	·068	14·71	47·96	·088	11·36	37·06	·25	4·00	13·05
·009	111·1	362·4	·029	34·48	112·5	·049	20·41	66·56	·069	14·49	47·27	·089	11·24	36·65	·26	3·85	12·54
·010	100·0	361·6	·030	33·33	108·7	·050	20·00	65·23	·070	14·29	46·59	·090	11·11	36·24	·28	3·57	11·65
·011	90·91	296·5	·031	32·26	105·2	·051	19·61	63·95	·071	14·08	45·94	·091	10·99	37·84	·30	3·33	10·87
·012	83·33	271·8	·032	31·25	101·9	·052	19·23	62·72	·072	13·89	45·30	·092	10·87	35·45	·35	2·86	9·319
·013	76·92	250·9	·033	30·30	98·84	·053	18·87	61·54	·073	13·70	44·68	·093	10·75	35·07	·40	2·50	8·154
·014	71·43	233·0	·034	29·41	95·93	·054	18·52	60·40	·074	13·51	44·07	·094	10·64	34·70	·45	2·22	7·248
·015	66·67	217·4	·035	28·57	93·18	·055	18·18	59·30	·075	13·33	43·49	·095	10·53	34·33	·50	2·00	6·523
·016	62·50	203·8	·036	27·78	90·60	·056	17·86	58·24	·076	13·16	42·91	·096	10·42	33·97	·55	1·82	5·930
·017	58·82	191·8	·037	27·03	88·15	·057	17·54	57·22	·077	12·99	42·36	·097	10·31	33·62	·60	1·67	5·436
·018	55·56	181·2	·038	26·32	85·83	·058	17·24	56·23	·078	12·82	41·81	·098	10·20	33·28	·65	1·54	5·018
·019	52·63	171·7	·039	25·64	83·63	·059	16·95	55·28	·079	12·66	41·29	·099	10·10	32·94	·70	1·43	4·659
·020	50·00	163·1	·040	25·00	81·54	·060	16·62	54·36	·080	12·50	40·77	·100	10·00	32·62	·75	1·33	4·349

TABLE 11. SUNSET AND SUNRISE

The time varies slightly from year to year, but Table 11(B) will give the Apparent or True (Sundial) time of both sunset or sunrise within a few minutes, in both northern and southern latitudes.

To find the Mean Time equivalent, add or subtract the value given for the Equation of Time (E). A further correction is required for longitude, of 4 minutes for each degree west or east of the prime meridian; added if west, subtracted if east.

To obtain the time of sunrise, subtract the time of sunset (from Table 11(B)) from 12 h 00 m, and adjust for both Equation of Time and longitude, as for sunset. Thus sunrise on May 25 in latitude 45° north, longitude 4° west of prime meridian, is at 04 h 38 m (12 h – 7 h 35 m, – 3 m for E, +16 m for longitude).

Note that the value of E given here is the negative of the Equation of Time in Table 1.

(A) Earliest and Latest Sunrise and Sunset in Different North Latitudes

There are two 'earliests' and 'latests' in low latitudes

Latitude	0°		10°		20°	30°	35°	40°	45°	50°	55°	60°
Rising. Earliest: a.m.	Nov. 4 5.40	May 16 5.53	May 30 5.37	Oct. 11 5.48	June 7 5.20	June 11 4.58	June 14 4.45	June 15 4.30	June 17 4.12	June 18 3.50	June 19 3.20	June 19 2.35
Latest: a.m.	Feb. 12 6.11	July 28 6.03	Aug. 24 5.51	Jan. 27 6.23	Jan. 18 6.38	Jan. 11 6.57	Jan. 8 7.09	Jan. 6 7.22	Jan. 3 7.39	Jan. 1 7.59	Dec. 29 8.26	Dec. 28 9.04
Setting. Earliest: p.m.	Nov. 2 5.47	May 14 6.00	Nov. 17 5.35	Apr. 10 6.10	Nov. 26 5.19	Dec. 3 5.00	Dec. 6 4.48	Dec. 8 4.35	Dec. 11 4.18	Dec. 13 3.58	Dec. 15 3.32	Dec. 17 2.53
Latest: p.m.	Feb. 10 6.18	July 25 6.10	July 12 6.25	Mar. 17 6.11	July 5 6.43	July 2 7.05	June 30 7.18	June 28 7.33	June 27 7.51	June 26 8.13	June 25 8.43	June 24 9.28

TABLE 11 (contd) (B) APPARENT (SUNDIAL) TIME OF SUNSET

Northern Latitudes				0°	10°	20°	30°	35°	40°	45°	50°	52°	54°	56°	58°	60°	Southern Latitudes			
Date	E	Date	E	h m	h m	h m	h m	h m	h m	h m	h m	h m	h m	h m	h m	h m	Date	E	Date	E
Dec. 21	−2	Dec. 21	−2	6 04	5 46	5 28	5 06	4 54	4 40	4 23	4 02	3 52	3 41	3 28	3 14	2 56	Jun. 21	+1	Jun. 21	+1
24	−1	19	3	6 04	5 47	5 28	5 07	4 55	4 40	4 23	4 03	3 53	3 42	3 29	3 14	2 57	24	2	18	+1
27	+1	16	5	6 04	5 47	5 28	5 07	4 55	4 40	4 24	4 03	3 54	3 43	3 30	3 15	2 58	27	3	16	0
30	2	14	6	6 04	5 47	5 28	5 07	4 55	4 41	4 25	4 04	3 55	3 44	3 31	3 16	2 59	30	3	13	0
Jan. 1	3	11	7	6 04	5 47	5 29	5 08	4 56	4 42	4 26	4 05	3 56	3 45	3 33	3 18	3 01	July 3	4	10	−1
4	+5	8	−8	6 04	5 47	5 29	5 08	4 57	4 43	4 27	4 07	3 57	3 46	3 35	3 21	3 04	6	+4	7	−2
7	6	5	10	6 04	5 47	5 30	5 09	4 58	4 44	4 28	4 09	4 00	3 49	3 38	3 24	3 08	9	5	3	2
10	7	2	11	6 04	5 48	5 31	5 11	4 59	4 46	4 30	4 12	4 03	3 53	3 41	3 28	3 13	12	5	May 31	3
13	8	Nov. 29	12	6 04	5 48	5 32	5 12	5 01	4 48	4 33	4 15	4 06	3 56	3 45	3 33	3 18	15	6	28	3
16	10	26	13	6 04	5 48	5 32	5 13	5 02	4 50	4 36	4 17	4 09	3 59	3 49	3 37	3 23	19	6	25	3
19	11	23	14	6 04	5 49	5 33	5 15	5 04	4 52	4 39	4 21	4 13	4 03	3 54	3 42	3 29	22	6	22	4
22	11	20	15	6 04	5 50	5 34	5 17	5 07	4 55	4 42	4 25	4 18	4 08	3 59	3 48	3 36	25	6	19	4
25	12	17	15	6 04	5 50	5 35	5 19	5 09	4 58	4 45	4 29	4 22	4 14	4 05	3 54	3 42	28	6	15	4
28	13	14	16	6 04	5 51	5 36	5 20	5 11	5 01	4 48	4 33	4 26	4 19	4 10	4 00	3 49	31	6	12	4
31	13	11	16	6 04	5 51	5 38	5 22	5 14	5 04	4 52	4 38	4 31	4 24	4 16	4 07	3 56	Aug. 3	6	9	4
Feb. 3	+14	8	−16	6 04	5 52	5 39	5 24	5 16	5 07	4 56	4 43	4 36	4 30	4 22	4 13	4 04	7	+6	6	−3
6	14	5	16	6 04	5 52	5 40	5 27	5 19	5 10	5 00	4 48	4 42	4 36	4 28	4 20	4 12	10	5	3	3
9	14	2	16	6 04	5 53	5 42	5 29	5 22	5 14	5 04	4 53	4 48	4 42	4 35	4 27	4 19	13	5	Apr. 30	3
12	14	Oct. 30	16	6 04	5 54	5 44	5 32	5 25	5 18	5 09	4 58	4 53	4 48	4 42	4 35	4 27	16	4	27	2
15	14	27	16	6 04	5 55	5 45	5 34	5 28	5 21	5 13	5 03	4 59	4 54	4 48	4 42	4 35	19	4	24	2
18	14	24	16	6 04	5 55	5 46	5 36	5 31	5 24	5 17	5 08	5 04	5 00	4 55	4 49	4 43	22	3	21	−1
21	14	21	15	6 03	5 56	5 48	5 39	5 34	5 28	5 21	5 14	5 10	5 06	5 01	4 56	4 51	26	2	18	0
24	13	18	15	6 03	5 56	5 50	5 42	5 37	5 32	5 26	5 19	5 16	5 13	5 08	5 04	4 59	29	+1	15	0
27	13	15	14	6 03	5 57	5 51	5 44	5 40	5 36	5 31	5 25	5 22	5 19	5 15	5 11	5 07	Sept. 1	0	12	+1
Mar. 2	12	12	13	6 03	5 58	5 53	5 47	5 43	5 40	5 36	5 30	5 28	5 26	5 22	5 19	5 15	4	−1	9	2
5	+12	9	−12	6 03	5 59	5 54	5 49	5 46	5 43	5 40	5 35	5 33	5 32	5 29	5 26	5 23	7	−2	5	+3
8	11	6	12	6 03	6 00	5 56	5 52	5 50	5 47	5 45	5 41	5 39	5 38	5 36	5 34	5 32	10	3	2	4
11	10	3	11	6 03	6 01	5 58	5 55	5 54	5 51	5 50	5 47	5 45	5 45	5 43	5 42	5 40	13	4	Mar. 30	5
14	10	Sept. 30	10	6 03	6 01	5 59	5 57	5 57	5 55	5 54	5 52	5 51	5 51	5 50	5 49	5 48	16	5	27	6
17	9	27	9	6 03	6 02	6 01	6 00	6 00	5 59	5 59	5 58	5 58	5 57	5 57	5 57	5 56	19	6	25	6
20	8	24	8	6 03	6 03	6 03	6 03	6 03	6 03	6 03	6 04	6 04	6 04	6 04	6 04	6 04	22	7	22	7
23	7	21	7	6 03	6 04	6 05	6 06	6 06	6 07	6 08	6 09	6 10	6 11	6 11	6 12	6 13	25	8	19	8
26	6	18	5	6 03	6 05	6 07	6 09	6 10	6 11	6 13	6 15	6 16	6 17	6 18	6 19	6 21	28	9	16	9
29	5	15	4	6 03	6 06	6 08	6 11	6 13	6 15	6 18	6 21	6 22	6 24	6 25	6 27	6 29	Oct. 2	10	13	10
Apr. 1	4	11	3	6 03	6 06	6 10	6 14	6 16	6 19	6 22	6 26	6 28	6 30	6 32	6 35	6 38	5	11	9	11
4	+3	8	−2	6 03	6 07	6 12	6 17	6 20	6 23	6 27	6 32	6 34	6 37	6 39	6 43	6 46	8	−12	6	+12
7	2	5	−1	6 03	6 08	6 13	6 20	6 23	6 27	6 32	6 38	6 40	6 44	6 46	6 50	6 54	11	13	3	12
10	2	2	0	6 03	6 08	6 14	6 22	6 26	6 31	6 36	6 43	6 46	6 50	6 53	6 57	7 02	13	13	Feb. 28	13
13	+1	Aug. 30	+1	6 03	6 09	6 16	6 24	6 29	6 35	6 41	6 48	6 52	6 56	7 00	7 05	7 10	16	14	25	13
16	0	27	2	6 03	6 10	6 18	6 27	6 32	6 39	6 46	6 54	6 58	7 02	7 07	7 12	7 18	19	15	22	14
19	−1	24	3	6 03	6 11	6 20	6 30	6 35	6 43	6 50	7 00	7 04	7 09	7 14	7 20	7 24	22	15	20	14
22	1	21	3	6 03	6 12	6 21	6 32	6 38	6 46	6 54	7 05	7 09	7 15	7 20	7 27	7 36	25	16	17	14
25	2	18	4	6 04	6 13	6 23	6 35	6 41	6 50	6 59	7 10	7 15	7 21	7 27	7 34	7 42	28	16	14	14
28	2	15	5	6 04	6 13	6 24	6 37	6 44	6 53	7 03	7 15	7 20	7 27	7 33	7 41	7 50	31	16	11	14
May 1	3	12	5	6 04	6 14	6 26	6 40	6 47	6 57	7 07	7 20	7 26	7 33	7 40	7 49	7 58	Nov. 3	16	8	14
4	−3	9	+6	6 04	6 15	6 27	6 42	6 50	7 00	7 11	7 25	7 31	7 39	7 47	7 56	8 06	6	−16	5	+14
7	3	6	6	6 04	6 15	6 28	6 44	6 53	7 03	7 15	7 30	7 36	7 44	7 53	8 02	8 14	9	16	2	14
10	4	3	6	6 04	6 16	6 31	6 46	6 56	7 07	7 19	7 35	7 42	7 50	7 59	8 09	8 22	12	16	Jan. 31	13
13	4	July 31	6	6 04	6 17	6 32	6 48	6 58	7 10	7 23	7 39	7 47	7 55	8 05	8 16	8 29	15	15	28	13
16	4	28	6	6 04	6 18	6 33	6 50	7 01	7 12	7 26	7 43	7 52	8 00	8 11	8 22	8 36	17	15	25	12
19	4	25	6	6 04	6 18	6 34	6 52	7 03	7 15	7 30	7 47	7 56	8 05	8 16	8 28	8 43	20	15	22	11
22	4	22	6	6 04	6 19	6 35	6 54	7 05	7 18	7 33	7 51	8 00	8 10	8 21	8 34	8 50	23	14	19	11
25	3	19	6	6 04	6 19	6 36	6 55	7 06	7 20	7 35	7 54	8 04	8 14	8 26	8 39	8 56	26	13	16	10
28	3	16	6	6 04	6 20	6 37	6 57	7 08	7 22	7 38	7 58	8 08	8 18	8 30	8 44	9 01	29	12	14	9
31	3	13	5	6 04	6 20	6 38	6 58	7 10	7 24	7 41	8 01	8 11	8 22	8 34	8 49	9 07	Dec. 2	11	11	8
June 3	−2	10	+5	6 04	6 20	6 38	6 59	7 11	7 26	7 42	8 03	8 14	8 25	8 38	8 53	9 12	5	−10	8	+6
6	2	7	5	6 04	6 21	6 39	7 00	7 13	7 27	7 44	8 05	8 16	8 28	8 41	8 57	9 16	7	9	5	5
9	1	4	4	6 04	6 21	6 39	7 01	7 13	7 28	7 46	8 07	8 18	8 30	8 44	9 00	9 19	10	8	2	4
12	−1	1	3	6 04	6 21	6 40	7 02	7 14	7 29	7 47	8 09	8 20	8 32	8 46	9 03	9 22	13	6	Dec. 31	3
15	0	June 28	3	6 04	6 21	6 40	7 02	7 15	7 30	7 48	8 10	8 21	8 33	8 48	9 04	9 24	16	5	28	+1
18	+1	25	2	6 04	6 21	6 40	7 02	7 15	7 30	7 48	8 11	8 22	8 34	8 48	9 05	9 26	19	3	25	0
21	+1	21	+1	6 04	6 22	6 41	7 03	7 16	7 31	7 49	8 12	8 23	8 35	8 49	9 06	9 27	21	−2	21	−2

TABLE 12. SUN'S LONGITUDE, RIGHT ASCENSION AND DECLINATION, AT 0 h

For R.A. on intermediate dates, add 4 minutes per day.

Date	Long.°	R.A. h	Dec.°	Date	Long.°	R.A. h	Dec.°	Date	Long.°	R.A. h	Dec.°	Date	Long.°	R.A. h	Dec.°	Date	Long.°	R.A. h	Dec.°
Jan. 1	280	—	-23	Mar. 5	344	23	-6	May 22	60	—	+20	Aug. 2	130	—	+18	Oct. 13	200	—	-7
5	284	19	23	11	350	—	-4	23	61	4	20	5	132	9	17	24	210	—	11
11	290	—	22	21	0	0	0	June 1	70	—	22	13	140	—	15	29	215	14	13
18	297	20	21	31	10	—	+4	7	76	5	23	21	147	10	12	Nov. 3	220	—	15
20	300	—	20	Apr. 6	16	1	6	11	80	—	23	24	150	—	11	10	227	15	17
30	310	—	18	10	20	—	8	22	90	6	23½	Sept. 3	160	—	8	13	230	—	18
Feb. 2	312	21	17	20	30	—	11	July 2	100	—	23	7	163	11	6	23	240	—	20
9	320	—	15	23	32	2	12	6	103	7	23	13	170	—	+4	25	242	16	21
17	327	22	12	May 1	40	—	15	13	110	—	22	24	180	12	0	Dec. 3	250	—	22
19	330	—	12	8	47	3	17	21	118	8	21	Oct. 3	190	—	-4	8	255	17	23
Mar.1	340	—	-8	11	50	—	+18	23	120	—	+20	10	196	13	-6	12	260	—	23
																22	270	18	-23½

TABLE 13. DEGREES CELSIUS (CENTIGRADE) CONVERTED TO DEGREES FAHRENHEIT

$$°F = (°C \times \tfrac{9}{5}) + 32 \qquad °C = (°F - 32) \times \tfrac{5}{9} \qquad °K = °C + 273$$

Note that intervals of $100°K = 100°C = 180°F$

°C	°F	°C	°F	°C	°F	°C	°F	°C	°F	°C	°F	°C	°F	°C	°F	°C	°F	°C	°F	°C	°F
-273	-460	-80	-112	10	50	110	230	210	410	310	590	410	770	750	1382	5500	9900	11000	19800	21000	37800
250	418	70	94	20	68	120	248	220	428	320	608	420	788	1000	1832	6000	10800	12000	21600	22000	39600
200	328	60	76	30	86	130	266	230	446	330	626	430	806	1500	2700	6500	11700	13000	23400	23000	41400
150	238	50	58	40	104	140	284	240	464	340	644	440	824	2000	3600	7000	12600	14000	25200	24000	43200
140	220	40	40	50	122	150	302	250	482	350	662	450	842	2500	4500	7500	13500	15000	27000	25000	45000
130	202	30	22	60	140	160	320	260	500	360	680	460	860	3000	5400	8000	14400	16000	28800	26000	46800
120	184	20	-4	70	158	170	338	270	518	370	698	470	878	3500	6300	8500	15300	17000	30600	28000	50400
110	166	-10	+14	80	176	180	356	280	536	380	716	480	896	4000	7200	9000	16200	18000	32400	30000	54000
100	148	0	32	90	194	190	374	290	554	390	734	490	914	4500	8100	9500	17100	19000	34200	35000	63000
-90	-130	+5	+41	100	212	200	392	300	572	400	752	500	932	5000	9000	10000	18000	20000	36000	40000	72000

TABLE 14. DEGREES KELVIN (ABSOLUTE) CONVERTED TO DEGREES CELSIUS (CENTIGRADE) AND DEGREES FAHRENHEIT

°K	°C	°F	°K	°C	°F	°K	°C	°F	°K	°C	°F	°K	°C	°F	°K	°C	°F
0	-273	-460	+500	227	441	4000	3700	6700	7500	7200	13,000	14,000	13,700	24,700	25,000	24,700	44,500
100	-173	-280	1000	727	1341	4500	4200	7600	8000	7700	13,900	15,000	14,700	26,500	30,000	29,700	53,500
200	-73	-99	1500	1200	2200	5000	4700	8500	9000	8700	15,700	16,000	15,700	28,300	35,000	34,700	62,500
255	-18	0	2000	1700	3100	5500	5200	9400	10,000	9700	17,500	17,000	16,700	30,100	40,000	39,700	71,500
273	0	+32	2500	2200	4000	6000	5700	10,300	11,000	10,700	19,300	18,000	17,700	31,900	45,000	44,700	80,500
300	+27	+81	3000	2700	4900	6500	6200	11,200	12,000	11,700	21,100	19,000	18,700	33,700	50,000	49,700	89,500
400	+127	+261	3500	3200	5800	7000	6700	12,100	13,000	12,700	22,900	20,000	19,700	35,500	60,000	59,700	107,500

TABLE 15. HOURS AND MINUTES AS DECIMALS OF A DAY

Hours:

½h	1h	1½h	2h	2½h	3h	3½h	4h	4½h	5h	5½h	6h	6½h	7h	7½h	8h	8½h	9h
·0208d	·0417	·0625	·0833	·1042	·1250	·1458	·1667	·1875	·2083	·2292	·2500	·2708	·2917	·3125	·3333	·3542	·3750

9½h	10h	10½h	11h	11½h	12h	12½h	13h	14h	15h	16h	17h	18h	19h	20h	21h	22h	23h
·3958d	·4167	·4375	·4583	·4792	·5000	·5208	·5417	·5833	·6250	·6667	·7083	·7500	·7917	·8333	·8750	·9167	·9583

Minutes:

1m	2m	3m	4m	5m	6m	7m	8m	9m	10m	11m	12m	13m	14m	15m	16m	17m
·0007d	·0014	·0021	·0028	·0035	·0042	·0049	·0056	·0062	·0069	·0076	·0083	·0090	·0097	·0104	·0111	·0118

18m	19m	20m	21m	22m	23m	24m	25m	26m	27m	28m	29m	30m	35m	40m	45m	50m	55m
·0125d	·0132	·0139	·0146	·0153	·0160	·0167	·0174	·0181	·0187	·0194	·0201	·0208	·0243	·0278	·0313	·0347	·0382

TABLE 16. DECIMALS OF A DAY AS HOURS AND MINUTES

The decimals of a minute in the first column should be added to the whole minutes given *in the same line* in columns 2–10, where greater accuracy is required.

d	h m	d	h m	d	h m	d	h m	d	h m	d	h m	d	h m	d	h m	d	h m	d	h m	d	min.
·01	0 14·4	·11	2 38	·21	5 2	·31	7 26	·41	9 50	·51	12 14	·61	14 38	·71	17 2	·81	19 26	·91	21 50	·001	1·44
·02	0 28·8	·12	2 52	·22	5 16	·32	7 40	·42	10 4	·52	12 28	·62	14 52	·72	17 16	·82	19 40	·92	22 4	·002	2·88
·03	0 43·2	·13	3 7	·23	5 31	·33	7 55	·43	10 19	·53	12 43	·63	15 7	·73	17 31	·83	19 55	·93	22 19	·003	4·32
·04	0 57·6	·14	3 21	·24	5 45	·34	8 9	·44	10 33	·54	12 57	·64	15 21	·74	17 45	·84	20 9	·94	22 33	·004	5·76
·05	1 12·0	·15	3 36	·25	6 0	·35	8 24	·45	10 48	·55	13 12	·65	15 36	·75	18 0	·85	20 24	·95	22 48	·005	7·20
·06	1 26·4	·16	3 50	·26	6 14	·36	8 38	·46	11 2	·56	13 26	·66	15 50	·76	18 14	·86	20 38	·96	23 2	·006	8·64
·07	1 40·8	·17	4 4	·27	6 28	·37	8 52	·47	11 16	·57	13 40	·67	16 4	·77	18 28	·87	20 52	·97	23 16	·007	10·08
·08	1 55·2	·18	4 19	·28	6 43	·38	9 7	·48	11 31	·58	13 55	·68	16 19	·78	18 43	·88	21 7	·98	23 31	·008	11·52
·09	2 9·6	·19	4 33	·29	6 57	·39	9 21	·49	11 45	·59	14 9	·69	16 33	·79	18 57	·89	21 21	·99	23 45	·009	12·96
·10	2 24·0	·20	4 48	·30	7 12	·40	9 36	·50	12 0	·60	14 24	·70	16 48	·80	19 12	·90	21 36	1·0	24 0	·010	14·40

TABLE 17. DECIMALS OF A DEGREE AS MINUTES AND SECONDS OF ARC

(A) To express a decimal of a degree in minutes and seconds of arc.

°	' "	°	' "	°	' "	°	' "	°	' "	°	' "	°	' "	°	' "	°	' "	°	' "
·01	0 36	·11	6 36	·21	12 36	·31	18 36	·41	24 36	·51	30 36	·61	36 36	·71	42 36	·81	48 36	·91	54 36
·02	1 12	·12	7 12	·22	13 12	·32	19 12	·42	25 12	·52	31 12	·62	37 12	·72	43 12	·82	49 12	·92	55 12
·03	1 48	·13	7 48	·23	13 48	·33	19 48	·43	25 48	·53	31 48	·63	37 48	·73	43 48	·83	49 48	·93	55 48
·04	2 24	·14	8 24	·24	14 24	·34	20 24	·44	26 24	·54	32 24	·64	38 24	·74	44 24	·84	50 24	·94	56 24
·05	3 0	·15	9 0	·25	15 0	·35	21 0	·45	27 0	·55	33 0	·65	39 0	·75	45 0	·85	51 0	·95	57 0
·06	3 36	·16	9 36	·26	15 36	·36	21 36	·46	27 36	·56	33 36	·66	39 36	·76	45 36	·86	51 36	·96	57 36
·07	4 12	·17	10 12	·27	16 12	·37	22 12	·47	28 12	·57	34 12	·67	40 12	·77	46 12	·87	52 12	·97	58 12
·08	4 48	·18	10 48	·28	16 48	·38	22 48	·48	28 48	·58	34 48	·68	40 48	·78	46 48	·88	52 48	·98	58 48
·09	5 24	·19	11 24	·29	17 24	·39	23 24	·49	29 24	·59	35 24	·69	41 24	·79	47 24	·89	53 24	·99	59 24
·10	6 0	·20	12 0	·30	18 0	·40	24 0	·50	30 0	·60	36 0	·70	42 0	·80	48 0	·90	54 0	1·0	60 0

(B) To find the decimal equivalent of an angle expressed in minutes and seconds of arc, take the decimal equivalent just *less* than the value to be converted; thus 33′ 48″ = 0·56° (approx.).

°	' "	°	' "	°	' "	°	' "	°	' "	°	' "	°	' "	°	' "	°	' "	°	' "
·01	0 18	·11	6 18	·21	12 18	·31	18 18	·41	24 18	·51	30 18	·61	36 18	·71	42 18	·81	48 18	·91	54 18
·02	0 54	·12	6 54	·22	12 54	·32	18 54	·42	24 54	·52	30 54	·62	36 54	·72	42 54	·82	48 54	·92	54 54
·03	1 30	·13	7 30	·23	13 30	·33	19 30	·43	25 30	·53	31 30	·63	37 30	·73	43 30	·83	49 30	·93	55 30
·04	2 6	·14	8 6	·24	14 6	·34	20 6	·44	26 6	·54	32 6	·64	38 6	·74	44 6	·84	50 6	·94	56 6
·05	2 42	·15	8 42	·25	14 42	·35	20 42	·45	26 42	·55	32 42	·65	38 42	·75	44 42	·85	50 42	·95	56 42
·06	3 18	·16	9 18	·26	15 18	·36	21 18	·46	27 18	·56	33 18	·66	39 18	·76	45 18	·86	51 18	·96	57 18
·07	3 54	·17	9 54	·27	15 54	·37	21 54	·47	27 54	·57	33 54	·67	39 54	·77	45 54	·87	51 54	·97	57 54
·08	4 30	·18	10 30	·28	16 30	·38	22 30	·48	28 30	·58	34 30	·68	40 30	·78	46 30	·88	52 30	·98	58 30
·09	5 6	·19	11 6	·29	17 6	·39	23 6	·49	29 6	·59	35 6	·69	41 6	·79	47 6	·89	53 6	·99	59 6
·10	5 42	·20	11 42	·30	17 42	·40	23 42	·50	29 42	·60	35 42	·70	41 42	·80	47 42	·90	53 42	1·0	59 42

TABLE 18. MEAN REFRACTION (after F. W. Bessel)

For temperature 10°C (50°F) and pressure 752 mm Hg (29·6 in.).

For other temperatures: *add* 1% per 3°C (5°F) below 10°C, *subtract* 1% per 3°C when higher than 10°C.

For other pressures: *add* 1·5% per 10 mm (3·5% per inch) if higher, *subtract* when lower, than 752 mm.

Values to be subtracted from the observed altitude of the object to obtain its true altitude, or conversely, added to the observed zenith distance to obtain the true zenith distance.

°	' "	°	' "	°	' "	°	' "	°	' "	°	' "
0	34 54	2	18 09	7	7 20	12	4 25	20	2 37	45	0 58
¼	31 50	3	14 15	8	6 30	13	4 05	25	2 03	50	0 48
½	29 03	4	11 39	9	5 49	14	3 47	30	1 40	65	0 27
¾	26 35	5	9 47	10	5 16	15	3 32	35	1 22	80	0 10
1	24 25	6	8 23	11	4 49	16	3 19	40	1 09	90	0 00

TABLE 19. RIGHT ASCENSION CONVERTED INTO DEGREES OF ARC

R. A. Hours & Minutes converted into Degrees of arc; 1 min. = ¼°. (Reads continuously *across* page.)

R.A. h	0 m °	4 m °	8 m °	10 m °	12 m °	15 m °	16 m °	20 m °	24 m °	28 m °	R.A. h	30 m °	32 m °	36 m °	40 m °	44 m °	45 m °	48 m °	50 m °	52 m °	56 m °	R.A. h
0	—	1	2	2½	3	3¾	4	5	6	7	0	7½	8	9	10	11	11¼	12	12½	13	14	0
1	15	16	17	17½	18	18¾	19	20	21	22	1	22½	23	24	25	26	26¼	27	27½	28	29	1
2	30	31	32	32½	33	33¾	34	35	36	37	2	37½	38	39	40	41	41¼	42	42½	43	44	2
3	45	46	47	47½	48	48¾	49	50	51	52	3	52½	53	54	55	56	56¼	57	57½	58	59	3
4	60	61	62	62½	63	63¾	64	65	66	67	4	67½	68	69	70	71	71¼	72	72½	73	74	4
5	75	76	77	77½	78	78¾	79	80	81	82	5	82½	83	84	85	86	86¼	87	87½	88	89	5
6	90	91	92	92½	93	93¾	94	95	96	97	6	97½	98	99	100	101	101¼	102	102½	103	104	6
7	105	106	107	107½	108	108¾	109	110	111	112	7	112½	113	114	115	116	116¼	117	117½	118	119	7
8	120	121	122	122½	123	123¾	124	125	126	127	8	127½	128	129	130	131	131¼	132	132½	133	134	8
9	135	136	137	137½	138	138¾	139	140	141	142	9	142½	143	144	145	146	146¼	147	147½	148	149	9
10	150	151	152	152½	153	153¾	154	155	156	157	10	157½	158	159	160	161	161¼	162	162½	163	164	10
11	165	166	167	167½	168	168¾	169	170	171	172	11	172½	173	174	175	176	176¼	177	177½	178	179	11
12	180	181	182	182½	183	183¾	184	185	186	187	12	187½	188	189	190	191	191¼	192	192½	193	194	12
13	195	196	197	197½	198	198¾	199	200	201	202	13	202½	203	204	205	206	206¼	207	207½	208	209	13
14	210	211	212	212½	213	213¾	214	215	216	217	14	217½	218	219	220	221	221¼	222	222½	223	224	14
15	225	226	227	227½	228	228¾	229	230	231	232	15	232½	233	234	235	236	236¼	237	237½	238	239	15
16	240	241	242	242½	243	243¾	244	245	246	247	16	247½	248	249	250	251	251¼	252	252½	253	254	16
17	255	256	257	257½	258	258¾	259	260	261	262	17	262½	263	264	265	266	266¼	267	267½	268	269	17
18	270	271	272	272½	273	273¾	274	275	276	277	18	277½	278	279	280	281	281¼	282	282½	283	284	18
19	285	286	287	287½	288	288¾	289	290	291	292	19	292½	293	294	295	296	296¼	297	297½	298	299	19
20	300	301	302	302½	303	303¾	304	305	306	307	20	307½	308	309	310	311	311¼	312	312½	313	314	20
21	315	316	317	317½	318	318¾	319	320	321	322	21	322½	323	324	325	326	326¼	327	327½	328	329	21
22	330	331	332	332½	333	333¾	334	335	336	337	22	337½	338	339	340	341	341¼	342	342½	343	344	22
23	345	346	347	347½	348	348¾	349	350	351	352	23	352½	353	354	355	356	356¼	357	357½	358	359	23

TABLE 20. DEGREES OF ARC CONVERTED INTO RIGHT ASCENSION

°	h	°	h	°	h	°	m	°	m	°	m
15	1	135	9	255	17	1	4	6	24	11	44
30	2	150	10	270	18	2	8	7	28	12	48
45	3	165	11	285	19	3	12	8	32	13	52
60	4	180	12	300	20	4	16	9	36	14	56
75	5	195	13	315	21	5	20	10	40	15	60
90	6	210	14	330	22						
105	7	225	15	345	23						
120	8	240	16	360	24						

Decimals of degree:	·1	·2	·3	·4	·5	·6	·7	·8	·9	1·0
min and sec of time:	24ˢ	48ˢ	1ᵐ 12ˢ	1ᵐ 36ˢ	2ᵐ 00ˢ	2ᵐ 24ˢ	2ᵐ 48ˢ	3ᵐ 12ˢ	3ᵐ 36ˢ	4ᵐ 00ˢ

TABLE 21. THE GREEK ALPHABET

A	α	Alpha	H	η	Eta	N	ν	Nu	T	τ	Tau
B	β	Beta	Θ	θ	Theta	Ξ	ξ	Xi	Y	υ	Upsilon
Γ	γ	Gamma	I	ι	Iota	O	o	Omicron	Φ	φ	Phi
Δ	δ	Delta	K	κ	Kappa	Π	π	Pi	X	χ	Chi
E	ε	Epsilon	Λ	λ	Lambda	P	ρ	Rho	Ψ	ψ	Psi
Z	ζ	Zeta	M	μ	Mu	Σ	σ	Sigma	Ω	ω	Omega

TABLE 22. SIDEREAL TIME, OR HOUR OF R.A., ON THE MERIDIAN

The table shows R.A. on meridian at the dates and times indicated. If time is after midnight, add 1 day to the date at the side.

Intermediate Dates: Add to the R.A. for the previous date the requisite number of minutes from the 7- or 8-day-interval table below.

7 Days Interval: 1 day   2 d   3 d   4 d   5 d   6 d   8 Days Interval: 1 day   2 d   3 d   4 d   5 d   6 d   7 d
Add minutes: 4 m   9 m   13 m   17 m   21 m   26 m   Add minutes: 4 m   8 m   12 m   15 m   19 m   23 m   26 m

Intermediate Minutes of Mean Time: add the same number of R.A. minutes to the previous R.A. hour. Thus Apr. 6 at 1709 h = R.A. 6 h 9 m.

U.T.	1700	1800	1900	2000	2100	2200	2300	0000	0100	0200	0300	0400	0500	0600
Date	h	h	h	h	h	h	h	h	h	h	h	h	h	h
Jan. 5	0	1	2	3	4	5	6	7	8	9	10	11	12	13
13	0½	1½	2½	3½	4½	5½	6½	7½	8½	9½	10½	11½	12½	13½
21	1	2	3	4	5	6	7	8	9	10	11	12	13	14
28	1½	2½	3½	4½	5½	6½	7½	8½	9½	10½	11½	12½	13½	14½
Feb. 5	2	3	4	5	6	7	8	9	10	11	12	13	14	15
13	2½	3½	4½	5½	6½	7½	8½	9½	10½	11½	12½	13½	14½	15½
20	3	4	5	6	7	8	9	10	11	12	13	14	15	16
28	3½	4½	5½	6½	7½	8½	9½	10½	11½	12½	13½	14½	15½	16½
Mar. 7	4	5	6	7	8	9	10	11	12	13	14	15	16	17
15	4½	5½	6½	7½	8½	9½	10½	11½	12½	13½	14½	15½	16½	17½
22	5	6	7	8	9	10	11	12	13	14	15	16	17	18
29	5½	6½	7½	8½	9½	10½	11½	12½	13½	14½	15½	16½	17½	18½
Apr. 6	6	7	8	9	10	11	12	13	14	15	16	17	18	19
14	6½	7½	8½	9½	10½	11½	12½	13½	14½	15½	16½	17½	18½	19½
22	7	8	9	10	11	12	13	14	15	16	17	18	19	20
29	7½	8½	9½	10½	11½	12½	13½	14½	15½	16½	17½	18½	19½	20½
May 7	8	9	10	11	12	13	14	15	16	17	18	19	20	21
15	8½	9½	10½	11½	12½	13½	14½	15½	16½	17½	18½	19½	20½	21½
22	9	10	11	12	13	14	15	16	17	18	19	20	21	22
30	9½	10½	11½	12½	13½	14½	15½	16½	17½	18½	19½	20½	21½	22½
June 6	10	11	12	13	14	15	16	17	18	19	20	21	22	23
14	10½	11½	12½	13½	14½	15½	16½	17½	18½	19½	20½	21½	22½	23½
22	11	12	13	14	15	16	17	18	19	20	21	22	23	0
29	11½	12½	13½	14½	15½	16½	17½	18½	19½	20½	21½	22½	23½	0½
Jul. 7	12	13	14	15	16	17	18	19	20	21	22	23	0	1
15	12½	13½	14½	15½	16½	17½	18½	19½	20½	21½	22½	23½	0½	1½
22	13	14	15	16	17	18	19	20	21	22	23	0	1	2
30	13½	14½	15½	16½	17½	18½	19½	20½	21½	22½	23½	0½	1½	2½
Aug. 6	14	15	16	17	18	19	20	21	22	23	0	1	2	3
14	14½	15½	16½	17½	18½	19½	20½	21½	22½	23½	0½	1½	2½	3½
22	15	16	17	18	19	20	21	22	23	0	1	2	3	4
29	15½	16½	17½	18½	19½	20½	21½	22½	23½	0½	1½	2½	3½	4½
Sept. 6	16	17	18	19	20	21	22	23	0	1	2	3	4	5
13	16½	17½	18½	19½	20½	21½	22½	23½	0½	1½	2½	3½	4½	5½
21	17	18	19	20	21	22	23	0	1	2	3	4	5	6
29	17½	18½	19½	20½	21½	22½	23½	0½	1½	2½	3½	4½	5½	6½
Oct. 6	18	19	20	21	22	23	0	1	2	3	4	5	6	7
14	18½	19½	20½	21½	22½	23½	0½	1½	2½	3½	4½	5½	6½	7½
21	19	20	21	22	23	0	1	2	3	4	5	6	7	8
29	19½	20½	21½	22½	23½	0½	1½	2½	3½	4½	5½	6½	7½	8½
Nov. 6	20	21	22	23	0	1	2	3	4	5	6	7	8	9
13	20½	21½	22½	23½	0½	1½	2½	3½	4½	5½	6½	7½	8½	9½
21	21	22	23	0	1	2	3	4	5	6	7	8	9	10
28	21½	22½	23½	0½	1½	2½	3½	4½	5½	6½	7½	8½	9½	10½
Dec. 6	22	23	0	1	2	3	4	5	6	7	8	9	10	11
14	22½	23½	0½	1½	2½	3½	4½	5½	6½	7½	8½	9½	10½	11½
21	23	0	1	2	3	4	5	6	7	8	9	10	11	12
29	23½	0½	1½	2½	3½	4½	5½	6½	7½	8½	9½	10½	11½	12½

TABLE 23. SEMI-DIURNAL ARCS

The table gives, for stars of particular Declinations, the length of their semi-diurnal arcs as observed from various latitudes; the arcs are also a measure of the time elapsed between rising or setting of the star and its transit over the observer's meridian.

Observers in the northern hemisphere read the star's Declination at the *top* of the column; those in the southern hemisphere at the foot.

Obsr's Lat.	N. Hemisphere: Stars with North Declination							Obsr's Lat.	N. Hemisphere: Stars with South Declination						Obsr's Lat.
	30°	25°	20°	15°	10°	5°	0°		5°	10°	15°	20°	25°	30°	
°	h m	h m	h m	h m	h m	h m	h m	°	h m	h m	h m	h m	h m	h m	°
5	6 11	6 8	6 7	6 5	6 4	6 2	6 0	5	5 58	5 56	5 55	5 53	5 52	5 49	5
10	6 23	6 19	6 15	6 11	6 7	6 4	6 0	10	5 56	5 53	5 49	5 45	5 41	5 37	10
15	6 36	6 29	6 22	6 16	6 11	6 5	6 0	15	5 55	5 49	5 44	5 38	5 31	5 24	15
20	6 49	6 39	6 30	6 22	6 15	6 7	6 0	20	5 53	5 45	5 38	5 30	5 21	5 11	20
25	7 2	6 49	6 39	6 29	6 19	6 9	6 0	25	5 51	5 41	5 31	5 21	5 11	4 58	25
30	7 19	7 2	6 49	6 36	6 23	6 12	6 0	30	5 48	5 37	5 24	5 11	4 58	4 41	30
35	7 35	7 16	6 59	6 43	6 28	6 14	6 0	35	5 46	5 32	5 17	5 1	4 44	4 25	35
40	7 55	7 32	7 11	6 52	6 34	6 17	6 0	40	5 43	5 26	5 8	4 49	4 28	4 5	40
45	8 18	7 51	7 25	7 2	6 41	6 20	6 0	45	5 40	5 19	4 58	4 35	4 9	3 42	45
50	8 53	8 15	7 43	7 14	6 49	6 24	6 0	50	5 36	5 11	4 46	4 17	3 45	3 7	50
55	9 39	8 47	8 5	7 30	6 58	6 29	6 0	55	5 31	5 2	4 30	3 55	3 13	2 21	55
60	11 22	9 35	8 36	7 51	7 11	6 35	6 0	60	5 25	4 49	4 9	3 24	2 25	0 38	60
	S. Hemisphere: Stars with South Declination								S. Hemisphere: Stars with North Declination						

TABLE 24. PRECESSION

Precession in R.A. for Ten Years. For northern objects use the upper line of R.A. Hours; for southern objects, the lower. The ± signs are added algebraically to the catalogue positions, like signs being added, unlike signs subtracted. For reckoning backwards, to an earlier date, reverse the + or − signs.

Hours of Right Ascension for NORTHERN Objects

Dec.	0, 12	1, 11	2, 10	3, 9	4, 8	5, 7	6	18	19, 17	20, 16	21, 15	22, 14	23, 13	Dec.
°	m	m	m	m	m	m	m	m	m	m	m	m	m	°
80	+0.51	+0.84	+1.14	+1.40	+1.60	+1.73	+1.77	−0.75	−0.70	−0.58	−0.38	−0.12	+0.19	80
70	0.51	0.67	0.82	0.94	1.04	1.10	1.12	−0.10	−0.08	−0.02	+0.08	+0.21	0.35	70
60	0.51	0.61	0.70	0.78	0.84	0.88	0.90	+0.13	+0.14	+0.18	+0.24	+0.32	0.41	60
50	0.51	0.58	0.64	0.70	0.74	0.77	0.78	+0.25	+0.26	+0.28	+0.32	+0.38	0.44	50
40	0.51	0.56	0.61	0.64	0.67	0.69	0.70	+0.33	+0.33	+0.35	+0.38	+0.42	0.46	40
30	0.51	0.54	0.58	0.60	0.62	0.64	0.64	+0.38	+0.39	+0.40	+0.42	+0.45	0.48	30
20	0.51	0.53	0.55	0.57	0.58	0.59	0.59	+0.43	+0.43	+0.44	+0.45	+0.47	0.49	20
10	0.51	0.52	0.53	0.54	0.55	0.55	0.55	+0.47	+0.47	+0.48	+0.48	+0.49	0.50	10
0	+0.51	+0.51	+0.51	+0.51	+0.51	+0.51	+0.51	+0.51	+0.51	+0.51	+0.51	+0.51	0.51	0
Dec.	0, 12	23, 13	22, 14	21, 15	20, 16	19, 17	18	6	5, 7	4, 8	3, 9	2, 10	1, 11	Dec.

Hours of Right Ascension for SOUTHERN Objects

Precession in Declination for Ten Years. Add algebraically to Declination.

Hours:	0, 24	1, 23	2, 22	3, 21	4, 20	5, 19	6, 18	7, 17	8, 16	9, 15	10, 14	11, 13	12
	′	′	′	′	′	′		′	′	′	′	′	′
	+3.3	+3.2	+2.9	+2.4	+1.7	+0.9	0	−0.9	−1.7	−2.4	−2.9	−3.2	−3.3

Example—The star α Ursæ Majoris is placed in 1920 in R.A. 10 h 58·9 m, Declination +62° 11′; find its approximate position in 1950.

Turn to the column headed by the nearest R.A. hour, 11. In this column the 10-year R.A. correction for 60° N is +0·61 m, for 70° N it is +0·67 m, giving about +0·62 m for the intermediate Dec. of the star.

R.A. of α Ursæ Majoris for 1920   is   10 h 58·9 m
Correction for 30 years (+0·62 × 3) is   +1·9 m

R.A. for 1950:   11 h 0·8 m

The star's Declination for 1920   is   +62° 11′
Correction for 30 years (−3′·2 × 3) is   −10′

Dec. for 1950:   +62° 1′

TABLE 25. CONVERSION OF HERSCHEL CATALOGUE DESIGNATIONS TO N.G.C. NUMBERS

The New General Catalogue has long superseded Herschel's Catalogue so, in order to identify a cluster or nebula in the Charts if only its N.G.C. number is known, the following Conversion Table by the late William H. Meyer, Jr., gives the N.G.C. number for all objects in the Charts bearing a Herschel designation.

The 'type' code is as follows:

c = open clusters;   g = globular clusters;   n = diffuse nebulæ;   p = planetary nebulæ;   s = galaxies.

N.G.C. No.	H.	Type
0 Hours		
16	15^4	s
23	147^3	s
129	79^8	c
136	35^6	c
205	18^5	s
225	78^8	c
253	1^5	s
278	159^1	s
288	20^6	g
1 Hour		
381	64^8	c
457	42^7	c
467	108^1	-
524	151^1	s
559	48^7	c
584	100^1	s
613	281^1	s
654	46^7	c
663	31^6	c
720	105^1	s
752	32^7	c
772	112^1	s
779	101^1	s
2 Hours		
821	152^1	s
869	33^6	c
884	34^6	c
891	19^5	s
908	153^1	s
936	23^4	s
949	154^1	s
1022	102^1	s
1023	156^1	s
1027	66^8	c
1052	63^1	s
1084	64^1	s
1097	48^5	s
3 Hours		
1201	109^1	s
1245	25^6	c
1309	106^1	s
1332	60^1	s
1342	88^8	c
1395	58^1	s
1407	107^1	s
1444	80^8	c
1491	258^1	n
4 Hours		
1501	53^4	p
1513	60^7	c
1514	69^4	p
1528	61^7	c
1535	26^4	p
1579	217^1	n
1637	122^1	s
1647	8^8	c
5 Hours		
1758	21^7	-
1778	61^8	c
1817	4^7	c
1857	33^7	c
1907	39^7	c
1931	261^1	n
2022	34^4	p
2024	28^5	n
2129	26^8	c
6 Hours		
2169	24^8	c
2186	25^7	c
2232	25^8	c
2234	9^8	c
2244	2^7	c
2251	3^8	c
2260	48^8	c
2281	71^8	c
2286	31^8	c
2301	27^6	c
2304	2^6	c
2318	14^7	c
7 Hours		
2331	40^8	c
2343	33^8	c
2353	34^8	c
2360	12^7	c
2362	17^7	c
2374	35^8	c
2392	45^4	p
2394	44^8	c
2395	11^8	c
2396	36^8	c
2403	44^5	s
2413	52^8	c
2420	1^6	c
2422	38^8	c
2430	46^8	c
2440	64^4	p
2482	10^7	c
2489	23^7	c
2506	37^6	c
8 Hours		
2539	11^7	c
2548	22^6	c
2627	63^7	c
2655	288^1	s
2681	242^1	s
2683	200^1	s
9 Hours		
2742	249^1	s
2768	250^1	s
2775	2^1	s
2781	66^1	s
2782	167^1	s
2784	59^1	s
2787	216^1	s
2830	113^1	s
2841	205^1	s
2859	137^1	s
2880	260^1	s
2903	56^1	s
2905	57^1	s
2964	114^1	s
2974	61^1	s
2976	285^1	s
2985	78^1	s
3003	26^5	s
3021	115^1	s
3077	286^1	s
3079	47^5	s
10 Hours		
3115	163^1	s
3147	79^1	s
3166	3^1	s
3169	4^1	s
3198	199^1	s
3206	266^1	s
3242	27^4	p
3245	86^1	s
3254	72^1	s
3294	164^1	s
3310	60^4	s
3344	81^1	s
3348	80^1	s
3379	17^1	s
3384	18^1	s
3395	116^1	s
3412	27^1	s
3414	362^2	s
3432	172^1	s
3445	267^1	s
3458	268^1	s
8 Hours		
3486	87^1	s
3489	101^2	s
11 Hours		
3504	88^1	s
3521	13^1	s
3549	220^1	s
3556	46^5	s
3593	29^1	s
3599	49^2	s
3607	50^2	s
3610	270^1	s
3613	271^1	s
3621	241^1	s
3631	226^1	s
3655	5^1	s
3665	219^1	s
3672	131^1	s
3675	194^1	s
3683	246^1	s
3690	247^1	s
3718	221^1	s
3735	287^1	s
3810	21^1	s
3813	94^1	s
3877	201^1	s
3887	120^1	s
3894	248^1	s
3898	228^1	s
3900	82^1	s
3923	259^1	s
3938	203^1	s
3941	173^1	s
3945	251^1	s
3949	202^1	s
3953	45^5	s
3962	67^1	s
3982	64^4	s
4026	223^1	s
4030	121^1	s
4036	253^1	s
4041	252^1	s
12 Hours		
4062	174^1	s
4085	224^1	s
4088	206^1	s
4096	207^1	s
4102	225^1	s
4111	195^1	s
4124	33^1	s
4128	263^1	s
4133	278^1	s
4138	196^1	s
4145	169^1	s
4147	19^1	g
4150	73^1	s
4151	165^1	s
4153	11^1	-
4179	9^1	s
4203	175^1	s
4214	95^1	s
4216	35^1	s
4220	209^1	s
4245	74^1	s
4250	264^1	s
4251	89^1	s
4258	43^5	s
4274	75^1	s
4278	90^1	s
4291	275^1	s
4314	76^1	s
4319	276^1	s
4361	65^1	p
4365	30^1	s
4369	166^1	s
4371	22^1	s
4377	12^1	s
4378	123^1	s
4386	277^1	s
4414	77^1	s
4435	28^1	s
4448	91^1	s
4449	213^1	s
4490	198^1	s
4494	83^1	s
4526	31^1	s
4546	160^1	s
4550	36^1	s
4559	92^1	s
4565	24^5	s
4570	32^1	s
4594	43^1	s
4596	24^1	s
4605	254^1	s
13 Hours		
4631	42^5	s
4643	10^1	s
4656	176^1	s
4665	142^1	s
4666	15^1	s
4697	39^1	s
4699	129^1	s
4725	84^1	s
4754	25^1	s
4762	75^2	s
4781	134^1	s
4782	135^1	s
4814	243^1	s
4856	68^1	s
4866	162^1	s
4900	143^1	s
13 Hours		
4958	130^1	s
5005	96^1	s
5033	97^1	s
5061	138^1	s
5247	297^2	s
5248	34^1	s
5273	98^1	s
5290	170^1	s
5297	180^1	s
5308	255^1	s
5322	256^1	s
5363	6^1	s
5377	187^1	s
5383	181^1	s
5389	240^1	s
14 Hours		
5466	9^6	g
5533	418^2	s
5557	99^1	s
5566	144^1	s
5576	146^1	s
5634	70^1	g
5676	189^1	s
5678	237^1	s
5713	182^1	s
5746	126^1	s
5813	127^1	s
15 Hours		
5846	128^1	s
5866	215^1	s
5879	757^2	s
5897	19^6	g
5907	759^2	s
5921	148^1	s
5982	764^2	s
16 Hours		
6171	40^6	g
6229	50^4	g
17 Hours		
6284	11^6	g
6287	195^2	g
6293	12^6	g
6304	147^1	g
6316	45^1	g
6356	48^1	g
6369	11^4	p
6412	41^6	s
6451	13^6	c
6543	37^4	p
18 Hours		
6522	49^1	g
6561	54^8	c
6568	30^7	c
6624	50^1	g
6633	72^8	c
6638	51^1	g
6645	23^6	c
6664	12^8	c
6712	47^1	g
19 Hours		
6755	19^7	c
6800	21^8	c
6802	14^6	c
6804	38^6	p
6818	51^4	p
6826	73^4	p
6830	9^7	c
20 Hours		
6866	59^7	c
6885	20^8	c
6905	16^4	p
6910	56^8	c
6934	103^1	g
6939	42^6	c
6940	8^7	c
6960	15^5	n
6992	14^5	n
7006	52^1	g
7008	192^1	p
21 Hours		
7009	1^4	p
7082	52^7	c
7086	32^6	c
22 Hours		
7209	53^7	c
7217	207^2	s
7243	75^8	c
7331	53^1	s
7380	77^8	c
23 Hours		
7479	55^1	s
7662	18^4	p
7789	30^6	c

The Table is reproduced by kind permission of *Sky and Telescope*.

TABLE 26. ATLASES, CHARTS AND CATALOGUES

	Epoch	Author(s)	Pubn	Scale mm per °	Coverage	App. lim. mag.
STAR CHARTS (VISUAL)						
Norton's Star Atlas (this volume, Charts I to XVI)	1950·0	A. P. Norton	1910 (16th edn 1973)	3·5	w.s.	6·5
Atlas Coeli Skalnate Pleso	1950·0	A. Bečvář	1948 (U.S.A. 1949)	7·5	w.s.	7·5
Atlas des Nordlichen Gestirnten Himmels [BD]	1855·0	F. W. A. Argelander	1863	20	+90° to −2°	9·0
Atlas der Himmelszone zwischen 1° und 23° südlicher Declination	1855·0	E. Schönfeld	1887	20	−1° to −23°	9·0
Cordoba Durchmusterung Charts	1875·0	J. M. Thome	1892 +	20	−22° to −90°	9·5
Atlas Stellarum Variabilium	1900·0	J. G. Hagen	1899	160	v.s.	14·0
Star Atlas of Reference Stars and Nonstellar Objects	1950·0	Smithsonian Astrophysical Observatory	1969	8·6	w.s.	9·0
STAR CHARTS (PHOTOGRAPHIC)						
Carte du Ciel (Astrographic Charts)	1900	Various observatories	1892 +	120	w.s. (n.y.c.)	14
Photographic Chart of the Sky	1900	J. Franklin-Adams	1914	15	w.s.	16
Palisa–Wolf Charts	1875	J. Palisa & M. Wolf	1908–31	37	210 g.a.	16
Palomar Sky Atlas	1950	National Geographic Society–Palomar Observatory	1952	54	+90° to −27° (red & blue)	20 (R) 21 (B)

	Epoch	Author(s)	Pubn	Coverage	App. lim. mag.	No. of stars listed
GENERAL CATALOGUES						
Astrographic Catalogue (*Carte du Ciel* project)	1900·0	Various	1892 + (in progress)	w.s. (n.y.c.)	14	
Astronomische Gesellschaft Katalog (AGK)	1875·0		Leipzig, 1890 +			
Zweiter Katalog der Astronomische Gesellschaft (AGK2)	1950·0	R. Schorr & A. Kohlschutter	Hamburg–Bergedorf, 1951	+90° to +50°		183,000
Bonner Durchmusterung des Nordlichen Himmels (BD)	1855·0	F. W. A. Argelander	Bonn, 1859–62; reprinted 1903	+90° to −2°	9·5	458,000
Durchmusterung	1855·0	E. Schönfeld	Bonn, 1886	−1° to −23°	9·5	
Cape Photographic Durchmusterung	1875·0	D. Gill & J. C. Kapteyn	Cape of Good Hope, 1896–1903	−19° to −90°	10	455,000
Catalogue of Bright Stars	1950·0	F. Schlesinger & L. F. Jenkins	New Haven, 1940 (2nd edn)	w.s.	6·5	9110
Cordoba Durchmusterung	1875·0	J. M. Thome	Cordoba, 1892 +	−22° to −90°	10	614,000
General Catalogue of 33342 Stars	1950·0	B. Boss	Washington, 1937	w.s.	7	33,342
Skalnate Pleso Atlas Catalogue	1950·0	A. Bečvář	Prague, 1959 (2nd edn)	w.s.	6·25	
Smithsonian Astrophysical Observatory Star Catalog	1950·0		Washington, 1966	w.s.	9	258,997
Yale Catalogues	1950·0		New Haven	+90° to +85° +60° to +50° +30° to −30°	9	
FUNDAMENTAL CATALOGUES						
Dritter Fundamentalkatalog des Berliner Astronomischen Jahrbuchs (FK3)	1950.0	A. Kopff	Berlin, 1934	w.s.	7	1535
Fourth Fundamental Catalogue (FK4)	1950.0	A. Kopff	Heidelberg, 1963	w.s.	7	1535
CIRCUMPOLAR CATALOGUES						
A Catalogue of Circumpolar Stars	1810.0	S. Groombridge (Ed. G. B. Airy)	London, 1838	n.p.r.		4243
New Reduction of Groombridge's Circumpolar Catalogue	1810.0	F. W. Dyson & W. G. Thackeray	London, 1905	n.p.r.		4243
ZODIACAL CATALOGUE						
Catalogue of 3539 Zodiacal Stars	1950·0	J. Robertson	Washington, 1940	z.b.		3539
DOUBLE STAR CATALOGUES						
General Catalogue of Double Stars	1880·0 & 1900·0	S. W. Burnham	Washington, 1906	+90° to −31°		13,665
New General Catalogue of Double Stars	1900·0 & 1950·0	R. G. Aitken	Washington, 1932	+90° to −30°		17,180
Southern Double Star Catalogue		R. T. A. Innes	Johannesburg, 1926–7	−19° to −90°		
VARIABLE STAR CATALOGUE						
General Catalogue of Variable Stars		B. V. Kukarkin *et al.*	Moscow, 1958 (2nd edn)			14,700

Note. Pubn = year of publication; App. lim. mag. = approximate limiting magnitude; w.s. = whole sky; n.p.r. = north polar region; z.b. = zodiacal band; v.s. = selected comparison fields for variable stars; g.a. = galactic areas; n.y.c. = not yet complete.

III. THE SOLAR SYSTEM

The solar system comprises the Sun and those bodies in its neighbourhood and under its gravitational influence. These are the nine planets, their 32 known satellites and many thousands of minor planets, comets and meteoroids.

THE SUN

The Sun is an ordinary star, but because it is so much nearer than the other stars, it is possible to study its surface features, even with relatively small instruments. It is, however, necessary to emphasize that special precautions are required when observing the Sun. On no account should attempts be made to observe it directly, even if filters are available. The safest technique is by projection—see below.

Physical and Orbital Data

Diameter: 1,392,000 km	Volume: $1{,}303{,}600 \times V_{\oplus}$
Mean Distance from Earth: 149,600,000 km	Mass: $332{,}946 \times M_{\oplus}$
Inclination of Axis to	Density: $1 \cdot 409 \, \text{g/cm}^3$
Perpendicular to Plane of Ecliptic: $7° \cdot 25$	Surface Gravity: $27 \cdot 90 \times g_{\oplus}$
Sidereal Period of Axial Rotation: $25 \cdot 380$ d	Escape Velocity: $617 \cdot 5$ km/s

Solar Motion. Observations of the proper motions of stars reveal a tendency for stars to diverge from a point in Hercules and to converge on a diametrically opposite point in Columba. This indicates that the Sun has a motion within the Galaxy, towards the point in Hercules (the *Solar Apex*) and away from that in Columba (the *Solar Antapex*). The velocity of this *Solar Motion* is believed to be about 19·5 km/s.

The approximate co-ordinates of the solar apex are R.A. 270° (18 h), Dec. 34° N, and of the solar antapex R.A. 90° (6 h), Dec. 34° S.

The visible disk is known as the *photosphere* and has a granular or 'rice-grain' structure in large telescopes. Even in instruments as small as 8 cm aperture, the surface will have a mottled appearance when observing conditions are good, but this mottling is of a coarser texture than the delicate granular structure seen in larger instruments. Further, it will be noticed that there is considerable *limb-darkening*, the limb having only about ⅔ of the brilliance of the centre of the disk. This is due to absorption—by the cooler outer photospheric layers—of radiation coming from within, the rays from the limb regions having passed through a much greater thickness of the solar 'atmosphere' than those from the centre of the disk. The limb-darkening is especially noticeable in solar photographs.

Sunspots can be seen as dark patches on the photosphere. They can vary in size from small 'pores' to groups that are so large that they are easily visible to the naked eye when the Sun's brilliance is sufficiently reduced by cloud, mist or atmospheric absorption. A sunspot has a central dark region or *umbra*, surrounded by a less dark region or *penumbra*. These regions are only dark by comparison with the remainder of the visible disk, being at a lower temperature than the photosphere. The temperature of the umbra (dependent upon its diameter) is usually at least 1000°K cooler than the photosphere at 5800°K. The temperature of the penumbra is only slightly lower than that of the photosphere, about 5500°K. The penumbra of a well developed sunspot is always larger than its umbra, usually exceeding it in area by a factor of about 5 to 1.

As a spot approaches the Sun's limb an apparent displacement of the umbra is often observed, as a result of which the penumbra becomes much broader on the side nearest to the limb. This is known as the *Wilson Effect* (it was first recorded by A. Wilson of Glasgow in 1774), and indicates that the umbra is depressed below the surrounding surface, generally by about 2000 km. It is now believed that the Wilson Effect is also partially due to the umbra being more transparent than the penumbra. Occasionally·a negative Wilson Effect is seen, in which case the spot may appear as a small notch in the edge of the Sun's disk when just coming into or going out of view.

42

Sunspots are never seen in the Sun's polar regions. They occur mainly in two zones between 10° and 30° latitude, north and south, and are rarely seen at latitudes less than 5° or greater than 45°. Sunspots have magnetic fields and the magnetic polarity, + or –, of the 'preceding' or leading spot of a group is opposite in the northern and southern hemispheres. The length of time any particular sunspot group may persist depends upon a number of factors; small groups may never really develop and may decay within a few days of their formation, whereas remnants of large groups have been known to survive for several months.

The Sun's Rotation may be traced by the daily motion of the spots across the disk from east to west, the 'synodic' rotational period averaging $27\frac{1}{4}$ days. Spots may therefore be seen for just under a fortnight, although they are considerably foreshortened for half this period when near the limb. The 'sidereal' period is 25·03 days near the equator, 25·19 days at 10° latitude, 25·65 days at 20°, 26·39 days at 30°, 27·37 days at latitude 40° and increases to about 30 days near the pole.

The mean sidereal rotation period at present used in the *A.E.* is 25·38 days (27·2753 days synodic) but a 25·2 day sidereal (27·1 days synodic) is perhaps nearer the true value, being that favoured in the recurrence of sunspots, faculæ, flocculi and prominences. Carrington's Series of Rotations (25·38 days), used for statistical purposes, has as zero meridian the solar prime meridian that passed through the ascending node at 0 h U.T. on 1854 January 1. Rotation No. 1 began on 1853 November 9, No. 1583 on 1971 December 31·40.

The Sun's axis of rotation is inclined $7\frac{1}{4}°$, and the Earth's axis of rotation $23\frac{1}{2}°$, from the vertical to the plane of the ecliptic. Hence, as the Earth revolves around the Sun the direction of the Sun's axis of rotation appears to change. It may be displaced by as much as $26\frac{1}{2}°$ east or west of the solar meridian as defined by

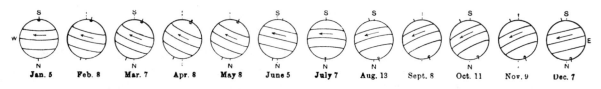

The distance of the Sun's visible pole from the limb has necessarily been exaggerated in the diagram. N, S, indicate the line of the hour circle. N showing North in an inverting telescope—nearest the horizon in the N. Hemisphere. In the S. Hemisphere, hold the book upside down.

FIGURE 8. Apparent motions of sunspots

the vertical to the plane of the ecliptic, and may be tilted towards or away from the observer by as much as $7\frac{1}{4}°$. Sunspots will therefore not normally travel in straight lines across the disk, but in curves as shown in Fig. 8. The variation of the position angle of the Sun's axis of rotation during the year (for the *North* pole) is approximately as given in Table 27, and the variation of the heliographic latitude of the centre of the Sun's disk (due to the component of the inclination of the Sun's axis in the direction of the Earth) is given in Table 28.

TABLE 27. VARIATION OF THE POSITION ANGLE OF THE SUN'S AXIS DURING THE YEAR

Jan. 5, July 7: 0°	July 7, Jan. 5: 0°
Jan. 16, June 26: 5° W	July 19, Dec. 26: 5° E
Jan. 27, June 15: 10° W	July 30, Dec. 16: 10° E
Feb. 8, June 5: 14° W	Aug. 13, Dec. 7: 14° E
Feb. 23, May 19: 20° W	Aug. 28, Nov. 20: 20° E
Mar. 7, May 8: 23° W	Sept. 8, Nov. 9: 23° E
Mar. 18, Apr. 26: 25° W	Sept. 21, Oct. 30: 25° E
April 8: 26°·3 W	Oct. 11: 26°·3 E

TABLE 28. VARIATION OF THE HELIOGRAPHIC LATITUDE OF THE CENTRE OF THE SUN'S DISK DURING THE YEAR

Dec. 7, June 6: 0°	June 6, Dec. 7: 0°
Dec. 15, May 28: 1°·0 S	June 14, Nov. 24: 1°·0 N
Dec. 23, May 20: 2°·0 S	June 22, Nov. 21: 2°·0 N
Jan. 1, May 11: 3°·0 S	July 1, Nov. 13: 3°·0 N
Jan. 10, May 2: 4°·0 S	July 11, Nov. 4: 4°·0 N
Jan. 19, Apr. 21: 5°·0 S	July 21, Oct. 25: 5°·0 N
Feb. 1, Apr. 8: 6°·0 S	Aug. 3, Oct. 12: 6°·0 N
Feb. 18, Mar. 21: 7°·0 S	Aug. 24, Sept. 22: 7°·0 N
Mar. 7: 7°·3 S	Sept. 9: 7°·3 N

The Sunspot Cycle. The degree of spottedness waxes and wanes over a period of about 11 years on average, although the actual value can vary between $7\frac{1}{2}$ and $16\frac{1}{2}$ years. The apparent 11-year cycle is really a half-cycle, for the spot-polarity changes after every minimum. The rise to maximum activity is normally more rapid than the decline, taking about $4\frac{1}{2}$ years. At times of sunspot minimum, no spots may be visible for weeks. Large spots can, however, appear at any part of the cycle, although they are most frequent at sunspot maximum.

Spörer's Law is the name given to the observed fact that the two spot zones simultaneously move slowly from high latitudes towards the solar equator as the solar cycle progresses. At minimum, the spot zones are at latitudes of only a few degrees north and south of the equator. The appearance of spots of opposite polarity at high latitudes at this time heralds the start of a new cycle and the number of spots belonging to the old cycle gradually decreases. The variation in latitude and number of the spots is shown in a striking manner by plotting the spots by date and latitude, producing a diagram which, from its shape, is known as the *Butterfly Diagram* (Fig. 9). It was first plotted by E. W. Maunder of the Royal Observatory, Greenwich, in 1904.

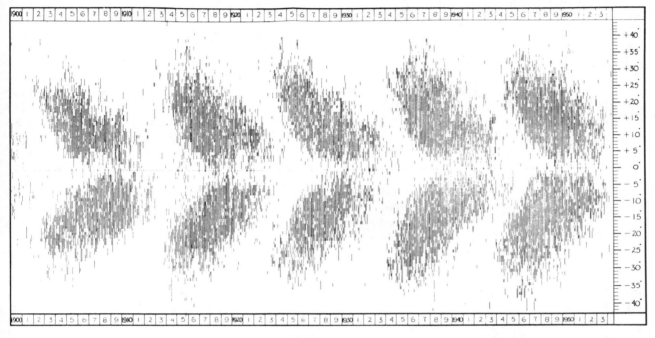

FIGURE 9. The 'Butterfly Diagram' for five complete solar cycles, 1900–1953

Objective Methods of Recording Sunspot Activity. There are two standard systems in use for recording the 'spottedness' of the Sun:

(*a*) *The Zürich (Wolf) Relative Sunspot Number (R).* $R = k(10g + f)$ where g = number of groups of spots, f = total number of spots, and k = a factor depending on the instrument used and the observer. The numbers vary from 0 to about 200 at a high maximum.

(*b*) *The Greenwich Sunspot Area* records the total area of all spots, corrected for foreshortening, in millionths of the Sun's visible hemisphere. It is useful to note that one millionth of the Sun's hemisphere is equal to about 3 million square kilometres. (For a sunspot to be visible to the unaided eye, its area must exceed 500 millionths.)

Both indexes of sunspot activity are listed for all available years in Table 29.

Faculæ. In addition to sunspots it may be possible to see irregular, more or less streaky patches, somewhat brighter than the normal Sun's surface. They are at elevations above the general level of the photosphere and exist mainly in the sunspot zones; they are intimately connected with sunspots. They are best seen near the limb of the disk, where they contrast well with the limb darkening. Faculæ usually appear before the formation of a spot and are still present long after the spot has disappeared.

Prominences are jets or clouds of glowing red gas (mostly hydrogen) which rise all round the Sun's limb from the *chromosphere,* a bright scarlet irregular ring of light (5″ to 15″ of arc in depth) seen only during total solar eclipses or in monochromatic light. The *reversing layer* is a relatively thin layer of gas lying directly above the photosphere which is responsible for the dark lines in the solar spectrum, caused by its absorbing certain portions of the bright light from the photospheric layers beneath and hence leaving gaps, or 'dark lines' at the wavelengths absorbed. In solar eclipses, just before the Sun disappears, it shows the bright emission lines of the chromosphere instead of the dark absorption lines—a phenomenon known as the *flash spectrum.*

TABLE 29. STATISTICS OF SUNSPOT ACTIVITY

R_Z: Zurich yearly means of daily Relative Sunspot Numbers. A_G: Greenwich yearly means of daily whole spot areas, corrected for foreshortening, in millionths of the Sun's visible hemisphere. Years of sunspot maximum are shown in bold type.

	1701	1702	1703	1704	**1705**	1706	1707	1708	1709	1710	1711	1712	1713	1714	1715
R_Z:	11	16	23	36	58	29	20	10	8	3	0	0	2	11	27

	1716	**1717**	1718	1719	1720	1721	1722	1723	1724	1725	1726	**1727**	1728	1729	1730
R_Z:	47	63	60	39	28	26	22	11	21	40	78	122	103	73	47

	1731	1732	1733	1734	1735	1736	1737	**1738**	1739	1740	1741	1742	1743	1744	1745
R_Z:	35	11	5	16	34	70	81	111	101	73	40	20	16	5	11

	1746	1747	1748	1749	**1750**	1751	1752	1753	1754	1755	1756	1757	1758	1759	1760
R_Z:	22	40	60	80·9	83·4	47·7	47·8	30·7	12·2	9·6	10·2	32·4	47·6	54·0	62·9

	1761	1762	1763	1764	1765	1766	1767	1768	**1769**	1770	1771	1772	1773	1774	1775
R_Z:	85·9	61·2	45·1	36·4	20·9	11·4	37·8	69·8	106·1	100·8	81·6	66·5	34·8	30·6	7·0

	1776	1777	**1778**	1779	1780	1781	1782	1783	1784	1785	1786	**1787**	1788	1789	1790
R_Z:	19·8	92·5	154·4	125·9	84·8	68·1	38·5	22·8	10·2	24·1	82·9	132·0	130·9	118·1	89·9

	1791	1792	1793	1794	1795	1796	1797	1798	1799	1800	1801	1802	1803	**1804**	1805
R_Z:	66·6	60·0	46·9	41·0	21·3	16·0	6·4	4·1	6·8	14·5	34·0	45·0	43·1	47·5	42·2

	1806	1807	1808	1809	1810	1811	1812	1813	1814	1815	**1816**	1817	1818	1819	1820
R_Z:	28·1	10·1	8·1	2·5	0·0	1·4	5·0	12·2	13·9	35·4	45·8	41·1	30·1	23·9	15·6

	1821	1822	1823	1824	1825	1826	1827	1828	1829	**1830**	1831	1832	1833	1834	1835
R_Z:	6·6	4·0	1·8	8·5	16·6	36·3	49·6	64·2	67·0	70·9	47·8	27·5	8·5	13·2	56·9

	1836	**1837**	1838	1839	1840	1841	1842	1843	1844	1845	1846	1847	**1848**	1849	1850
R_Z:	121·5	138·3	103·2	85·7	64·6	36·7	24·2	10·7	15·0	40·1	61·5	98·5	124·7	96·3	66·6

	1851	1852	1853	1854	1855	1856	1857	1858	1859	**1860**	1861	1862	1863	1864	1865
R_Z:	64·5	54·1	39·0	20·6	6·7	4·3	22·7	54·8	93·8	95·8	77·2	59·1	44·0	47·0	30·5

	1866	1867	1868	1869	**1870**	1871	1872	1873	1874	1875	1876	1877	1878	1879	1880
R_Z:	16·3	7·3	37·6	74·0	139·0	111·2	101·6	66·2	44·7	17·0	11·3	12·4	3·4	6·0	32·3
A_G:									604	249	126	108	22	38	441

	1881	1882	**1883**	1884	1885	1886	1887	1888	1889	1890	1891	1892	**1893**	1894	1895
R_Z:	54·3	59·7	63·7	63·5	52·2	25·4	13·1	6·8	6·3	7·1	35·6	73·0	85·1	78·0	64·0
A_G:	681	1000	1154	1079	807	380	179	89	78	99	569	1214	1464	1282	974

	1896	1897	1898	1899	1900	1901	1902	1903	1904	**1905**	1906	1907	1908	1909	1910
R_Z:	41·8	26·2	26·7	12·1	9·5	2·7	5·0	24·4	42·0	63·5	53·8	62·0	48·5	43·9	18·6
A_G:	543	514	375	111	75	29	62	350	490	1191	778	1082	697	694	264

	1911	1912	1913	1914	1915	1916	**1917**	1918	1919	1920	1921	1922	1923	1924	1925
R_Z:	5·7	3·6	1·4	9·6	47·4	57·1	103·9	80·6	63·6	37·6	26·1	14·2	5·8	16·7	44·3
A_G:	64	37	7	152	697	724	1537	1118	1052	618	420	252	55	276	830

	1926	1927	**1928**	1929	1930	1931	1932	1933	1934	1935	1936	**1937**	1938	1939	1940
R_Z:	63·9	69·0	77·8	64·9	35·7	21·2	11·1	5·7	8·7	36·1	79·7	114·4	109·6	88·8	67·8
A_G:	1262	1058	1390	1242	516	275	163	88	119	624	1141	2074	2019	1579	1039

	1941	1942	1943	1944	1945	1946	**1947**	1948	1949	1950	1951	1952	1953	1954	1955
R_Z:	47·5	30·6	16·3	9·6	33·2	92·6	151·6	136·3	134·7	83·9	69·4	31·5	13·9	4·4	38·0
A_G:	658	423	295	126	429	1817	2637	1977	2129	1222	1136	404	146	35	553

	1956	**1957**	1958	1959	1960	1961	1962	1963	1964	1965	1966	1967	**1968**	1969	1970
R_Z:	141·7	190·2	184·8	159·0	112·3	53·9	37·5	27·9	10·2	15·1	47·0	93·8	105·9	105·5	104·5
A_G:				2879	1659	614	458	288	56						

	1971	1972	1973	1974	1975	1976	1977	1978	1979	1980	1981	1982	1983	1984	1985
R_Z:	66·6														
A_G:															

Filaments are long dark prominences seen in projection on the Sun's disk in monochromatic light (usually that of hydrogen).

Flocculi, also known as *plages*, are seen on spectroheliograms in one particular wavelength of light (normally calcium or hydrogen); they are small irregular clouds of either of these elements and can be seen all over the disk.

Solar Flare. A brief increase in luminosity of a localized region of the chromosphere, usually directly above a sunspot group, often accompanied by emission of ultra-violet and X-ray radiation, and also charged particles which cause strong disturbances in the Earth's ionosphere approximately one day later.

The Corona, normally seen well only at times of solar eclipse, has the appearance of an irregular pearly ring of light surrounding the Sun. It is a tenuous layer of gas, mostly ionized hydrogen and free electrons, at a temperature of approximately 1,000,000°K. Its shape varies with the 11-year sunspot cycle, but in detail its shape depends on the solar activity at the time of the eclipse. Generally, at sunspot maximum it is more or less distributed regularly around the Sun, whilst at sunspot minimum there are often large streamers, several degrees in length, near the solar equator, with tufts or plumes of light near the poles. The brightness of the corona falls off rapidly with distance from the Sun.

Observation of the Sun

It is extremely dangerous to attempt to view the Sun unless proper precautions are taken; blindness may be the penalty of rashness or ignorance. A perfectly safe method is to support a smooth, white card

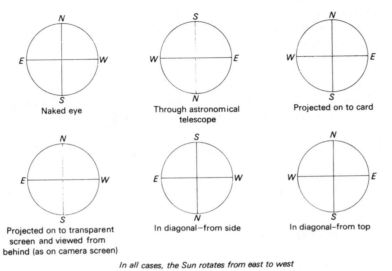

In all cases, the Sun rotates from east to west

FIGURE 10

at the distance of about a foot from the eye-piece, and to focus the image of the Sun projected on to it. The screen should be held in a covered frame-work or box, and the picture of the Sun viewed through a hole in one of the sides.

The orientation of the cardinal points varies with the method of projection used, as can be seen in Fig. 10.

Observing Sunspots. In studying their motion across the disk from east to west the position of the Sun's axis must be taken into consideration, as the apparent path varies according to the time of the year. The spots only move in straight lines across the disk around June 6 and December 7, on which dates alone the solar equator is presented as a straight line which bisects the visible disk with both poles exactly on the limb. At all other times one pole alone is visible—very near the limb owing to foreshortening—and the solar equator lies on one side or other of the apparent centre of the disk, and is curved downwards or upwards, as are also the paths of the spots: maximum curvature northwards, about March 7; southwards, about September 9. See Tables 21 and 22 above.

The *Astronomical Ephemeris* and the *B.A.A. Handbook* give the following information necessary for determining the position of the spot on the Sun:

P, the position angle of the northern end of the Sun's axis
(+ve if east of the north point, – ve if west);
B_0, the heliographic latitude of the centre of the disk
(+ve if the equator is curved southwards, – ve if curved northwards);
L_0, the heliographic longitude of the centre of the disk.

Observing Prominences, by the spectroscope. The edge of the Sun's image should be made to fall on the nearly-closed slit of the spectroscope—which must be one of considerable dispersive power. The telescope should then be driven so as to keep the image in the same position. The spectroscope is next focused on one of the hydrogen lines of the spectrum, and, on the slit being opened, the prominence will be seen. Good views may be obtained in this way, using a 7·5 cm (3 in.) telescope with a spectroscope having several prisms.

THE MOON

General

The Moon occupies a special position so far as we are concerned, since it is the only body which has been reached by Man. Before the Space Age, our knowledge of the lunar surface was drawn largely from observations made by amateur observers. The situation now is, of course, very different; the Moon has been studied not only by the *Apollo* astronauts who have landed there, but also by means of the many thousands of close-range photographs taken from vehicles such as the U.S. *Orbiters* and the Russian *Luna* probes. Undoubtedly this restricts the scientific value of observations carried out from Earth. However, the Moon remains the most interesting of all celestial bodies from the viewpoint of the owner of a small telescope, because there is so much detail to be seen.

Orientation. Until recently all lunar maps and drawings were presented with south at the top, west being to the left in the telescopic view (i.e. Mare Crisium to the western limb, Grimaldi to the eastern). East and west have now been reversed, according to the official decision of the International Astronomical Union, and the new orientation is followed in the maps given here. However, it was also decided to print all maps and drawings with north at the top; this has not been adopted in the maps given here, because it is not what the observer will actually see through his telescope (from the Earth's northern hemisphere).

Nomenclature. The system of nomenclature for the Moon was introduced by Riccioli in 1651, though it has of course been greatly adapted and extended. In general, craters are named after famous persons of the past (Ptolemy, Tycho, Kepler, Newton, etc.) with smaller craters distinguished by letters; thus Kepler A is a smaller crater near Kepler. The system used here is that approved by the International Astronomical Union. It has also been extended to cover the Moon's far side, never visible from Earth.

Earthshine. Popularly known as 'the Old Moon in the New Moon's arms'. It is due to light reflected on to the Moon from the Earth, and is very noticeable during the crescent stage.

The Surface Features

The lunar map reproduced on pp. 48 and 49 covers that part of the Moon visible from Earth. The averted hemisphere, first photographed by the Soviet vehicle *Lunik 3* in 1959 and since charted in great detail by the *Orbiters*, contains no major maria, though there are craters in profusion.

Maria. These are the darker and smoother portions of the surface, still known as 'seas' because they were originally thought to be expanses of water. They are of two main kinds: basically circular (Mare Imbrium, Mare Crisium) and irregular (Mare Frigoris). Most of the major maria form a connected system. The complicated and important Mare Orientale is an exceptional feature, but is barely visible from Earth, since it lies right on the limb.

Mountains. The Moon is a mountainous world, and there are many high peaks, loftier in relation to the lunar globe than are the mountains of Earth. However, the main 'ranges' form the boundaries of the regular maria; thus the spectacular Apennines make up part of the border of the Mare Imbrium. Isolated peaks are also very common; Pico and Piton, in the neighbourhood of the dark-floored Plato, are excellent examples. The heights of the elevations are found by measurements of the shadows which they cast, though there is of course no convenient standard of reference such as sea-level on the Earth.

Walled Formations. The whole Moon is dominated by the walled structures which are known generally as *craters*. These range from vast enclosures over 250 km in diameter down to tiny features too small to be seen from Earth. There is no universal agreement as to their origin, or, for that matter, the origin of the maria. Some authorities believe them to have been produced by internal forces, while others attribute them to meteoritic impact. No doubt both forces have operated; the question at issue is which force has played the major rôle.

Locating Table for Lunar Map

This Table gives the selenographic longitude and latitude, respectively, of the co-ordinate grid intersection that is nearest to each crater on the accompanying Lunar Map (pp. 48–49). This permits quick location of features that are known by name only.

#	Name	Long	Lat
1.	Abenezra	+ 10	− 20
2.	Abulfeda	+ 10	− 10
3.	Agatharchides	− 30	− 20
4.	Agrippa	+ 10	0
5.	Albategnius	0	− 10
6.	Alexander	+ 10	+ 40
7.	Aliacensis	0	− 30
8.	Almanon.	+ 20	− 20
9.	Alpetragius	0	− 20
10.	Alphonsus	0	− 10
11.	Apianus	+ 10	− 30
12.	Apollonius	+ 60	0
13.	Arago	+ 20	+ 10
14.	Archimedes	0	+ 30
15.	Archytas	0	+ 60
16.	Aristarchus	− 50	+ 20
17.	Aristillus	0	+ 30
18.	Aristoteles	+ 20	+ 50
19.	Arzachel	0	− 20
20.	Asclepi	+ 20	− 50
21.	Atlas	+ 50	+ 50
22.	Autolycus	0	+ 30
23.	Azophi	+ 10	− 20
24.	Baco	+ 20	− 50
25.	Bailly	− 70	− 70
26.	Barocius	+ 20	− 40
27.	Bayer	− 30	− 50
28.	Beaumont	+ 30	− 20
29.	Bernouilli	+ 60	+ 30
30.	Berzelius	+ 50	+ 40
31.	Bessel	+ 20	+ 20
32.	Bettinus	− 40	− 60
33.	Bianchini	− 30	+ 50
34.	Biela	+ 50	− 50
35.	Billy	− 50	− 10
36.	Birmingham	− 10	+ 60
37.	Birt	− 10	− 20
38.	Blancanus	− 20	− 60
39.	Blanchinus	0	− 30
40.	Boguslawsky	+ 50	− 70
41.	Bohnenberger	+ 40	− 20
42.	Bond, W. C.	0	+ 60
43.	Bonpland	− 20	− 10
44.	Borda	+ 50	− 20
45.	Boscovitch	+ 10	+ 10
46.	Bouguer	− 40	+ 50
47.	Boussingault	+ 70	− 70
48.	Bulliadus	− 20	− 20
49.	Burckhardt	+ 60	+ 30
50.	Bürg	+ 30	+ 40
51.	Calippus	+ 10	+ 40
52.	Campanus	− 30	− 30
53.	Capella	+ 30	− 10
54.	Capuanus	− 30	− 30
55.	Cardanus	− 70	− 10
56.	Casatus	− 30	− 70
57.	Cassini	0	+ 40
58.	Catharina	+ 20	− 20
59.	Cavalerius	− 70	+ 10
60.	Cavendish	− 50	− 20
61.	Celsius	+ 20	− 30
62.	Cepheus	+ 50	+ 40
63.	Chacornac	+ 30	+ 30
64.	Cichus	− 20	− 30
65.	Clairaut	+ 10	− 50
66.	Clausius	− 40	− 40
67.	Clavius	− 10	− 60
68.	Cleomedes	+ 60	+ 30
69.	Colombo	+ 50	− 10
70.	Condamine	− 30	+ 50
71.	Condorcet	+ 70	+ 10
72.	Conon	0	+ 20
73.	Cook	+ 50	− 20
74.	Copernicus	− 20	+ 10
75.	Crüger	− 70	− 20
76.	Curtius	0	− 70
77.	Cuvier	+ 10	− 50
78.	Cyrillus	+ 30	− 10
79.	Damoiseau	− 60	0
80.	Daniell	+ 30	+ 30
81.	Davy	− 10	− 10
82.	Dawes	+ 30	+ 20
83.	De Gasparis	− 50	− 30
84.	Delambre	+ 20	0
85.	De la Rue	+ 50	+ 60
86.	Delauney	0	− 20
87.	Delisle	− 30	+ 30
88.	Deluc	0	− 50
89.	Descartes	+ 20	− 10
90.	Diophantus	− 30	+ 30
91.	Dollond	+ 10	− 10
92.	Doppelmayer	− 40	− 30
93.	Eichstädt	− 70	− 20
94.	Encke	− 40	0
95.	Endymion	+ 60	+ 50
96.	Epigenes	0	+ 70
97.	Eratosthenes	− 10	+ 10
98.	Euclides	− 30	− 10
99.	Eudoxus	+ 20	+ 40
100.	Euler	− 30	+ 20
101.	Fabricius	+ 40	− 40
102	Faraday	+ 10	− 40
103.	Fermat	+ 20	− 20
104.	Fernelius	0	− 40
105.	Firmicus	+ 60	+ 10
106.	Flamsteed	− 40	0
107.	Fontenelle	− 20	+ 60
108.	Fracastorius	+ 30	− 20
109.	Fra Mauro	− 20	− 10
110.	Franklin	+ 50	+ 40
111.	Furnerius	+ 60	− 40
112.	Gambart	− 10	0
113.	Gassendi	− 40	− 20
114.	Gauricus	− 10	− 30
115.	Gaus	+ 70	+ 40
116.	Gay-Lussac	− 20	+ 10
117.	Geber	+ 10	− 20
118.	Geminus	+ 60	+ 30
119.	Gemma Frisius	+ 10	− 30
120.	Goclenius	+ 50	− 10
121.	Godin	+ 10	0
122.	Goodacre	+ 10	− 30
123.	Grimaldi	− 70	− 10
124.	Gruithuisen	− 40	+ 30
125.	Guericke	− 10	− 10
126.	Gutenberg	+ 40	− 10
127.	Hahn	+ 70	+ 30
128.	Hainzel	− 30	− 40
129.	Halley	+ 10	− 10
130.	Hansteen	− 50	− 10
131.	Harpalus	− 40	+ 50
132.	Hase	+ 60	− 30
133.	Heinsius	− 20	− 40
134.	Helicon	− 20	+ 40
135.	Hell	− 10	− 30
136.	Heraclitus	+ 10	− 50
137.	Hercules	+ 40	+ 50
138.	Herigonius	− 30	− 10
139.	Herodotus	− 50	+ 20
140.	Herschel	0	− 10
141.	Herschel, J.	− 40	+ 60
142.	Hesiodus	− 20	− 30
143.	Hevelius	− 70	0
144.	Hippalus	− 30	− 20
145.	Hipparchus	0	0
146.	Horrebow	− 40	+ 60
147.	Horrocks	0	0
148.	Hortensius	− 30	+ 10
149.	Humboldt, W.	+ 70	− 30
150.	Hypatia	+ 20	0
151.	Isidorus	+ 30	− 10
152.	Jansen	+ 30	+ 10
153.	Janssen	+ 40	− 40
154.	Julius Caesar	+ 10	+ 10
155.	Kepler	− 40	+ 10
156.	Kies	− 20	− 30
157.	Kirch	− 10	+ 40
158.	Klaproth	− 30	− 70
159.	Klein	0	− 10
160.	Krafft	− 70	+ 20
161.	Landsberg, C.	− 30	0
162.	Lagrange	− 70	− 30
163.	Lalande	− 10	0
164.	Lambert	− 20	+ 30
165.	Landsberg	− 30	0
166.	Langrenus	+ 60	− 10
167.	Lassell	− 10	− 20
168.	Lee	− 40	− 30
169.	Lehmann	− 60	− 40
170.	Letronne	− 40	− 10
171.	Leverrier	− 20	+ 40
172.	Lexell	0	− 40
173.	Licetus	+ 10	− 50
174.	Lilius	+ 10	− 50
175.	Lindenau	+ 30	− 30
176.	Linné	+ 10	+ 30
177.	Littrow	+ 30	+ 20
178.	Lohrmann	− 70	0
179.	Longomontanus	− 20	− 50
180.	Lubiniezky	− 20	− 20
181.	Maclear	+ 20	+ 10
182.	Macrobius	+ 50	+ 20
183.	Mädler	+ 30	− 10
184.	Magelhaens	+ 40	− 10
185.	Maginus	− 10	− 50
186.	Mairan	− 40	+ 40
187.	Manilius	+ 10	+ 10
188.	Manzinus	+ 30	− 70
189.	Maraldi	+ 30	+ 20
190.	Marius	+ 70	− 40
191.	Maskelyne	+ 30	0
192.	Maupertuis	− 30	+ 50
193.	Maurolycus	+ 10	− 40
194.	Mayer, Tobias	− 30	+ 20
195.	Menelaus	+ 20	+ 20
196.	Mercator	− 30	− 30
197.	Mersenius	− 50	− 20
198.	Messala	+ 60	+ 40
199.	Messier	+ 50	0
200.	Metius	+ 40	− 40
201.	Meton	+ 20	+ 70
202.	Milichius	− 30	+ 10
203.	Miller	0	− 40
204.	Monge	+ 50	− 20
205.	Moretus	0	− 70
206.	Mösting	− 10	0
207.	Mutus	+ 30	− 60
208.	Nasireddin	0	− 40
209.	Neander	+ 40	− 30
210.	Nearchus	+ 40	− 60
211.	Nicolai	+ 30	− 40
212.	Oken	+ 70	− 50
213.	Orontius	0	− 40
214.	Palisa	− 10	− 10
215.	Pallas	0	0
216.	Parrot	0	− 10
217.	Parry	− 20	− 10
218.	Peirce	+ 50	+ 20
219.	Petavius	+ 60	− 20
220.	Philolaus	− 30	+ 70
221.	Phocylides	− 60	− 50
222.	Piazzi	− 70	− 40
223.	Picard	+ 60	+ 10
224.	Piccolomini	+ 30	− 30
225.	Pickering, W. H.	+ 50	0
226.	Pictet	− 10	− 40
227.	Pitatus	− 10	− 30
228.	Pitiscus	+ 30	− 50
229.	Plana	+ 30	+ 40
230.	Plato	− 10	+ 50
231.	Playfair	+ 10	− 20
232.	Plinius	+ 20	+ 20
233.	Pontanus	+ 10	− 30
234.	Pontécoulant	+ 70	− 60
235.	Posidonius	+ 30	+ 30
236.	Prinz	− 50	+ 30
237.	Proclus	+ 50	+ 20
238.	Protagoras	+ 10	+ 50
239.	Ptolemaeus	0	− 10
240.	Purbach	0	− 30
241.	Pythagoras	− 60	+ 60
242.	Pytheas	− 20	+ 20
243.	Rabbi Levi	+ 20	− 30
244.	Ramsden	− 30	− 30
245.	Regiomontanus	0	− 30
246.	Reichenbach	+ 50	− 30
247.	Reiner	− 60	+ 10
248.	Reinhold	− 20	0
249.	Repsold	− 70	+ 50
250.	Rhaeticus	0	0
251.	Rheita	+ 50	− 40
252.	Riccioli	− 70	0
253.	Römer	+ 40	+ 30
254.	Ross	+ 20	+ 10
255.	Rothmann	+ 30	− 30
256.	Sacrobosco	+ 20	− 20
257.	Santbech	+ 50	− 20
258.	Sasserides	− 10	− 40
259.	Saussure	0	− 40
260.	Scheiner	− 30	− 60
261.	Schickard	− 50	− 40
262.	Schiller	− 40	− 50
263.	Schröter	− 10	0
264.	Seleucus	− 70	+ 20
265.	Sharp	− 40	+ 50
266.	Simpelius	+ 20	− 70
267.	Snellius	+ 60	− 30
268.	Sosigenes	+ 20	+ 10
269.	Stadius	− 10	+ 10
270.	Stevinus	+ 60	− 30
271.	Stöfler	+ 10	− 40
272.	Strabo	+ 50	+ 60
273.	Struve	+ 60	+ 40
274.	Struve, Otto	− 70	+ 20
275.	Tacitus	+ 20	− 20
276.	Taruntius	+ 50	+ 10
277.	Theaetetus	+ 10	+ 40
278.	Thebit	0	− 20
279.	Theophilus	+ 30	− 10
280.	Timaeus	0	+ 60
281.	Timocharis	− 10	+ 30
282.	Torricelli	+ 30	0
283.	Triesnecker	0	0
284.	Tycho	− 10	− 40
285.	Ukert	0	+ 10
286.	Vendelinus	+ 60	− 20
287.	Vieta	− 60	− 30
288.	Vitello	− 40	− 30
289.	Vitruvius	+ 30	+ 20
290.	Vlacq	+ 40	− 50
291.	Walter	0	− 30
292.	Weiss	− 20	− 30
293.	Werner	0	− 30
294.	Wilhelm I	− 20	− 40
295.	Wilkins	+ 20	− 30
296.	Wurzelbauer	− 20	− 30
297.	Zach	0	− 60
298.	Zagut	+ 20	− 30
299.	Zuchius	− 50	− 60
300.	Zupus	− 50	− 20

MAP OF THE MOON

This map of the moon is based on the original drawing by Karel Andel, published in 1926 as *Mappa Selenographica*. A grid of selenographic co-ordinates has been superimposed. The positions of the numbered craters to the nearest 10 degrees of longitude and latitude are given in the locating table on page 47.

The coordinate grid and identifications are by Sky Publishing Corp. of Cambridge, Massachusetts, USA, and are used by permission.

MOUNTAINS AND VALLEYS

a. Alpine Valley	n. Laplace Prom.
b. Alps Mts.	o. Leibnitz Mts.
c. Altai Mts.	p. Pico
d. Apennine Mts.	q. Piton
e. Carpathian Mts.	r. Pyrenees Mts.
f. Caucasus Mts.	s. Rheita Valley
g. D'Alembert Mts.	t. Riphæus Mts
h. Doerfel Mts.	u. Rook Mts.
i. Haemus Mts.	v. Spitzbergen
j. Harbinger Mts.	w. Straight Range
k. Heraclides Prom.	x. Straight Wall
l. Hyginus Cleft	y. Taurus Mts.
m. Jura Mts.	z. Teneriffe Mts.

LUNAR CRATERS

1. Abenezra	57. Cassini
2. Abulfeda	58. Catharina
3. Agatharchides	59. Cavalerius
4. Agrippa	60. Cavendish
5. Albategnius	61. Celsius
6. Alexander	62. Cepheus
7. Aliacensis	63. Chacornac
8. Almanon	64. Cichus
9. Alpetragius	65. Clairaut
10. Alphonsus	66. Clausius
11. Apianus	67. Clavius
12. Apollonius	68. Cleomedes
13. Arago	69. Colombo
14. Archimedes	70. Condamine
15. Archytas	71. Condorcet
16. Aristarchus	72. Conon
17. Aristillus	73. Cook
18. Aristoteles	74. Copernicus
19. Arzachel	75. Crüger
20. Asclepi	76. Curtius
21. Atlas	77. Cuvier
22. Autolycus	78. Cyrillus
23. Azophi	
	79. Damoiseau
24. Baco	80. Daniell
25. Bailly	81. Davy
26. Barocius	82. Dawes
27. Bayer	83. De Gasparis
28. Beaumont	84. Delambre
29. Bernouilli	85. De la Rue
30. Berzelius	86. Delauney
31. Bessel	87. Delisle
32. Bettinus	88. Deluc
33. Bianchini	89. Descartes
34. Biela	90. Diophantus
35. Billy	91. Dollond
36. Birmingham	92. Doppelmayer
37. Birt	
38. Blancanus	93. Eichstädt
39. Blanchinus	94. Encke
40. Boguslawsky	95. Endymion
41. Bohnenberger	96. Epigenes
42. Bond, W. C.	97. Eratosthenes
43. Bonpland	98. Euclides
44. Borda	99. Eudoxus
45. Boscovitch	100. Euler
46. Bouguer	
47. Boussingault	101. Fabricius
48. Bullialdus	102. Faraday
49. Burckhardt	103. Fermat
50. Bürg	104. Fernelius
	105. Firmicus
51. Calippus	106. Flamsteed
52. Campanus	107. Fontenelle
53. Capella	108. Fracastorius
54. Capuanus	109. Fra Mauro
55. Cardanus	110. Franklin
56. Casatus	111. Furnerius

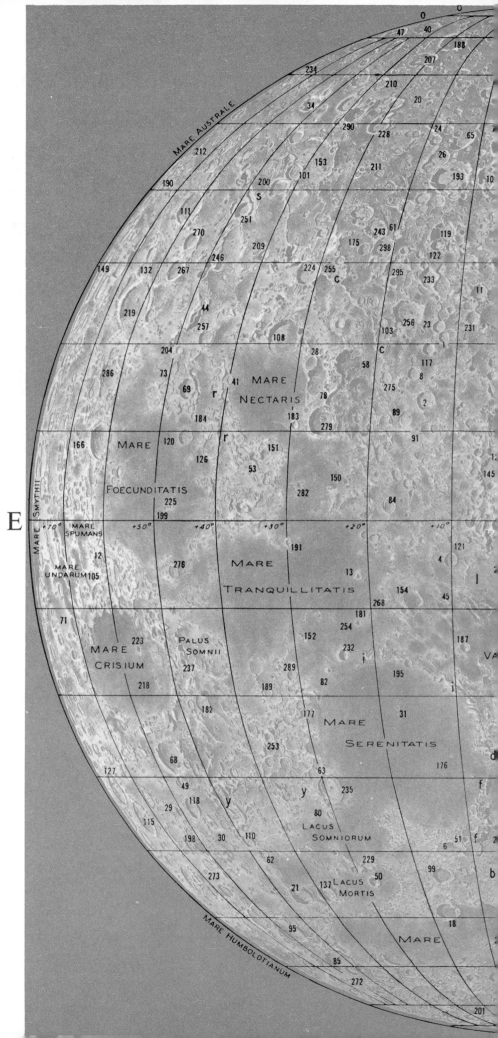

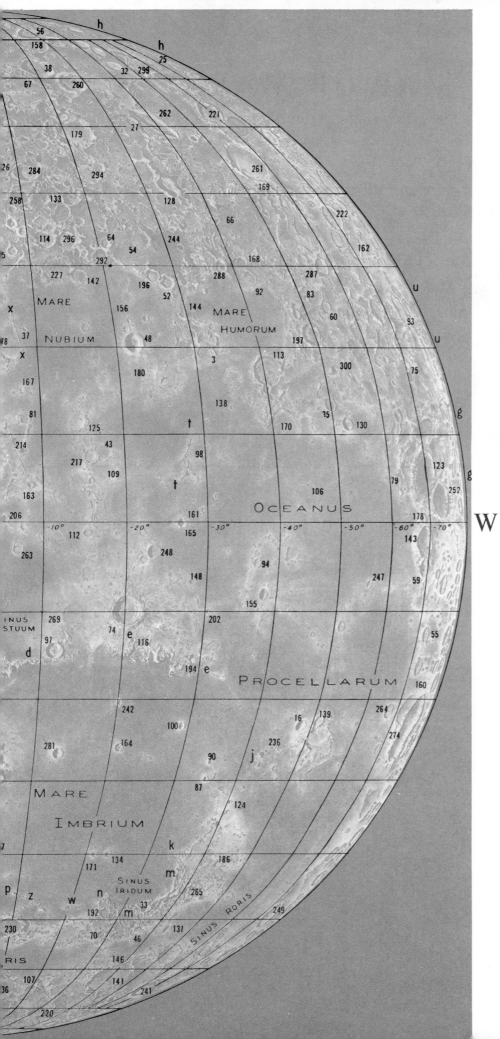

MAP OF MARS

and list of named features, as adopted by the International Astronomical Union

S

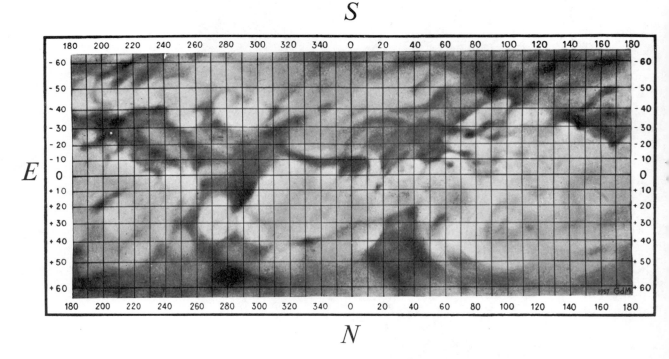

N

Planetographic Co-ordinates of Principal Features

Co-ordinates are given in the order (longitude, latitude), thus: (30°, +45°)

Acidalium Mare (30°, +45°)	Copaïs Palus (280°, +55°)	Libya (270°, 0°)	Protei Regio (50°, −23°)
Aeolis (215°, −5°)	Coprates (65°, −15°)	Lunæ Lacus (65°, +15°)	Protonilus (315°, +42°)
Aeria (310°, +10°)	Cyclopia (230°, −5°)	Margaritifer Sinus (25°, −10°)	Pyrrhæ Regio (38°, −15°)
Aetheria (230°, +40°)	Cydonia (0°, +40°)	Memnonia (150°, −20°)	Sabaeus Sinus (340°, −8°)
Aethiopis (230°, +10°)	Deltoton Sinus (305°, −4°)	Meroe (285°, +35°)	Scandia (150°, +60°)
Amazonis (140°, 0°)	Deucalionis Regio (340°, −15°)	Meridiani Sinus (0°, −5°)	Serpentis Mare (320°, −30°)
Amenthes (250°, +5°)	Deuteronilus (0°, +35°)	Moab (350°, +20°)	Sinaï (70°, −20°)
Aonius Sinus (105°, −45°)	Diacria (180°, +50°)	Mœris Lacus (270°, +8°)	Sirenum Mare (155°, −30°)
Arabia (330°, +20°)	Dioscuria (320°, +50°)	Nectar (72°, −28°)	Sithonius Lacus (245°, +45°)
Araxes (115°, −25°)	Edom (345°, 0°)	Neith Regio (270°, +35°)	Solis Lacus (90°, −28°)
Arcadia (100°, +45°)	Electris (190°, −45°)	Nepenthes (260°, +20°)	Styx (200°, +30°)
Argyre (25°, −45°)	Elysium (210°, +25°)	Nereidum Fretum (55°, −45°)	Syria (100°, −20°)
Arnon (335°, +48°)	Eridania (220°, −45°)	Niliacus Lacus (30°, +30°)	Syrtis Major (290°, +10°)
Auroræ Sinus (50°, −15°)	Erythræum Mare (40°, −25°)	Nilokeras (55°, +30°)	Tanaïs (70°, +50°)
Ausonia (250°, −40°)	Eunostos (220°, +22°)	Nilosyrtis (290°, +42°)	Tempe (70°, +40°)
Australe Mare (40°, −60°)	Euphrates (335°, +20°)	Nix Olympica (130°, +20°)	Thaumasia (85°, −35°)
Baltia (50°, +60°)	Gehon (0°, +15°)	Noachis (330°, −45°)	Thoth (255°, +30°)
Boreum Mare (90°, +50°)	Hadriacum Mare (270°, −40°)	Ogygis Regio (65°, −45°)	Thyle I (180°, −70°)
Boreosyrtis (290°, +55°)	Hellas (290°, −40°)	Olympia (200°, +80°)	Thyle II (230°, −70°)
Candor (75°, +3°)	Hellespontica Depressio (340°, −6°)	Ophir (65°, −10°)	Thymiamata (10°, +10°)
Casius (260°, +40°)	Hellespontus (325°, −50°)	Ortygia (0°, +60°)	Tithonius Lacus (85°, −5°)
Cebrenia (210°, +50°)	Hesperia (240°, −20°)	Oxia Palus (18°, +8°)	Tractus Albus (80°, +30°)
Cecropia (320°, +60°)	Hiddekel (345°, +15°)	Oxus (10°, +20°)	Trinacria (268°, −25°)
Ceraunius (95°, +20°)	Hyperboreus Lacus (60°, +75°)	Panchaïa (200°, +60°)	Trivium Charontis (198°, +20°)
Cerberus (205°, +15°)	Iapigia (295°, −20°)	Pandoræ Fretum (340°, −25°)	Tyrrhenum Mare (255°, −20°)
Chalce (0°, −50°)	Icaria (130°, −40°)	Phæthontis (155°, −50°)	Uchronia (260°, +70°)
Chersonesus (260°, −50°)	Isidis Regio (275°, +20°)	Phison (320°, +20°)	Umbra (290°, +50°)
Chronium Mare (210°, −58°)	Ismenius Lacus (330°, +40°)	Phlegra (190°, +30°)	Utopia (250°, +50°)
Chryse (30°, +10°)	Jamuna (40°, +10°)	Phœnicis Lacus (110°, −12°)	Vulcani Pelagus (15°, −35°)
Chrysokeras (110°, −50°)	Juventæ Fons (63°, −5°)	Phrixi Regio (70°, −40°)	Xanthe (50°, +10°)
Cimmerium Mare (220°, −20°)	Læstrygon (200°, 0°)	Promethei Sinus (280°, −65°)	Yaonis Regio (320°, −40°)
Claritas (110°, −35°)	Lemuria (200°, +70°)	Propontis (185°, +45°)	Zephyria (195°, 0°)

It is not easy to divide the walled structures into definite classes, and the following system—developed from that of Neison—is only one of many.

(*a*) Walled Plains, of large size (over 70 km in diameter). These have, in general, low walls and moderately sunken floors which often lack any central mountain structures. Examples are Ptolemæus, Grimaldi, Clavius and Plato.

(*b*) Ring Plains, essentially similar to the walled plains but of smaller size. Examples are Firmicus and Crüger.

(*c*) Craters, with higher walls, more deeply sunken floors, and—in many cases—central mountains or mountain groups. Examples are Tycho, Copernicus, Kepler and Alpetragius.

(*d*) Small craters, essentially similar to the major craters, but with more sharply-defined walls; usually below about 25 km in diameter. Bessel, on the Mare Serenitatis, is a good example.

(*e*) Craterlets, below about 10 km in diameter.

(*f*) Small features, with hardly perceptible walls and floors which are only slightly depressed below the outer surface.

(*g*) Chain-craters, which have been described as resembling 'strings of beads'. They are of small size, and are often associated with rills. For instance, the so-called Rheita Valley is really a crater-chain.

The distribution of the walled structures is interesting. They tend to appear in lines (Ptolemæus–Alphonsus–Arzachel), groups (Archimedes–Aristillus–Autolycus) or pairs (Abenezra–Azophi). Where one crater breaks into another, it is usually the smaller structure which is the intruder. Some formations have had their 'seaward' walls badly damaged, or even obliterated (Hippalus, Littrow). Wargentin, almost 90 km in diameter, is 'filled', with a raised floor; it is the only large example of what may be termed a plateau.

Rays. The rays, systems of bright streaks associated with certain craters, dominate the scene near Full Moon, though they are obscure under low angles of illumination. The most important ray-systems are those of Tycho and Copernicus. Among others, there are rays associated with Kepler, Olbers and Anaxagoras. Some small craters are surrounded by bright patches; Euclides is a good example.

Valleys. These are, of course, common on the Moon, but not many of them are spectacular. The most striking is the Alpine Valley, which is over 120 km long. Other so-called valleys, such as that of Rheita, are in fact made up of chains of craters whose intervening walls have been reduced or destroyed.

Rilles (German, *rillen*), also known as **Clefts.** Deep, often winding features which are usually attributed to collapse. Some of them are visible with small telescopes, notably the Ariadæus Rill and the neighbouring Hyginus Rill (which has craterlike enlargements along it). Some craters, such as Alphonsus, Gassendi, Mersenius and Hevel, have complicated rill-systems on their floors; and there are areas which are very rich in rills—such as that of Prinz, on the plain not far from the brilliant crater Aristarchus. In August 1971 astronauts Scott and Irwin, from *Apollo 15*, drove to the edge of the great rill near Mount Hadley, in the foothills of the Apennines, and took photographs showing that its walls reveal obvious stratification.

Faults are also to be found. The most evident is the so-called Straight Wall, over 120 km long, in the Mare Nubium. The surface to the west drops by approximately 800 feet at an angle of approximately 40°. Before Full Moon, the 'Wall' appears as a dark line because of the shadow it casts; after Full the feature reappears as a bright line.

Domes are gentle swellings, often crowned by summit craterlets. They tend to occur in groups; for instance, near Arago and on the floor of Capuanus.

This description is necessarily very brief, but suffices to show the great variety of features visible on the Moon's surface.

Time-Dependent Phenomena

The Moon is to all intents and purposes a changeless world; reports of alterations in structures (notably Linné, on the Mare Serenitatis) are generally discounted. However, in recent years there has been systematic observation of the occasional signs of activity known as T.L.P.s, or Transient Lunar Phenomena. In general these take the form of faint, short-lived reddish patches, or of local obscurations. Areas particularly subject to them are Aristarchus, Gassendi and Alphonsus. Many cases of T.L.P.s have been catalogued, though their interpretation is still a matter for debate.

Diameters of Walled Formations

It is not easy to give precise diameters for the walled formations, if only because so few of them are completely regular. The following list is merely designed as a guide to the scale of the features shown on the Lunar Map. The diameters are given in kilometres.

1st Quadrant (NE)		2nd Quadrant (NW)		3rd Quadrant (SW)		4th Quadrant (SE)	
Apollonius	48	Anaxagoras	51	Alpetragius	43	Abenezra	43
Aristillus	56	Archimedes	80	Billy	51	Albategnius	129
Aristoteles	96	Aristarchus	37	Birt	18	Alfraganus	19
Atlas	88	Beer	13	Bullialdus	62	Catharina	88
Autolycus	38	Bessarion	10	Clavius	230	Curtius	80
Bessel	19	Bianchini	40	Euclides	11	Delambre	51
Cleomedes	125	Birmingham	105	Fra Mauro	80	Fabricius	88
Dionysius	19	Copernicus	90	Gassendi	88	Furnerius	129
Endymion	125	Eratosthenes	61	Grimaldi	192	Goclenius	51
Eudoxus	64	Harpalus	35	Hell	32	Langrenus	133
Firmicus	56	Helicon	24	Phocylides	96	Mädler	32
Littrow	35	Hevel	111	Ptolemæus	147	Magelhæns	40
Macrobius	66	Kepler	35	Riccioli	160	Maurolycus	109
Menelaus	32	Lambert	29	Scheiner	113	Metius	80
Picard	33	Marius	35	Schickard	215	Moretus	120
Plinius	48	Pallas	48	Schröter	32	Petavius	160
Posidonius	100	Philolaus	74	Tycho	87	Piccolomini	90
Proclus	29	Plato	96	Walter	144	Theophilus	103
Theætetus	26	Xenophanes	108	Wargentin	88	Webb	22

Libration

As the Moon has a synchronous or captured rotation, it keeps essentially the same hemisphere turned Earthward, though the various librations mean that it is possible to examine a total of 59% of the surface (though, of course, never more than 50% at any one time). Features in the so-called libration zones are seen as extremely foreshortened, and until the Space Age they were inaccurately mapped. They have now, however, been photographed in great detail by the orbiting probes.

Objects near the Moon's north pole are best placed for observation when the Moon has its greatest south latitude (about 5°), and vice versa for the south pole; those near the east limb when the Moon has its actual longitude east of (i.e. greater than), and those near the west limb when it is west of (i.e. less than) the mean longitude. The dates when any object near the limb will be nearest the centre, and thus best placed for observation from Earth, can be obtained from the *Astronomical Ephemeris*, by finding the times when the most favourable libration in latitude is about 6° and that in longitude about 7°; the Moon may, however, be below the horizon, or the phase unsuitable.

At each recurring phase, the Moon's latitude and longitude will have altered, and we view the object and its shadow from a different position; the total alteration may amount to over 20°. Except at rare intervals, therefore, we do not re-observe objects under the same conditions, due to libration. These effects are, of course, most marked for objects which lie close to the Moon's limb.

The libration on any date can be found from the *Astronomical Ephemeris* (columns Earth's Selenographic Latitude and Longitude in the Moon's Physical Ephemeris). When the libration in longitude is +ve, the mean centre of the disk is displaced to the west, and the Mare Crisium is furthest from the limb. When the libration is −ve, the mean centre is displaced to the east, and the Mare Crisium is nearest the limb. Similarly, when the libration in latitude is +ve, the mean centre is displaced to the south, and Plato is furthest from the limb; and *vice versa*.

The Mean Centre of the Moon's near-side—the intersection of the lunar prime meridian and the lunar equator—is situated in the Sinus Medii, within the triangle formed by the craters Herschel, Schröter and Triesnecker and equidistant from them. The position of a nearby crater, Mösting A, was for many years observed with meridian instruments at national observatories in order to monitor the Moon's libratory movements. It is an 8 km crater that can be located in all conditions of solar illumination from about the 8th to the 22nd day of every lunation. It lies roughly at the centre of a smaller triangle formed by the craters Herschel, Lalande and Mösting, adjoining the eastern rim of the ruined ring plain Flammarion.

The lunar prime meridian passes through the centre of Walter, the eastern rim of Ptolemæus and the western rim of Aristillus. The lunar equator passes through Landsberg, Rhæticus and the southern part of Mare Spumans.

Observing the Moon

The changing aspect of illumination produces apparent changes in the appearance of the surface which are remarkably striking. A crater is at its most spectacular when close to the terminator, so that its floor is partly or wholly shadow-filled; under higher lighting it may become very obscure. For instance, the large crater Maginus is difficult to locate near the time of Full Moon. The only craters which are always readily identifiable under any conditions of illumination are those which are exceptionally bright (Aristarchus, Kepler, etc.) or have dark floors (Plato, Grimaldi, etc.).

When setting out to identify the various features, it is therefore wise to begin not at Full Moon, when there are virtually no shadows, but when the Moon is at the crescent, half or somewhat gibbous stage. A full description of the Moon's surface is beyond the scope of the present work, but various detailed atlases are available. Strongly recommended for identification purposes is *The Amateur Astronomer's Photographic Lunar Atlas*, by Henry Hatfield (London, 1970).

The Position of the Terminator on the Moon's equator, corresponding to various ages, can be obtained from the Sun's Co-longitude column of the Moon's Physical Ephemeris, in the *Astronomical Ephemeris*, as follows:

Sun's Co-longitude	Position of Terminator
From	
0° to 90°, the figures in the Table give—	the longitude of the terminator W of the central meridian (Sun rising)
90° to 180°, subtract the Sun's co-longitude from 180°: answer—	the longitude of the terminator E of the central meridian (Sun setting)
180° to 270°, subtract 180° from the Sun's co-longitude: answer—	the longitude of the terminator W of the central meridian (Sun setting)
270° to 360°, subtract the Sun's co-longitude from 360°: answer—	the longitude of the terminator E of the central meridian (Sun rising)

Repetition of the same phase of illumination, near the same hour, may be expected in about 2 and 15 lunations, on the average, but there are variations—corresponding with the lengths of different lunations, which vary to and fro between $29\frac{1}{4}$ and $29\frac{3}{4}$ days. The mean lunation is just over $29\frac{1}{2}$ days, and hence, on the average, in the second lunation the similar phase falls in daylight; in the third, it is $1\frac{1}{2}$ hours later in the evening than the first, and so on. One mean lunation = 29 d 12 h 44 m; 2 lunations, 59 d $1\frac{1}{2}$ h; and 15 lunations, 442 d 23 h. The mean interval from perigee to perigee, or mean anomalistic period, is 27·55455 days, and does not recur at the same phase till after 14 lunations (about 1·13 years), or about $1\frac{1}{2}$ months later in the following year, so that the 'most favourable' conditions generally disappear for a period.

Best Altitude Conditions. For any given age of the Moon, there is a certain time in the year about which the altitude conditions are at their most favourable, though the actual date is modified by the Moon's changes in latitude. This is because the Moon's average path coincides with the ecliptic, so that on any given day its altitude above the observer's horizon at culmination will, on average, be the same as that of the Sun at noon on the date when the Sun has similar R.A. The following table indicates, approximately, the most favourable dates, with respect to altitude, for the principal phases, as observed from the northern hemisphere. (For southern hemisphere, transpose April/October, July/January.)

	Moon 3–4 d old	First Quarter	Full Moon	Last Quarter	25–26 d old
Most favourable:	End of April	Vernal Equinox	Winter Solstice	Autumnal Equinox	End of July
Least favourable:	End of October	Autumnal Equinox	Summer Solstice	Vernal Equinox	End of January

THE PLANETS AND THEIR SATELLITES

There are nine principal planets in orbit around the Sun, and a large number of *minor planets*, or asteroids. They can be grouped in different ways for various purposes, and it is worth setting out some of the groupings more frequently encountered in order to prevent any possible confusion.

The term *major planets* is used to denote the four 'giant' planets, Jupiter, Saturn, Uranus and Neptune. The corresponding term is *terrestrial planets*, used to denote Mercury, Venus, Earth and Mars. In discussions of the internal structure of the planets Pluto is often included in this group, which it more nearly resembles than the gaseous major planets. The term *minor planets* is these days confined to the much smaller bodies otherwise known as *asteroids*.

Another division of the planets is based on their position in the solar system relative to the orbit of the Earth: the two planets with orbits inside that of the Earth, Mercury and Venus, are termed *inferior planets* and those with orbits outside it—Mars, Jupiter, Saturn, Uranus, Neptune and Pluto—are together termed *superior planets*.

Primary, Secondary. When two or more bodies are orbiting around a common centre of gravity the principal, i.e. most massive, one is closest to the centre of the system and is termed the *primary*, the others being *secondaries*. Thus the Sun is the primary member of the solar system and the planets are secondaries. In its own system Jupiter, for example, is the primary and its satellites are secondaries.

Apparition. This is the term used to denote a period of time during which a particular planet is observable; its duration is not fixed, but varies with the planet and with the circumstances prevailing at the time. It is however a most convenient concept—especially in expressions such as 'the forthcoming apparition of Mars'.

Bode's Law. A mathematical relationship between the mean distances of the planets from the Sun, demonstrated by the German astronomer J. E. Bode in 1772; it is also attributed to Bode's contemporary J. B. Titius. The relationship had been noted, though not formalized, by Kepler more than a century earlier.

Bode's Law is based upon the progression 0, 3, 6, etc. To each number in the series 4 is added; the resulting figures, divided by ten, then represent remarkably closely the mean distances of most of the planets in Astronomical Units. The series provides for a planet at the mean distance of the minor planets, but appears to break down beyond the distance of Neptune, Pluto being close to the position predicted for Neptune.

TABLE 30. DISTANCES OF THE PLANETS

Planet:	Mercury	Venus	Earth	Mars	Minor planets	Jupiter	Saturn	Uranus	Neptune	Pluto
Distance calculated from Bode's Law (A.U.):	0·4	0·7	1·0	1·6	2·8	5·2	10·0	19·6	38·8	77·2
Actual mean distance (A.U.):	0·39	0·72	1·00	1·52	2·65 (average)	5·20	9·54	19·2	30·1	39·5

Planetary Motion

The planets, and indeed all orbiting bodies, obey the three *laws of planetary motion* established by Johannes Kepler between 1609 and 1618:

1. The orbit of a planet is an ellipse, with the Sun at one of the foci.

2. A planet moves in its orbit at such a speed that its radius vector sweeps out equal areas in equal intervals of time.

3. The revolution period squared is proportional to the mean distance (from the Sun) cubed.

Elliptical Orbits. A particular orbit is defined by its major axis (*AB* in Fig. 11) and minor axis (*DE*) which intersect at the centre (*C*). They are usually measured in Astronomical Units, and the value of the semi-axis is used in each case. In Fig. 11 *S* represents the focus occupied by the Sun, and *F* the

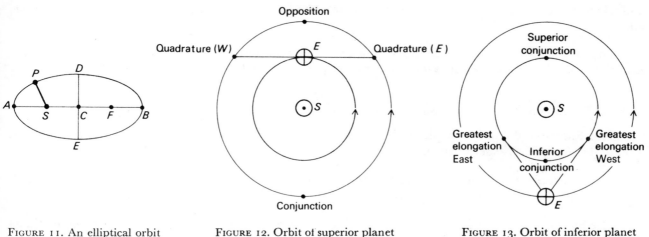

FIGURE 11. An elliptical orbit (schematic: not to scale)

FIGURE 12. Orbit of superior planet

FIGURE 13. Orbit of inferior planet

'empty focus'. If P represents the position of the orbiting planet at a given instant, PS is its *radius vector*; A represents the position of the planet's perihelion, and B its aphelion. The *eccentricity* of the orbit is measured by the ratio SC/AC: this is a very small quantity for most of the planets, whose orbits are near-circular, ranging from 0·0068 for Venus to 0·0934 for Mars. Only Mercury (0·2056) and Pluto (0·2494) have orbits which depart appreciably from circularity.

Orbital Elements. Seven elements are required to define a planetary orbit: the semi-major axis, a; the eccentricity, e; the inclination between the planes of the orbit and the ecliptic, i; the longitude of the ascending node, Ω; the longitude of perihelion, ϖ; the epoch, T; the mean motion, n.

Nodes. The nodes of a planet's orbit are the points where the orbit intersects the plane of the ecliptic. The ascending node is where the planet passes from south to north and the descending node where it passes from north to south through the plane.

Planetary Positions

Certain important relative positions of a planet and the Earth in their orbits are best understood by reference to Figs. 12 and 13.

Conjunction, Opposition, Quadrature, Elongation, Syzygy. A superior planet (Fig. 12) is said to be in *conjunction* when it has the same geocentric longitude as the Sun—that is, when it is on the far side of its orbit, in line with and far beyond the Sun as seen from the Earth. The opposite point in its orbit, when it again lies on a line through the Earth and the Sun but with the Earth this time between the Sun and the planet, which is therefore closer to the Earth than at conjunction, is termed *opposition*. There are two positions in the orbit of a superior planet termed *quadrature*—when the angle Sun–planet–Earth is exactly 90°.

In the case of an inferior planet (Fig. 13) the position on the far side of the Sun when all three bodies are in line is termed *superior conjunction*, and that when they are in line with the planet between the Earth and the Sun *inferior conjunction*. In this case the positions of quadrature are termed *Greatest Elongation East* and *Greatest Elongation West*, since these are the points in its orbit when the planet reaches its maximum distance from the Sun as viewed from the Earth.

The Moon is said to be in *syzygy* when in conjunction or opposition, i.e. when New or Full.

Perihelion, Aphelion. A planet or comet is said to be at *perihelion* when at that point in its orbit closest to the Sun, and at *aphelion* when at the point farthest from the Sun.

Perigee, Apogee. A planet or the Moon is said to be at *perigee* when at the point closest to the Earth and at *apogee* when farthest from the Earth.

Perijove, Apojove, etc. Satellites of Jupiter are said, when closest to the primary, to be at *perijove* and when farthest at *apojove*; corresponding terms are used for other planets, e.g. *perisaturnium, aposaturnium*, etc.

Appulse is the close approach (in terms of their apparent positions) of one celestial body to another. It is usually used for the close approach of two planets, or of a planet and the Moon or a star.

Orbital Periods of Planets and Satellites

The Sidereal Period of a planet is the time taken by the planet to make one complete circuit around the star sphere, as seen from the Sun.

The Anomalistic Period of a planet is the time interval between successive passages of the planet through perihelion or aphelion. It is practically the same as the planet's sidereal period.

The Synodic Period of a planet is the time interval between successive oppositions (or conjunctions) with the Sun, as seen from the Earth, and is the average interval between successive apparations of the planet.

The Synodic Period of a Satellite is the time interval between successive elongations or conjunctions with its primary.

Orbital Motions

The orbital motion of a planet or comet around the Sun, or of a satellite around its primary, is described as *direct* when from west to east, *retrograde* when from east to west. The apparent movements of the planets against the background stars are similarly described. A planet is at a *stationary point* when changing from direct to retrograde motion, and vice versa.

Rotation Periods

The periods of axial rotation of the planets are of considerable importance to the observer. They are known with considerable accuracy for Mars (solid surface) and Jupiter (gaseous 'surface'), and with less precision for the gaseous surfaces of Saturn, Uranus and Neptune. In the case of Mercury (solid surface) and Venus (gaseous atmosphere) the axial rotation periods now adopted were determined by means of radar observations. A precise definition of the axial rotation period of a planet would be the interval between successive passages of a meridian on its surface across the centre of the true disk as seen from the Earth. As we cannot observe the solid surfaces of some of the planets we have to substitute for this ideal definition a hypothetical concept, adopting an axial rotation period that seems to agree with observed features and predicting the times of transit of a purely hypothetical prime meridian. The situation is further complicated in the case of the giant, gaseous planets, as a rotating body of gas becomes compressed along its axis of rotation and takes on the form of an oblate spheroid. The rates of rotation of the surface layers vary with latitude, being greatest at the equator. Thus, in the case of Jupiter, on which several well defined currents with differing rates of rotation are known, a double system of longitudes has had to be adopted, one for the rapidly rotating equatorial current and one for the remainder of the planet.

Central Meridian. This is a useful concept when dealing with the determination of longitudes of observed surface features. It is not a meridian in the conventional sense, having a fixed position on the surface of the rotating planet, but is the imaginary line which bisects the visible disk of the planet from pole to pole, and is used as a reference against which the changing longitudes of the planetary features are measured as they pass 'beneath' it.

Planetary Radiation

The *Insolation* of a planet is the total radiation it receives from the Sun; of this the planet reflects much solar radiation of short wave-length (i.e., the ultra-violet, visible and shortest infra-red wave-lengths, up to say 14,000 Å) and absorbs the rest, subsequently re-radiating it as *planetary radiation* of long wave-length —i.e., invisible low-temperature heat rays (infra-red) which may include the planet's own radiation, if

57

any. As an atmosphere acts as a blanket, the planetary radiation of planets with no atmosphere will be high; that of those with atmospheres will tend to be low. The Moon and Mercury, both atmosphere-less, re-emit 74% of the solar radiation received; Mars, which has a thin atmosphere, about 50%. Venus, with a dense atmosphere, re-emits only about 8%—very similar to the 6% emitted by the gaseous planets Jupiter and Saturn.

Albedo. Strictly, the proportion of the total amount of the sunlight falling upon a planet which is reflected by the planet (in all directions). The true albedo may vary over the planet's surface, but for practical purposes the mean albedo is used. In calculating the mean albedo it is assumed that the planet's surface is spherical and that the incident light-rays are parallel. Comparisons of their mean albedos are an important factor in studies of the nature of the planetary surfaces. Those planets which have dense atmospheres have much higher albedos than those with transparent or no atmospheres, where the reflection takes place at the solid surface. The albedos of the principal members of the solar system are as follows:

TABLE 31. ALBEDOS OF THE PLANETS

Planet:	Mercury	Venus	Earth	Moon	Mars	Jupiter	Saturn	Uranus	Neptune	Pluto (estimated)
Albedo:	0·06	0·76	0·36	0·07	0·16	0·73	0·76	0·93	0·84	0·14

Planetary Temperatures

These are difficult to measure directly from Earth, and will vary with the altitude of the Sun from particular points on the planet's surface. They will also depend on the depth, density and composition of the planet's atmosphere, if any.

The surface temperature on the Moon varies greatly throughout the lunar day; under a vertical Sun it is more than 100°C, whilst during the long lunar night it sinks to less than −150°C.

The temperature at the surface of Mercury is more than 400°C—above the melting point of lead; the dark-side temperature has not been measured but must be very low, comparable to that of the Moon. The temperature at the observed surface of Venus—i.e. in its upper atmosphere—is only about −23°C, but space-probes indicate the tremendously high temperature near the surface of about 475°C. This indicates the 'greenhouse effect' of the dense atmosphere.

Mars has a vertical-Sun temperature ranging from about 25°C at perihelion to about −10°C at aphelion. The temperatures at the visible, outer layers of the gaseous outer planets are, of course, very low: Jupiter, −130°C; Saturn, −150°C; Uranus, −190°C and Neptune, −220°C. The temperature of Pluto cannot be measured, but is probably lower than −240°C.

Planetary Magnitudes

These are measured in the same scale as the apparent magnitudes of stars. The magnitude of a planet is very variable, depending upon its distance from both the Sun and the Earth, and upon its phase.

Opposition Magnitude. This is the apparent magnitude of a superior planet when in opposition; the planet is then nearest to the Earth and brightest and, in theory, is only then seen with its disk fully illuminated. Ordinarily the term denotes the brightness at mean opposition distance, as the planet's distance and brightness vary at different oppositions. The mean opposition visual magnitudes of the outer planets are as follows:

Mars	Jupiter	Saturn	Uranus	Neptune	Pluto
−2·0	−2·6	+0·7 (Rings closed)	+5·5	+7·8	+14·0

The visual magnitudes of the inner planets at mean greatest elongation are:

Mercury	Venus
0·0	−4·4

58

Phase

The proportion of the illuminated hemisphere of a planet or the Moon visible from Earth at a given time. Usually expressed as a decimal fraction, 'full phase' being taken as 1·000. The inferior planets show a full range of phases similar to those of the Moon; the superior planets show phases only from gibbous to full—the least phase of Mars being 0·84.

Transits of Inferior Planets

These occur when an inferior planet is at or near one of its nodes when at inferior conjunction: the planet is seen to pass, in silhouette, across the Sun's disk.

Transits of Mercury take place when inferior conjunction occurs within a few days of May 7 (descending node) or November 9 (ascending node). November transits occur rather more frequently than May transits, being possible after intervals of 7, 13 and 46 years, whereas May transits can occur only after intervals of 13 and 46 years. Transits during the remainder of this century will occur on 1973 November 9, 1986 November 12 and 1999 November 14.

Transits of Venus occur when inferior conjunction is within a few days of June 7 (descending node) or December 8 (ascending node). Five synodic periods of Venus being almost 8 years, transits take place in pairs 8 years apart. Such pairs of transits occur at intervals of $105\frac{1}{2}$ and $121\frac{1}{2}$ years alternately; the next pair of June transits will occur in 2004 and 2012, and the next December pair in 2117 and 2125.

Visibility of the Planets

The planets vary enormously in the ease and frequency with which they can be observed. This is due not only to their actual size, but also to their distance from the Earth at the time of observation, which depends on the relative positions of the Earth and the planet in their orbits—which in turn are constantly varying. The planet's declination also governs its visibility from a particular observing site.

Only Mercury, Venus, Mars, Jupiter and Saturn are naked-eye objects. Uranus (mag. $5\frac{1}{2}$) and the minor planet Vesta (mag. $6\frac{1}{2}$) are just bright enough to be found with the naked eye with the aid of charts; Neptune (mag. $7\frac{3}{4}$) and several more of the minor planets can be found with the aid of binoculars and accurate charts. Pluto (mag. 14) can seldom be seen with telescopes with apertures of less than 30 cm (12 in.).

All the planets, except Pluto which has a relatively eccentric orbit, remain close to the ecliptic, and within the twelve constellations of the Zodiac. Their positions on any particular night can be found by looking up their co-ordinates (Right Ascension and Declination) in *The Astronomical Ephemeris* or an almanac such as the *Handbook of the British Astronomical Association* or the *Yearbook of Astronomy*, both of which are published annually. Using these co-ordinates the position of the planet among the fixed stars can then be found from the appropriate map in this Atlas.

Unlike the Moon, which souths about 50 minutes later each day, on average, the superior planets usually south earlier each night. Thus they are seen to approach the Sun when east of it and visible in the early part of the night, and to recede from the Sun when west of it and seen in the early hours of the morning. Jupiter and Saturn are lost to view in normal telescopes for some six to eight weeks annually, being too close to the Sun. Mars and the minor planets, which have long synodic periods, disappear only every other year but for much longer periods—several months.

The superior planets are best seen when they are in opposition and south at about midnight; the inferior planets, Mercury and Venus, are best seen when at Greatest Elongation from the Sun, G.E. East when seen in the western sky in the evening, G.E. West when seen in the eastern sky before sunrise.

Oppositions and elongations may occur at any time of the year, but the closer they occur to a particular date the larger and brighter is the planet. In the case of the superior planets, this date is that on which the Earth's heliocentric longitude is the same as that of the perihelion of the planet; many years elapse, however, before the most favourable conditions recur for a particular planet.

The Paths of the Planets. If we could watch the movements of the planets from the vicinity of the Sun, their paths would seem to be virtually unchanging; the orbit of each planet would appear to intersect the orbit of the Earth in two fixed points which are termed the nodes. As seen from the Earth these 'heliocentric' orbits are the average path of the planet, but they deviate from the average path due to the Earth's own motion around its orbit.

Planets attain their greatest heliocentric latitude when 90° in longitude from their nodes. They remain rather longer on that side of the ecliptic in which their aphelion lies, because the distance along the orbit from node to node through aphelion is longer than that through perihelion and the planet's orbital velocity is smaller. If the angular distance between the node and perihelion is greater than about 180° aphelion will be in the north celestial hemisphere; if it is less than 180° it will be in the south. In the former case the altitude at favourable oppositions is best for observers in the southern hemisphere of the Earth, in the latter case for observers in the northern hemisphere. Favourable oppositions occur in the northern hemisphere for Mercury, Venus, Uranus and Pluto, and in the southern hemisphere for Mars, Jupiter, Saturn and Neptune.

As seen from the Earth the superior planets (Mars excepted—see below) reach a maximum latitude north or south of the ecliptic close to the inclinations of their orbits. The remoter the planet is from the Sun the closer its geocentric path is to the heliocentric path referred to above.

Due to its proximity the position of Mars may deviate from its heliocentric path by as much as 5° at perihelic oppositions; the effect is negligible for the more distant planets, not exceeding $\frac{1}{4}$° even in the case of Jupiter.

The mean daily motion of the Earth in its orbit is about 1°; this exceeds that of Mars by about $\frac{1}{2}$° and those of the outer planets by nearly a degree. It will be understood from this that for a period before and after opposition the Earth is 'overtaking' the outer planet, which will therefore appear to move backwards against the background stars. The outer planet's apparent motion therefore includes a large loop (*retrograde motion*) each year; the largest loop of retrogression is that of Mars, which may retrogress for as much as 18°.

Mercury attains a maximum distance from the Ecliptic of about 5°; it is always so close to the Sun that even when favourably situated it can readily be observed for only about half an hour with the naked eye, or up to about two hours with a telescope, immediately after sunset or before sunrise. It is also seen only at very low altitudes, especially by observers in high latitudes. Due to its highly eccentric orbit the distance of Mercury from the Sun at Greatest Elongation (G.E.) varies between 18° and 28°; the latter value applies only when Mercury is at aphelion, when it is south of the celestial equator and best seen by southern observers.

For observers in temperate latitudes Mercury is best placed for observation as an evening star when G.E. East occurs in early April for northern observers, early October for southern observers, and as a morning star when G.E. West occurs in early October (northern observers), early April (southern observers).

Mercury shows phases, being 'Full' only at superior conjunction when the apparent diameter is only 4″·7; at inferior conjunction the diameter may be as much as 12″·7 but the phase is new and the planet cannot be seen. At G.E. the phase is, of course, such that just half of the illuminated hemisphere is presented towards the Earth. The magnitude of Mercury at G.E. varies between −1·2 and +1·1.

The mean synodic period of Mercury—the interval between successive inferior conjunctions—is 116 days; G.E. East occurs about 22 days before inferior conjunction and G.E. West about 22 days after. Thus the interval between eastern and western elongations is about 44 days, and between western and eastern elongations about 72 days.

It will be appreciated that the periods during which Mercury can be observed can be extended considerably by the use of a well adjusted equatorial telescope provided with accurate setting circles, which enable the planet to be located in daylight.

Venus, the brightest of the planets, is very much farther from the Sun and is therefore much more often available for study than Mercury. It can often be seen in broad daylight, and after dark will cast a shadow when particularly bright.

Inferior conjunctions of Venus occur at intervals of 584 days; greatest elongations occur about 72 days before and after inferior conjunction, when the planet reaches a distance from the Sun of 45 to 47°. The interval between eastern and western elongations is thus a little over 20 weeks, and that between western and eastern elongations about 63 weeks—14$\frac{1}{2}$ months.

At superior conjunction, when the planet shows full phase, the apparent diameter is only about 11″; at inferior conjunction it is over 60″. At elongation, when the phase is 50%, the apparent diameter is about 25″. Maximum brightness occurs about 36 days from inferior conjunction, that is, about 5 weeks after G.E. East and 5 weeks before G.E. West. At such times Venus is the brightest object in the heavens save for the Sun and Moon, reaching a stellar magnitude of up to − 4·4. This maximum brightness is achieved about every eight years, when the planet reaches perihelion at the end of December. At such times it is south of the equator, and is best seen, as a morning star, by observers in the southern hemisphere. The most favourable time for observers in the northern hemisphere to study Venus is when it reaches perihelion in mid-March; although the magnitude is then rather less than at a December perihelion, the planet reaches a much greater altitude above the horizon.

Mars, although the planet which has most captured the popular imagination, is not in fact an easy object to observe. Its surface features are beyond the reach of all but the most powerful telescopes except for two or three months every other year, and except at very favourable apparitions Mars presents such a small disk that useful work can be done only with the aid of fairly large apertures.

The interval between oppositions of Mars is longer than the synodic period of any other planet—780 days, or a little under 26 months; thus oppositions occur, on average, about two months later every alternate year. The planet's distance at opposition varies between 101 million km at aphelic oppositions, which occur in February, and 56 million km at perihelic oppositions which occur in August. The apparent diameter of the planet's disk at perihelic oppositions is about 25″, whereas at aphelic oppositions the apparent diameter is little more than half this figure. When at perihelion Mars has a high southern declination, so that it is best seen by observers in the southern hemisphere. At opposition the planet is a very bright naked-eye object despite its small diameter; at perihelic oppositions Mars reaches a magnitude of − 2·8, brighter even than Jupiter. Even at aphelion the opposition magnitude is − 1·0.

Like all the outer planets Mars exhibits a phase effect, and always appears gibbous except near opposition. The minimum phase occurs at quadrature, when only 84% of the visible disk is illuminated.

Favourable oppositions of Mars occur at intervals of 15 to 17 years, the last very favourable one being that of 1971 August.

Mars has two tiny satellites, but they are of mag. 12 and can be seen only with powerful telescopes.

Jupiter is from many points of view the best of the planets for observers with moderate-sized telescopes; a fine sight even with a 7·5 cm (3 in.) refractor, and much useful observational work can be done with a 10 cm (4 in.) refractor or 15 cm (6 in.) reflector.

The mean synodic period is 399 days, so that oppositions occur about one month later each year. The distance at opposition varies from about 670 million km at aphelic oppositions to only 590 million km at perihelic oppositions, which occur about every twelve years, in September or October. The apparent diameter of the planet is never less than about 30″, and reaches 46″ to 48″ at most oppositions. The opposition magnitude does not vary very much, ranging between − 2·5 and − 2·3.

As the axis of rotation of Jupiter is almost perpendicular to the plane of its orbit—the inclination is only 3°—the equatorial regions of the planet are always presented towards the Earth, and the polar regions are never well seen.

A great deal of fine structure can be recorded with moderate apertures, and the rates of differential rotation of the planet have been very well determined. There is an equatorial current some 20° wide which has a rotation period of 9 h 50 m 30 s; longitudes expressed on the basis of this period are known as 'System I' longitudes. For the rest of the planet System II longitudes are used, based on a rotation period of 9 h 55 m 41 s. In fact there are a number of different currents, with rotation periods differing from this figure by several seconds. The belts are also known to drift slightly in latitude, so that latitude determinations are a valuable activity for observers having suitable equipment. (A good clock-driven equatorial refractor with a filar micrometer is the best equipment for this rather specialized work.)

Eight of Jupiter's twelve satellites are very faint, with magnitudes between 13 and 19; the four Galilean satellites, however, can be seen quite easily with small telescopes, and would all be easy naked-eye objects but for their proximity to the brilliant planet.

As the four brightest satellites (magnitudes 5–6) all orbit the planet in its equatorial plane, which is inclined to the plane of the Earth's orbit by only a little over one degree, they are frequently seen to pass in front of the disk of Jupiter ('in transit'), accompanied by their shadows, or to be occulted or eclipsed by it. The timing of these phenomena is a fascinating occupation, open even to those observers who only have the use of very modest telescopes, and is also very useful, as the timings can be used to improve our knowledge of the dynamics of the Jovian system. For a few months every six years or so, as the Earth passes through the plane of the satellites, the satellites can be seen to eclipse and occult each other.

Saturn, although the second largest planet, is so much farther away that it is a much inferior telescopic object to Jupiter. Its distance at opposition varies from 1197 million km at perihelion to about 1654 million km at aphelion. At opposition the apparent diameter is seldom more than 20″ and at conjunction may be as little as 14″. Thus, although with its unique ring system Saturn is a beautiful object to observe even with a fairly small telescope such as a 7·5 cm (3 in.) refractor, an instrument of aperture 25 cm (10 in.) or more is needed to reveal much surface detail.

The mean synodic period of Saturn is 378 days, i.e. oppositions occur about a fortnight later each year. The planet is observable, at some part of the night, for 9 to 10 months every year. Oppositions vary tremendously, however, in suitability for observation from a particular location, as the planet's declination varies between 26° N and 26° S. During one sidereal revolution of the planet, occupying $29\frac{1}{2}$ years, it is therefore usual for an observer at one station to experience relatively favourable apparitions for about fourteen years, followed by an equal period of unfavourable apparitions. Oppositions occurring in winter are the most favourable for observers in the northern hemisphere and the least favourable for southern observers.

Unlike Jupiter, Saturn's equatorial plane is inclined to the plane of its orbit by quite a large angle—about $26\frac{3}{4}°$—which means that one hemisphere is frequently tilted towards the Earth, permitting the polar regions of the planet to be observed. This also results in the rings presenting a constantly changing aspect. Twice during each sidereal revolution of the planet, when the Earth passes through the ring-plane, they are edge-on to the Earth and generally disappear from view. They can be observed very close to the date of passage with powerful instruments, however. These occasions provide valuable opportunities for study of the cross-section of the rings during the period preceding and following the edgewise presentation. Occasionally a satellite may be seen apparently 'speared' on the thin line of the near-edgewise ring.

Owing to the great distance of the planet, spots and other recognizable fine structure are but rarely seen in its belts; this makes it difficult to establish the rotation periods in various latitudes, although it is known that the planet rotates differentially in a manner very similar to Jupiter. A rotation period of 10 h 14 m is fairly well established for the equatorial region, but the rotation in higher latitudes is not well known. In latitudes of 30 to 40° north or south of the planet's equator the few spots observed suggest a rotation period of about 10 h 38 m, and in latitudes above 60° it may exceed 11 h.

Of the ten satellites of Saturn, the brightest are Titan (8·4) and Rhea (9·8); most of the others are fainter than tenth magnitude; some of the fainter satellites—notably Iapetus—are variable, however, and well repay regular observation with adequate apertures.

With the exceptions of the outermost satellites, Iapetus and Phœbe, all the satellites orbit Saturn roughly in the plane of its equator. The high tilt of this plane to the planet's orbital plane means that satellite phenomena cannot be observed all the time as in the case of Jupiter, but only during four or five apparitions centred on each passage of the Earth through the ring-plane, the number of phenomena increasing with proximity to the date of passage. In each sidereal revolution of the planet ($29\frac{1}{2}$ years) there are thus two periods of about ten years when no satellite phenomena can be observed. For a short period around the time of the Earth's passage through the ring-plane mutual phenomena of the satellites can be observed, but these are rare and usually require a powerful telescope for successful observation.

Uranus, Neptune and Pluto are not good subjects for serious observation. Both Uranus and Neptune can be seen as tiny disks in, say, a good 10 cm (4 in.) refractor, but little surface detail can be seen on either even with very powerful instruments. Pluto cannot be satisfactorily resolved into a disk even with the world's largest telescopes, so that even its diameter is not known with certainty.

Users of small telescopes will find it both enjoyable and good practice to follow the motion of Uranus (mag. +5·5) and Neptune (mag. +7·8) against the background stars; they can be found by plotting their co-ordinates taken from one of the almanacs referred to above on a chart traced from the relevant map, or by reference to the special charts published annually in the *Handbook of the British Astronomical Association*.

Pluto is too faint (mag. +14) to be observed at all except with a large instrument.

Description of the Planets

TABLE 32. PLANETARY ORBITAL DATA
(Epoch 1950 Jan. 0·5 ET)

	Mean Distance from Sun (A.U.)	(km × 10⁶)	Eccentricity	at Epoch 1950·0 °	of Perihelion °	of Ascending Node °	Inclination to Plane of the Ecliptic °	Mean Orbital Velocity (km/s)	
MERCURY	0·3870987	57·91	0·2056289	33·16835	76·6774	47·7386	7·0038	47·87	☿
VENUS	0·7233322	108·21	0·0067864	81·57200	130·8674	76·2297	3·3941	35·02	♀
EARTH	1·0000000	149·60	0·0167209	99·58840	102·0805	—	—	29·79	⊕
MARS	1·5236915	227·94	0·0933791	144·33520	335·1384	49·1720	1·8500	24·13	♂
JUPITER	5·2028039	778·34	0·0484550	316·15933	13·5170	99·9432	1·3060	13·06	♃
SATURN	9·5388437	1427·01	0·0556402	158·30359	92·0685	113·2202	2·4903	9·65	♄
URANUS	19·181871	2869·6	0·0472421	98·30862	169·8515	73·7399	0·7729	6·80	♅
NEPTUNE	30·057924	4496·7	0·0085840	194·95248	44·1586	131·2283	1·7745	5·43	♆
PLUTO	39·439	5898·9	0·2502	165·60256	223·5224	109·6336	17·1428	4·73	♇

Heliocentric Mean Longitudes columns: at Epoch 1950·0, of Perihelion, of Ascending Node.

TABLE 33. PLANETARY PERIODS AND MOTIONS

	Sidereal Period (d)	(Trop. yrs)	Mean Synodic Period (d)	Sidereal Period of Axial Rotation (d)	Inclination of Equatorial Plane to Orbital Plane °	Sidereal Mean Daily Motion per day °	per year °	
MERCURY	87·969	0·2408	115·88	58·7	0·0	4·092339	—	☿
VENUS	224·701	0·6152	583·92	243·0 (h)	178·0	1·602130	—	♀
EARTH	365·256	1·00004	—	23·93	23·45	0·985609	360·0	⊕
MARS	686·980	1·8809	779·94	24·62	23·98	0·524033	191·5	♂
JUPITER	4332·59	11·862	398·88	9·84	3·07	0·083091	30·2	♃
SATURN	10,759·20	29·458	378·09	10·23	26·73	0·033460	12·2	♄
URANUS	30,685·0	84·013	369·66	10·82	97·88	0·011732	4·2	♅
NEPTUNE	60,190·2	164·795	367·49	15·80 (d)	28·80	0·005981	2·1	♆
PLUTO	90,465·2	247·69	366·72	6·390	?	0·003979	1·2	♇

TABLE 34. PHYSICAL DATA FOR THE PLANETS

	Equatorial (km)	Polar (km)	Volume (⊕ = 1)	Mass (⊕ = 1)	Mean Density (g/cm³)	Surface Gravity (⊕ = 1)	Escape Velocity (km/s)	
MERCURY	4870	—	0·056	0·056	5·50	0·381	4·27	☿
VENUS	12,100	—	0·8572	0·8150	5·25	0·9032	10·36	♀
EARTH	12,756	12,714	1·0000	1·0000	5·517	1·0000	11·18	⊕
MARS	6790	6750	0·1504	0·1074	3·94	0·3799	5·03	♂
JUPITER	142,800	133,500	1318·7	317·89	1·330	2·643	60·22	♃
SATURN	119,300	107,700	743·6	95·14	0·706	1·159	36·25	♄
URANUS	47,100	43,800	47·1	14·52	1·70	1·11	22·4	♅
NEPTUNE	48,400	47,400	53·7	17·25	1·77	1·21	23·9	♆
PLUTO	5900	—	0·10	0·10	5·5	0·47	5·1	♇

Diameter columns: Equatorial (km), Polar (km).

TABLE 35. PLANETARY SATELLITE DATA

	Mean Distance from Primary (A.U.)	(km)	Mean Sidereal Period (d)	Mean Synodic Period (d)	Inclin. of Orbit °	Diam. (km)	Reciprocal Mass (Planet = 1)	Mean Density (g/cm³)	Mean Visual Opposition Magnitude	
EARTH										**EARTH**
I Moon	0·0025695	384,390	27·321661	29·5306	23·4	3476	81·30	3·3	− 12·7	I
MARS										**MARS**
I Phobos	0·0000625	9350	0·318910	0·3191	1·1	13	?	?	11·6	I
II Deimos	0·0001570	23,487	1·262441	1·2648	1·8	8	?	?	12·8	II
JUPITER										**JUPITER**
V	0·0012099	181,000	0·498179	0·4983	0·4	200	?	?	13·0	V
I Io	0·0028193	421,770	1·769138	1·7699	0·0	3659	26,200	2·82	4·8	I
II Europa	0·0044857	671,030	3·551181	3·5573	0·5	2900	40,300	3·7	5·2	II
III Ganymede	0·0071552	1,070,400	7·154553	7·1664	0·2	5000	12,200	2·4	4·5	III
IV Callisto	0·0125845	1,882,700	16·689018	16·7536	0·2	4500	19,600	2·0	5·5	IV
VI	0·076723	11,478,000	250·5662	265·947	28	100	?	?	13·7	VI
X	0·078345	11,720,000	259·2188	275·715	29	20	?	?	18·6	X
VII	0·078455	11,735,000	259·6528	276·206	28	30	?	?	16·0	VII
XII	0·142	21,243,500	631	551	147	20	?	?	18·8	XII
XI	0·151	22,589,500	692	597	163	20	?	?	18·1	XI
VIII	0·157	23,487,000	744	635	148	20	?	?	18·8	VIII
IX	0·158	23,637,000	758	645	157	20	?	?	18·3	IX
SATURN										**SATURN**
X Janus	0·00106	158,580	0·7490	0·7493	0·0	300	?	?	14·0	X
I Mimas	0·0012406	185,590	0·942422	0·9425	1·5	500	15,000,000	1	12·1	I
II Encaladus	0·0015916	238,100	1·370218	1·3704	0·0	600	7,000,000	1	11·8	II
III Tethys	0·0019703	294,760	1·887803	1·8881	1·1	1000	910,000	1·1	10·3	III
IV Dione	0·0025235	377,510	2·736916	2·7376	0·0	1000	490,000	3·2	10·4	IV
V Rhea	0·0035241	527,200	4·517503	4·5194	0·3	1300	250,000	2·0	9·8	V
VI Titan	0·0081660	1,221,600	15·945448	15·9691	0·3	4800	4150	2·3	8·4	VI
VII Hyperion	0·0099115	1,482,700	21·276657	21·3188	0·6	500	5,000,000	3	14·2	VII
VIII Iapetus	0·023798	3,560,200	79·33085	79·9201	14·7	1100	300,000	3	11·0	VIII
IX Phœbe	0·086575	12,952,000	550·337	523·54	150	200	?	?	16·5	IX
URANUS										**URANUS**
V Miranda	0·000872	130,450	1·41349	1·4136	0·0	300	1,000,000	5	16·5	V
I Ariel	0·0012820	191,790	2·520384	2·5206	0·0	800	67,000	5	14·4	I
II Umbriel	0·0017860	267,180	4·144183	4·1448	0·0	600	170,000	4	15·3	II
III Titania	0·0029303	438,370	8·705876	8·7083	0·0	1100	20,000	6	14·0	III
IV Oberon	0·0039187	586,230	13·463262	13·4692	0·0	1000	34,000	5	14·2	IV
NEPTUNE										**NEPTUNE**
I Triton	0·0023747	355,260	5·876844	5·8979	159·9	3700	750	5·1	13·5	I
II Nereid	0·0371797	5,561,900	359·881	362·04	27·7	300	?	?	18·7	II

Mercury is best observed in broad daylight, since when the planet is visible with the naked eye it will be low down in the sky. However, locating Mercury in daylight is very difficult without a large telescope equipped with accurate setting circles, and the fact that the planet is so near the Sun precludes casual 'sweeping around' with a low magnification.

Even when at its best, small telescopes will show nothing on Mercury's surface, though the phase is evident enough. With large instruments some dark patches may be seen, but maps of the planet are still of dubious accuracy, and that drawn by E. M. Antoniadi forty years ago probably remains the best. However, a Venus–Mercury probe is now being planned, and it is hoped to obtain close-range pictures of Mercury within the next few years.

Mercury has virtually no atmosphere, and the temperature conditions are extreme. The rotation period has been shown by radar observations to be $58\frac{1}{2}$ days; it was formerly believed that the rotation was synchronous with the orbital revolution period (88 days). As yet nothing definite is known about the nature of the surface features, though it is quite likely that the probe pictures will show craters of the same basic type as those of the Moon or Mars.

Venus, like Mercury, is best observed under daylight conditions, though good views can also be obtained when the Sun is below the horizon and Venus still remains reasonably high in the sky. The phase is visible with any small telescope, or, for that matter, with good binoculars; but even powerful instruments will show little detail upon the brilliant disk. Vague patches are sometimes visible, but represent what may be termed 'cloud' phenomena in the upper part of the planet's atmosphere. The true surface is permanently concealed.

Until investigations with space-probes became possible, little was known about the nature of the surface. Even the rotation period remained unknown. It now seems that Venus spins in approximately 243 days (longer than the sidereal period of 224·7 days) and in a retrograde direction. Information drawn from the Russian soft-landing probes indicates that the surface temperature is over 400 degrees Centigrade, and that the surface atmospheric pressure is approximately 90 times that at sea-level on Earth. The main constituent of the atmosphere is carbon dioxide. It seems, therefore, that Venus is too hostile to support life.

The calculated phase sometimes differs slightly from the observed phase; this has become known as 'Schröter's effect', though its cause is not certainly known; some authorities regard it as due to observational error, while others attribute it to atmospheric effects. The so-called Ashen Light, or faint visibility of the hemisphere which is unilluminated by the Sun, has also caused controversy.

Mars, perhaps the most interesting of all the planets, is not so easy to study as might be imagined. Small and moderate instruments will show details well only when the planet is fairly near opposition; and, moreover, not all oppositions are equally favourable.

The main features visible are the white polar caps, formerly regarded as due to some icy or frosty deposit but now more generally attributed to solid carbon dioxide; the dark patches, once thought to be due to organic matter—though this now seems rather improbable; and the reddish-ochre tracts which are commonly called 'deserts'. Maps of the surface are extremely accurate, and some of the dark regions, such as the Syrtis Major in the southern hemisphere and the Mare Acidalium in the northern, are comparatively easy to see. The rotation period of Mars is approximately half an hour longer than ours; therefore, any feature will come to the central meridian of the planet half an hour later each night.

The seasonal cycle, connected with the shrinkage of the polar cap in Martian spring and summer, can be followed. 'Clouds' can also be seen from time to time in the planet's atmosphere, and occasionally there are widespread obscurations, due probably to dusty material held in suspension. However, the Martian atmosphere is very tenuous (ground pressure about 7 millibars) and is made up chiefly of carbon dioxide.

Pictures obtained from space-probes have shown that Mars, like the Moon, has craters on its surface, though there are also 'chaotic' areas with jumbled ridges and valleys. Crater structures cannot, of course, be seen as such from Earth. The *Mariner 9* photographs of 1971–72 have revealed huge volcanic structures.

The celebrated 'canals', studied so closely by Lowell from 1895 to 1916, appear to be either highland ridges or else chains of roughly aligned craters. Apparently the dark areas are not depressions, as used to be thought; some of them, notably the Syrtis Major, are elevated. We are still uncertain as to the nature of the dark regions, and it is too early to decide whether there is or is not any primitive life on Mars. Fortunately, the problem should be solved by means of the soft-landing Mars probes now being planned for the next few years. On the whole, it seems that any life is unlikely.

The two satellites of Mars, Phobos and Deimos, are too small to be seen except with large telescopes. They are quite different in nature from our Moon, and it has been suggested, though without proof, that they are captured asteroids. Phobos, photographed from the probes *Mariners 7* and *9*, is irregular in shape; it is 23 km long, but only 18 km broad. Deimos is also of irregular shape.

Jupiter is by far the most rewarding planet to observe with the kind of telescope normally available to amateurs. With an apparent disk usually more than 40″, a diameter superseded only occasionally by Venus when a narrow crescent, it is a fine sight even in quite small telescopes. Serious observation can be carried out with a 15 cm (6 in.) reflector or a good 10 cm (4 in.) refractor.

The outer layers, at least, of all four major planets are entirely gaseous, so that the features we observe are not permanent markings; in simple analogy they can best be described as cloud formations in the 'atmospheres' of these planets. It must be remembered, however, that these planets do not have a thin atmosphere like that of the Earth or Mars; they are extremely dense, and consist of a treacly, entirely opaque mass of very dense, poisonous gases many thousands of miles in depth. Just as the terrestrial meteorologist learns about the structure and changes of the Earth's atmosphere from global studies of the cloud formations in it and their movements over long periods of time, so too observations of the movements and changing shapes of features in the outer layers of the major planets provide the raw material from which the physicist can begin to deduce the nature of the planet's sub-surface layers, and the mechanisms in them which give rise to the features observed at the visible surface.

The surface features display the differential rotation characteristic of a gaseous body. There is a great equatorial current embracing the Equatorial Zone, the southern component of the North Equatorial Belt (NEB_S) and the northern component of the South Equatorial Belt (SEB_N): the adopted mean rotation period for this current is 9 h 50 m 30·003 s; longitudes based upon this rotation period are termed 'System I longitudes'. There are numerous distinct currents in higher latitudes, but their rotation periods differ only by seconds, and so a single standard rotation period of 9 h 55 m 40·632 s is adopted for all regions of the planet outside System I; longitudes referred to this rotation period are described as 'System II'.

As soon as the telescope is turned on to the planet, its disk is seen to be crossed by a number of dusky belts; some of them are quite prominent, although their intensities vary and a belt which is very prominent at one apparition may be very faint or even absent altogether at the next. Under good seeing conditions less obvious features will be seen—some of the belts will be seen to have fine structure, and both light and dark spots and streaks may be observed. Such features often prove, if observed for several days, to have quite rapid movements relative to the more stable background features.

Quite the most remarkable feature observed on Jupiter is the Great Red Spot—a huge oval marking situated in the South Tropical Zone, nearly 50,000 km in length and 13,000 km wide. Its northern edge usually extends into the southern component of the South Equatorial Belt, but nowhere touches it, as the Red Spot is always situated in a great bay, larger than the spot itself, in the side of the belt. This bay, known as the Red Spot Hollow, must have considerable significance in attempts to interpret the physical nature of the Spot and the matter surrounding it; it has frequently been seen to interact with other features in a most puzzling manner.

Records of the Red Spot or a feature very similar to it can be traced back to 1664, when it was observed by Robert Hooke. During the next fifty years or so it faded and even disappeared altogether from time to time, only to reappear for a further period. It finally disappeared in 1713 and was not seen again for 120 years.

The Red Spot visible today was first seen in 1831, and has seldom been absent since. Even when it has been invisible, the Red Spot Hollow has remained to mark its position.

From its rediscovery in 1831 to 1882 the Spot was a deep brick red colour, hence its name, but its colour then faded. There have been revivals since, notably in 1920, 1926 and 1936, but none of these have been so spectacular as the latest, which lasted from 1960 to 1972; during this time the Spot has been extremely prominent, and has usually been a deep pink and quite often distinctly red in colour.

The relation between the Red Spot and the Hollow in the SEB might be taken to imply that they occupy a fixed position on the planet. This is not the case, however, for long series of measurements of the longitude of the Spot/Hollow combination—largely carried out by amateur observers—show that they display considerable motion relative to the other surface features, of a very erratic nature. Although some movement in latitude has been observed, it is very small; in longitude, however, the total movement back and forth during the past eighty years exceeds 1000°—equivalent to more than three circuits of the planet.

The South Tropical Zone has often been the location of other interesting phenomena; in 1901 a grey streak formed across the Zone, linking the South Equatorial Belt and the South Temperate Belt; this feature, never previously observed, rapidly spread in longitude until it stretched half way round the globe of the planet. Bright patches formed at its ends, giving it the characteristic concave ends which became its hallmark. Although it faded from time to time, and varied considerably in length, the 'South Tropical Disturbance' was observed for nearly forty years before it finally disappeared. A similar feature has appeared for short periods during several apparitions since, but never in such an active or prominent form as the original Disturbance. During its lifetime the Disturbance generally had a rotation period rather shorter than that of the Red Spot, causing it to overtake this feature on a number of occasions. This always led to remarkable activity in the area: the dark matter of the Disturbance accelerated so as to cross the Red Spot region in a few days instead of the six weeks or so that it would have taken at its usual pace. It was also remarkable in that the Disturbance material was never seen to move directly across the Red Spot region, but instead appeared to flow around it, following the dark border of the Red Spot Hollow. No satisfactory explanation has ever been forthcoming for this peculiar behaviour. In the apparitions of 1919–20, 1928, 1931, 1932–3 and 1934 the Disturbance was also associated with remarkable series of dark spots which appeared to form at a fixed location and then drifted rapidly around the zone, never actually crossing the Disturbance but instead reversing direction and travelling back along the undisturbed part of the Zone.

The other principal form of activity observed on the planet is the outbreaks which occasionally occur in the Equatorial Belts. Both Equatorial Belts have been the subject of these major disturbances, the South Equatorial Belt being especially prone. The upheavals usually follow a long period of quiescence; they commence with the appearance of a series of dark and light spots, usually formed at a particular longitude, which rapidly drift away around the Belt. Typically, the dark spots drift in one direction and the light spots in the opposite direction. In major outbreaks the Belt concerned rapidly assumes a complicated structure, and gives the appearance of great turbulence.

It is difficult to deduce the kind of activity taking place at the visible surface and below it that would give rise to such phenomena, but at least until Earth-based observation can be supplemented by close examination by robot spacecraft this kind of observed feature is all the evidence we have for the theorist to work on. Traditionally an important field of activity for amateur observers, it is important that it should be continued so as to extend the detailed chronicle of Jovian activity obtained by visual observation during more than eighty years.

Jupiter has twelve known satellites, of which only four are brighter than mag. 13. These are easily seen with a small telescope, and are among the earliest telescopic discoveries, having been first recorded by Galileo in 1610. Their surfaces have certain markings that are apparently permanent, but very large telescopes are needed to record such detail. The main interest in the satellites is the observation of their eclipses, occultations and transits referred to above (p. 60).

Saturn is, apart from its unique system of rings, broadly similar to Jupiter. Due to its great distance and much smaller apparent diameter much less detail has been recorded, however; the globe has a similar system of parallel belts and zone, but fine detail is not easily seen even with quite large apertures, and features sufficiently well defined to permit the determination of their longitude by the timing of their central meridian transits are rare. It is therefore extremely important that the planet should be monitored constantly, in order to ensure that any such feature that does appear is not missed, and that its longitude is reliably determined. If it is sufficiently long-lived a succession of such determinations will enable a rotation period to be deduced, adding significantly to our meagre knowledge of the planet's constitution and activity. From time to time very large white oval spots have been seen, especially in the equatorial region, and although they are rare such features may appear without warning at any time.

TABLE 36. DIAMETER OF SATURN'S RING SYSTEM

		Angular Diameter at Mean Opposition Distance	Actual Diameter	Ratio
		"	(km)	
RING A:	outer edge	43·96	272,300	1·0000
	inner edge	38·69	239,600	0·8801
[Cassini's Division]				
RING B:	outer edge	37·80	234,200	0·8599
	inner edge	29·24	181,100	0·6652
RING C:	inner edge	24·12	149,300	0·5487

Few surface markings have both lasted long enough and been sufficiently well observed to permit reliable rotation periods to be established; as a result no continuing system of longitudes has been adopted for Saturn. There is substantial evidence to support the adoption of a rotation period of 10 h 14 m in the equatorial regions. Few determinations have been made but it seems probable that a rotation period of about 10 h 40 m would be appropriate for higher latitudes on the planet.

The rings of Saturn are themselves a rewarding subject of observation; the ring has three main components, two bright rings separated by Cassini's Division, and the faint 'crêpe ring' which adjoins the inner edge of the bright ring. The outer ring is known as Ring A, the inner bright ring as Ring B, and the crêpe ring, which adjoins the inner edge of Ring B, is termed Ring C. Ring B is clearly seen to have two distinct components, the outer part of the ring being noticeably brighter than the inner part. A number of minor 'divisions' have been recorded in the rings, although they are probably not true gaps. The rings being not solid but composed of myriads of tiny particles, the 'divisions' are believed to mark 'ripples' or thinly populated zones in the ring. They should be looked for by observers with powerful instruments, as they have provided valuable material for study. Many of the divisions that have been recorded have been shown to occur at specific distances from the planet from which the ring particles would be drawn away by the regularly repeated pull of certain of the planet's satellites.

Twice in the course of Saturn's $29\frac{1}{2}$-year sidereal period, at intervals of $13\frac{3}{4}$ and $15\frac{3}{4}$ years alternately, the Earth passes through the plane of the rings. (The disparity in the intervals arises from the eccentricity of Saturn's orbit.) The Earth can pass through the ring-plane up to three times on each occasion. When these passages occur (the last were in 1950 and 1966; the next will be in 1980) the rings are, for short intervals, extremely difficult or even impossible to observe. This is caused by three distinct circumstances: (i) the very thin ring-system is presented exactly edge-on to the Earth; (ii) the rings are exactly edge-on to the Sun, neither face being illuminated; (iii) the unilluminated face is presented toward the Earth. It is usual for observers to lose sight of the rings completely, but this is not always the case: in 1966, for example, some observers were able, with some difficulty, to follow the rings throughout the period.

Saturn has ten satellites, two of which are brighter than tenth magnitude and three fainter than 14th magnitude. New observers with large instruments will find it a useful exercise to plot the movements of some of them, but little can be done in the way of useful observation save the estimation of their magnitudes; this is difficult to do reliably without photometric equipment, however, partly due to the proximity of the brightly illuminated planet. Timing of the satellite phenomena which occur at certain apparitions is very valuable (see p. 71).

Uranus. Owing to its distance little detail can be observed on Uranus even with large telescopes. It presents a disk of a pale greenish colour, and has two parallel equatorial belts similar to those of Jupiter and Saturn which can be seen with apertures of 25–30 cm (10–12 in.). These often appear to be at a surprising angle, or even vertical, due to the high inclination of the planet's axis of rotation.

There are five satellites, all fainter than the 13th magnitude.

Neptune shows a bluish disk in telescopes of moderate aperture, no detail can be seen save with very powerful instruments, which suggest that it has belts similar to those of the other major planets, bordering the usual bright equatorial zone. Little can be done by the amateur observer, except for the instructive exercise of plotting its path against the background stars. Neptune has two satellites, but these are difficult objects, being of 13th and 18th magnitude.

Pluto is too small and too distant for any real assessment of its physical characteristics to be made; even the diameter of its apparent disk has only been measured, with difficulty, with the world's most powerful telescopes. It is believed to have a constitution more like that of the terrestrial planets than the other outer planets.

Observing the Planets

Intending observers should realize that in order to carry out effective observation, which will contribute a little towards increased knowledge of the planets, it is essential to become completely familiar with systematic methods of observation which have long been adopted by all serious bodies of observers, and to follow these procedures rigorously. To become a successful planetary observer requires patience and self-discipline; the observer must also be constantly on his guard against subjectivity—the danger of recording what he thinks *should* be visible rather than what he can actually detect. This is not meant to impute dishonest motives to the observer—observers of many years' experience know how easy it is to be genuinely misled in this way. Those who have the responsibility of collating planetary observations made by a large number of observers are aware of the problem, and are reluctant to take on trust any observation that is not independently confirmed, preferably by more than one other observer. This is one reason for the adoption of rigid procedures, which may at times seem onerous to the individualist observer, but which if consistently followed will greatly increase the value of his work. In any case, the self-imposed disciplines of good observing habits in time bring their own pleasure.

There are some simple 'rules' about observing which may seem obvious when stated in print, but which nevertheless are important and are worth setting out for the benefit of the novice.

Firstly, obtain a suitable observing book and use it regularly; try as far as possible to enter observing notes and records straight into it—unless you are a very disciplined person odd notes made on scraps of paper are all too often left 'to be copied in later', sometimes being lost and left out of the record altogether. A suitable book will depend to some extent on personal preference, but should have a fairly large page size. Some observers prefer plain pages, and others lined; the latter does not interfere with drawings which are usually done on special blank outlines and so are pasted into the observing book anyway.

TABLE 37. OBSERVATIONAL DATA FOR THE PLANETS

	Angular Equatorial Diameter						Oblateness	Albedo	Mean Visual (Opposition) Magnitude	
	at Unit Distance (1 A.U.)	at Minimum Distance	at Mean Distance	at Maximum Distance	at Mean Inf. Conj. Distance	at Mean Oppn. Distance				
	"	"	"	"	"	"				
MERCURY	6·68	12·9	6·4	4·5	11·37	—	0	0·06	0·0	☿
VENUS	16·82	66·0	16·0	9·6	60·32	—	0	0·76	−4·4	♀
EARTH	—	—	—	—	—	—	1/297	0·36	—	⊕
MARS	9·36	25·7	6·1	3·5	—	17·87	1/169·8	0·16	−2·0	♂
JUPITER	196·94	50·1	37·9	30·4	—	46·86	1/15·4	0·73	−2·6	♃
SATURN	166·66	20·9	17·3	15·0	—	19·27	1/9·5	0·76	+0·7	♄
URANUS	68·56	3·7	3·3	3·1	—	3·57	1/14·3	0·93	+5·5	♅
NEPTUNE	73·12	2·2	2·1	2·0	—	2·30	1/48·4	0·84	+7·8	♆
PLUTO	8·2	—	—	—	—	0·21	—	0·14	+14·9	♇

The date and times of commencement of each observing session should be recorded, in Universal Time (U.T.)—that is, Greenwich Mean Time: NOT British Standard or any other variant imposed by government, and not Local Time for the place of observation. The aperture of the telescope used, and the eyepiece power(s), should also be given. Some note of the prevailing weather conditions is also valuable, especially so if it can include readings of a good-quality external thermometer (dry bulb) and mercury barometer.

The 'seeing' is difficult to assess until the observer has gained considerable experience. Numerous sophisticated systems have been proposed, but really experienced observers consider that seeing scales should be kept as simple as possible, and recommend that laid down by E. M. Antoniadi, one of the greatest planetary observers of all time. This simply provides a numerical scale of five levels, each with a guide to the conditions:

I: Perfect seeing, without a quiver;
II: Slight undulations, with moments of calm lasting several seconds;
III: Moderate seeing, with larger air tremors;
IV: Poor seeing, with constant troublesome undulations;
V: Very bad seeing, scarcely allowing the making of a rough sketch.

When planetary drawings are made, it is important to finish these as quickly as is consistent with making a good job; as much of the detail as possible should be drawn *at the telescope*; some 'working up' indoors will be necessary but should be kept to a minimum and completed as soon as possible after leaving the telescope.

69

There are several fields of planetary observation which the observer can tackle when he has gained some experience; photography and colour-filter observations come immediately to mind. Details of these, and many other aspects of planetary observation, can be found in works such as *Practical Amateur Astronomy* (Faber, 1970).

Observing the Inferior Planets. For a number of reasons, neither of the inferior planets can be regarded as good objects to observe. In the case of *Mercury*, its proximity to the Sun and small observed disk render it difficult to observe at all most of the time, and quite large apertures are required to show any but the most prominent of the dark markings, even though these appear to be permanent features on the solid surface of the planet.

Whilst *Venus* presents a much larger disk, and being much more distant from the Sun is readily observable for months at a time, it is nevertheless a very disappointing object due to its dense, opaque atmosphere which totally hides the solid surface from our view. The only features seen on the disk are occasional faint dusky markings, which must be transient atmospheric features.

Observers with powerful instruments should seize any opportunity of observing Mercury in good conditions, producing a careful drawing of all features reliably seen. Their relative positions on the disk must be carefully recorded—the fact that the planet can only be observed for a few days when at elongation makes the interpretation of such drawings and the construction of maps of the surface features very difficult. The planet rotates very slowly on its axis, one revolution every 58½ days, but for many decades the appearance recorded by visual observers was so unchanging that it was believed to have an axial rotation equal to its period of orbital revolution—about 88 days. A 30 cm (12 in.) reflector is sufficient to permit the phase of Mercury to be accurately measured—preferably with a micrometer—and the exact date of dichotomy (50% phase) determined. Results suggest that there is no Schröter's Effect as observed for Venus (see below), but further observations would be valuable confirmation.

Observation of the occasional faint markings on Venus seem to be of little value; the absence of any visible features of the solid surface meant that even the period of axial rotation remained unknown until the development of radar measurements. Another effect of the presence of the deep atmosphere seems to be the Schröter Effect—that the moment of dichotomy (when the terminator exactly bisects the observed disk) occurs earlier than predicted at evening elongations of the planet and later at morning elongations.

It is usual to adopt a standard size for drawings of Venus of two inches (app. 50 mm) to the planet's diameter; in this case it is not usual to use prepared blanks, partly because the phase is quite different from one night to the next (an appropriate outline should be drawn lightly in pencil before going to the telescope), and partly because Venus frequently displays an uneven terminator, which would be difficult to draw on a blank with a black surround.

The terminator should be carefully studied, as it frequently has indentations, and on occasion the cusps (horns of a crescent phase) seem to extend beyond the average curve of the terminator. Another feature that should be looked out for is the *Ashen Light*. This is sometimes seen when Venus is in a fairly narrow crescent phase, the unilluminated portion of the disk being faintly visible as if very dimly lit. It is very difficult not to be subjective in observing this feature, for the eye tends to connect up the cusps and lead one to imagine that the entire disk can be seen when in fact it cannot. The most useful observations of the Ashen Light are those made with an occulting bar in the telescope field to hide the illuminated crescent (a curved bar of appropriate radius is best); if when the bright crescent is hidden behind the occulting bar the rest of the disk can still be seen, the observer can be confident that he is recording a real phenomenon.

From time to time areas of the already bright planet appear even brighter; such patches should be looked for and when seen their position carefully recorded. The cusps are frequently seen to be much brighter than the rest of the disk—these cusp 'caps' may account for the apparent projection of the cusps referred to above, due to a diffraction effect. The cusp caps are sometimes seen to be surrounded by a dark collar, similar to the 'blue band' surrounding the polar caps of Mars at times; it is generally believed that the collar is purely a contrast effect, but if seen it is worth recording.

Colour filters are often used in the observation of Venus, but such observations are of value only when carried out very systematically on a carefully controlled basis, and are properly the province of the very experienced observer.

Observing Transits of the Inferior Planets. The rare transits of Mercury, and even rarer transits of Venus, are both interesting and useful phenomena to observe. Accurate timing of the instants of ingress and egress of the planet onto the Sun's disk provide a valuable check of its orbital elements.

The times required are those of 1st contact (ingress of preceding limb of planet), 2nd contact (ingress of following limb), 3rd contact (egress of preceding limb), 4th contact (egress of following limb). Timing may be difficult, especially in the case of Venus, whose silhouetted disk is significantly smaller than the true disk due to irradiation and refraction of the Sun's light through the planet's atmosphere. This causes a *black drop* to link the silhouetted following limb of the planet and the Sun's limb for a few seconds following apparent 2nd contact: a similar effect may be seen a few seconds prior to 3rd contact.

The atmosphere of Venus is often seen as a bright ring of light surrounding the black disk during transit, and extending beyond the Sun's limb between 1st and 2nd contacts, and between 3rd and 4th contacts. This is due to refraction of the Sun's light in the planet's atmosphere.

Observing Mars. The first thing to be said is that Mars is not an easy planet to observe. In the first place, little can be done with telescopes with apertures of less than 20 cm (8 in.); and during unfavourable apparitions even a 30 cm (12 in.) reflector reveals only a limited amount of detail.

Nevertheless, Mars well repays study with suitable instruments; it is the only planetary body apart from the Moon on which we can observe extensive detail *of the solid surface*. Until 1965 our entire knowledge of the planet was based upon a few photographs made with very large telescopes, which in any case show only the broad detail, and the drawings made over many years by a great many devoted visual observers, by far the majority of them being amateurs. With the *Mariner 4* spacecraft of 1965, however, a new era of Martian study began; now the surface is being mapped from spacecraft television pictures with a resolution that could not possibly be achieved by telescopic observation from Earth. Drawing the planet as seen through the telescope is thus no longer a valuable contribution to the mapping of the planet's surface features. This is not to say that there is no longer any value in visual or photographic observation with Earth-based equipment, however, for having an atmosphere Mars, like the Earth, is troubled with inclement weather: the surface features are frequently obscured by clouds, at both high and low altitudes, and by gigantic dust storms that may obliterate a quarter of the visible surface or more. Further, many of the observed features vary in outline, in colour and in intensity; some of these variations seem to be related to the passing of the seasons of the Martian year, whilst others seem to be completely erratic and unpredictable. It is clear, therefore, that *regular*, systematic observation of Mars throughout an apparition may still be of considerable value, especially in the recording of these time-dependent phenomena.

Disk drawings are clearly an important means of recording the appearance of the planet at a given time; they should be made on prepared blanks on which the terminator has been drawn for the correct phase effect. The standard blanks have a diameter of two inches (approx. 50 mm). It is important, so far as possible, to reproduce the relative intensities of the various features as accurately as possible, also their exact position on the disk and their outlines, as these are the characteristics that may vary. Drawings in colour can be useful, but should not be attempted by the inexperienced observer. Many experienced observers stick to black and white drawings of the planet, owing to the difficulty of reproducing accurately the faint tints observed at the telescope. Colour drawings are in any case difficult to evaluate, especially as colour sensitivity varies considerably between individuals. Observations using colour filters can also be useful, but again only when carried out by experienced observers; the observer must be able to decide when the conditions are just not good enough for reliable observations to be made using filters—which is all too frequently the case.

The principal surface features can be identified by the standard map and nomenclature adopted by the International Astronomical Union and reproduced on p. 50.

Observing Jupiter and Saturn. By far the most valuable kind of observation that can be made of these planets is the regular determination of the positions of any spots or other features recognizable in the various belts and zones. To fix the position of such a feature in *latitude* is not easy; fortunately the rapid rotation of these planets ensures that most features remain in their particular longitudinal current, which do not vary very much in latitude. The latitudes of the edges of the belts should be checked at regular intervals, however; this can be done by the measurement of photographs or drawings made with great care by very experienced observers, but by far the most reliable method is direct measurement at the telescope, using a micrometer. To make such measurements satisfactorily requires a good telescope, a 12·5 cm (5 in.) refractor or 25 cm (10 in.) reflector is probably the minimum usable aperture; it should be equatorially mounted with a clock drive. The micrometer used should be a good filar micrometer whose scale value has been carefully determined. This work really falls in the province of the very experienced observer, and therefore no detailed exposition of the actual techniques used is given here.

The field in which all amateur observers with, say, a 15 cm (6 in.) reflector or 10 cm (4 in.) refractor can play a part, is the determination of the *longitudes* of surface features. Many spots drift quite rapidly in longitude, so that regular observation of them provides a most interesting and extremely valuable record. Thanks to the rapid rotation of the major planets we have a ready means of measuring the longitude. Looking at Jupiter through the telescope, it is easy to imagine the *Central Meridian*—the imaginary line which bisects the visible disk, perpendicular to the belts. This imaginary line marks, of course, the direction of the Earth as it would be seen from the centre of Jupiter; if we now imagine parallels of longitude on the surface of Jupiter, similar to those on a terrestrial globe, the rotation of the planet carries these parallels past the Central Meridian. In this way a spot or other surface marking can be seen to appear at one limb of the planet (known as the 'following limb'), slowly cross the disk past the Central Meridian and disappear at the ('preceding') limb. Observations of the longitude of such a spot simply consist of accurately recording the time at which it transits (crosses) the Central Meridian. With practice the observer can time the central-meridian passage of a feature to the nearest minute with complete reliability, and this accuracy is entirely sufficient. The observations are used in conjunction with those made by many other observers, and the positions and rotation periods (which may be such as to indicate a drift in longitude) determined. Such observations are extremely valuable, especially when carried out by the same observer regularly over a long period of time. The most valuable observations of Jupiter have been made by very dedicated observers.

Spots and other fine structure can be seen only very rarely in the case of Saturn; when they are seen it is especially important to time their central-meridian transit, as a few such observations may enable a rotation period to be determined which will fill an important gap in our knowledge of this distant planet.

It is important to ensure that features timed crossing the Central Meridian are fully identified in the observing log. The best way of ensuring this is to number transit observations serially throughout an apparition, and to list the transits made on a given night with the appropriate serial number and a detailed description, followed by the observed time of transit; the serial numbers should also be used to identify the features on an outline sketch of the surface features observed. Attention to this aspect will greatly increase the value of the observations when they come to be compared and collated with those of other observers.

Disk drawings are important, but in fact rather less so than the determinations of longitudes by the transit method. Their main value, in fact, is in supplementing the records of transits, and to provide a record of the changing appearance of the surface of the planet throughout each apparition. Most observers draw the full disk only once or twice during a night's observation, perhaps supplementing this with detail drawings of particularly interesting features.

Drawings are best made on printed blanks, in which an area of the correct outline is left white with a black surround. In the case of Jupiter the standard blank has an equatorial diameter of 2 inches (approx. 5 cm), and allows for the polar flattening of about $\frac{1}{15}$. In the case of Saturn, the adopted dimension is 4 inches (approx. 10 cm) for the diameter of Ring A—this is equivalent to about 1·8 inches (approx. 4·5 cm) for the equatorial diameter of the globe. Unfortunately the apparent shape of Saturn is constantly varying, depending on the tilt of the ring system at the time, so that it is not possible to use a single standard blank. The appropriate outline, depending on the value of B (the Saturnicentric latitude of the Earth relative to the ring-plane), is usually traced from a set of standard stencils.

Another useful kind of observation, provided that it is carried out systematically and regularly, is the estimation of the relative intensities of the various parts of the globe—and, in the case of Saturn, the various components of the ring system. This is done by assessing the intensities on a numerical scale from 0 (brightest) to 10 (darkest). Two fixed points on the scale have been adopted: for Jupiter, 2 for the Equatorial Zone and 10 for a deep shadow or dark sky background, and for Saturn, 1 for the outer part of Ring B and 10 for the absolute blackness of a deep shadow or dark sky background. Fractions such as $\frac{1}{2}$, or even $\frac{1}{4}$, may be used to denote intermediate intensities, but these should be rarely used and intensities quoted to a tenth are quite meaningless.

All observations should be fully documented, the date, time (U.T.) of the observation, instrument and power used, all being essential to the permanent record. Detailed notes of all important features noted should be added to the record *at the time of observation*.

In order to record properly observations of the surface feature of these planets, it is essential to use the adopted nomenclature, which is summarized in Fig. 14.

Observations of satellite phenomena, both of Jupiter and Saturn, are very valuable. The most important activity in this field is the accurate timing of each phase of the phenomenon, using a reliable

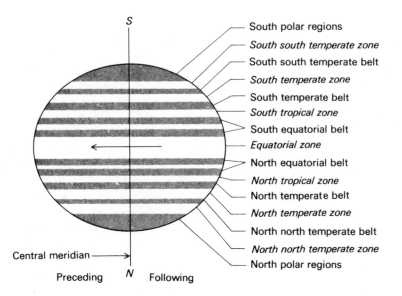

FIGURE 14. Nomenclature of surface markings on Jupiter (and Saturn)

watch which ideally should be compared with a wireless time signal or the Post Office speaking clock, as soon as possible before the observation and again immediately after. Many observers find a split-action stop-watch invaluable in this work, where timings to the nearest second at least are required, and a few use an electrical chronograph with which seconds pulses from an astronomical clock are recorded, the instants when each phase of the phenomenon occurs being added to the record also by means of a hand-tapper.

The magnitudes of the satellites—especially the five innermost satellites of Saturn, which are variable —are worth estimating. Titan is also suspected of being variable. The largest variation is that of Iapetus, which varies by more than two magnitudes, being brightest at western and faintest at eastern elongation.

The techniques used in this work are essentially those used by observers of variable stars. Visual estimations are difficult to make satisfactorily, however, due to the lack of a permanent sequence of comparison stars, and usually to a dearth of suitable stars in the telescope field when using a sufficiently high power to reveal the satellites. The most reliable method is photo-electric photometry, which unfortunately requires rather sophisticated equipment whose purchase or construction is beyond the reach of many amateurs.

OTHER MEMBERS OF THE SOLAR SYSTEM

The Minor Planets

These bodies, sometimes called asteroids, are small worlds; even Ceres, the largest of them, is only 685 km in diameter, and of the rest only Vesta (590 km) and Pallas (450 km) exceed 400 km. Only Vesta is ever visible with the naked eye, being closer to the Sun (and hence to the Earth) than Ceres.

The total number of minor planets is very great, and 40,000 may be a conservative estimate. Most of them keep to the region of the Solar System between the orbits of Mars and Jupiter, and most are true dwarfs—a few miles in diameter, and probably not even approximately spherical. They are so numerous that keeping track of them all is a difficult matter; new discoveries are made every year, but it often happens that a newly-found minor planet is insufficiently observed, so that its orbit cannot be accurately worked out. All minor planet discoveries are now made photographically.

The most interesting objects are those whose orbits carry them away from the main swarm. Thus No. 433 Eros, discovered by Witt in 1898, may approach the Earth to within 24 million km; the next approach is due in 1975. At its approach of 1931 it was exhaustively studied by observatories all over the world, since determination of its orbit could lead to a more accurate value for the astronomical unit.

However, better methods are now available, and Eros has lost its scientific importance in this respect. It is irregular in shape, with a longer diameter of about 27 km. Other minor planets have been known to approach even more closely; thus in 1937 Hermes, with an estimated diameter of only one mile, passed the Earth at a distance of only 780,000 km. Other 'Earth-grazers' are Amor, Apollo and Adonis. Icarus, discovered photographically by W. Baade in 1949, passes within the orbit of Mercury; No. 944 Hidalgo has its aphelion almost at the orbit of Saturn, and the so-called Trojan minor planets move in approximately the same orbit as Jupiter. (They are in no danger of collision with the giant planet, being in two groups keeping station in different parts of the orbit.)

TABLE 38. THE FIRST FIVE MINOR PLANETS

Object	Year of Discovery	Sidereal Period	Mean Distance from Sun	Orbital Inclination	Diameter	Maximum Apparent Magnitude
		y	km	° ′	km	
1 Ceres	1801	4·60	413,400,000	10 36	685	7·4
2 Pallas	1802	4·61	414,100,000	34 48	450	8·7
3 Juno	1804	4·36	398,700,000	13 00	240	8·0
4 Vesta	1807	3·63	352,800,000	7 08	590	6·0
5 Astræa	1845	4·14	385,000,000	5 20	180	9·9

TABLE 39. SOME INTERESTING CLOSE-APPROACH MINOR PLANETS

Object	Year of Discovery	Sidereal Period	Distance from Sun (Maximum)	(Minimum)	Diameter	Orbital Inclination	Orbital Eccentricity
		y	A.U.	A.U.	km	° ′	
433 Eros	1898	1·76	1·81	1·11	27	10 8	0·22
719 Albert	1911	4·16	3·98	1·19	3	10 8	0·54
887 Alinda	1918	4·00	3·88	1·16	3	9 0	0·54
1221 Amor	1932	2·67	2·75	1·09	8	11 9	0·44
— Apollo	1932	1·81	2·33	0·64	2½	6 4	0·57
— Adonis	1936	2·76	3·50	0·43	1½	1 5	0·78
— Hermes	1937	1·47	1·90	0·68	1½	4 7	0·47
1566 Icarus	1949	1·12	1·97	0·19	1½	23 0	0·83

The origin of the minor planets is not known with any certainty. They may be the débris left after the formation of the principal planets; alternatively, it has been suggested that they are the remnants of a former planet (or planets) which disintegrated. There seems to be no essential difference between an asteroid and a large meteoroid.

Telescopically, a minor planet looks exactly like a star, and the only way to identify it is by its position and its movement from night to night. Magnitude estimates are of some interest, and may be made in the same way as for variable stars.

The *nomenclature* of minor planets is quite a complex matter. Many of the earliest known asteroids have proper names, drawn both from classical mythology and contemporary life (e.g. Ceres, Apollo; Victoria, Rockefellia). New asteroids are sometimes given names, which are very convenient for reference, but *all* new discoveries are allocated a provisional designation at once. If subsequent observation proves the discovery to be genuinely a new minor planet, and not a re-discovery of one known previously, it is given a definitive number once its orbital elements have been satisfactorily determined.

For the provisional designation, originally a single letter sufficed, and the year; but in 1893, the double form AA to AZ, BA to BZ, etc., was introduced (I being omitted), this new series being continued right on until ZZ was reached, instead of beginning the alphabet afresh each year. A second alphabet was begun in 1907, with the year (1907 AA, etc.), and a third in 1916; this terminated with UA, 1924 Dec. 31, when a new system was started to enable belated discoveries to be inserted in approximately their proper place.

Under the present system of temporary nomenclature, the double alphabet begins afresh each year; the discoveries of Jan. 1–15 are AA, AB, AC, etc.; of Jan. 16–31, BA, BB, BC, etc.; of Feb. 1–15, CA, CB, etc., the year being prefixed in each case.

The first letters of the suffix for each half-month are:

January:	A, B;	May:	J, K;	September: R, S;
February:	C, D;	June:	L, M;	October: T, U;
March:	E, F;	July:	N, O;	November: V, W;
April:	G, H;	August:	P, Q;	December: X, Y.

When the orbit of a new asteroid is determined the provisional designation is replaced by a permanent number, usually symbolized thus: ⑭ .

Comets

Comets vary in brightness. Most of them never become bright enough to be seen without optical aid; all the short-period comets come into this category. Brilliant comets have very long revolution periods, and therefore cannot be predicted. They have been rather uncommon in the 20th century, though Bennett's Comet of 1970 was a spectacular object for some weeks.

A comet is generally seen first as a small, misty object, superficially rather like a nebula, but of course with definite individual motion; however, even a very bright comet may sometimes escape detection at first if it approaches in the line of sight of the Sun.

A comet consists of a *coma* or head, containing a *nucleus* which may appear almost stellar; and there may be a *tail*, which always points more or less away from the Sun. Many comets have tails both of dusty material and of gas. It has been suggested that the tail is produced by the evaporation of icy materials in the nucleus when the comet approaches perihelion; when the comet recedes after its nearest approach to the Sun, the tail decreases.

Periodic comets have known periods, and can always be predicted; few of them develop tails. They are given the prefix P and are given a permanent name—generally the name of their discoverer (P/Holmes, P/Faye) or joint-discoverers (P/Pons–Brooks, P/Tempel–Swift); less commonly by the computer of their orbits (P/Halley, P/Encke, P/Crommelin). Some periodic comets have been lost, and have presumably disintegrated. (One, P/Biela, divided into two parts prior to its last two returns (1846, 1852) and no longer exists as a comet. It is, however, associated with an annual meteor shower.) There are other comets similarly associated with meteor showers, and it is thought that much meteoric débris is spread along cometary orbits.

In addition to the permanent name, all newly discovered comets—whether new or previously known—are given a provisional designation comprising the year and a letter (a, b, etc.) indicating the order of discovery within that year, i.e. Comet 1972a, Comet 1972b, and so on. Subsequently, when the comet's orbit has been accurately determined, it is given a definitive number which lists comets in the order of perihelion passage during the year. This is in the form 1972 I, 1972 II, etc., and replaces the provisional designation.

Observing Comets. The two main fields of observing activity are seeking new comets and studying (visually or photographically) the physical structure of known ones.

For *comet seeking* a telescope of fairly large aperture and short focal length, with a low-power eye-piece giving a large field of view, should be used. The observer should slowly 'sweep' (i.e. move the telescope in a horizontal direction) for some distance, a careful watch being kept all the time. At the end of the sweep the telescope is *slightly* raised or lowered, and an overlapping sweep is taken in the opposite direction. This process is repeated continuously. Should a nebulous-looking object be noticed, the comet-hunter must consult a catalogue of nebulæ to see if the object can be identified. If not, he should draw a careful sketch of its position among the neighbouring stars. If during the course of several hours any movement can be detected, and the place of the suspected object does not agree with that of any known comet, its position should be determined as accurately as means will allow, and a telegram giving particulars sent to the nearest national observatory.

Visual observations of comet structure are best drawn in white paint on black paper. Care should be taken to reproduce accurately the relative sizes and intensities of the head, tail, and any 'beard' or 'spike' that may be present. If the comet has an extended tail it will often have brighter streamers or condensations within it, which should also be carefully drawn. It is important to include all nearby stars, accurately positioned, and drawn with a variable scale of diameters to indicate their respective brightness: this will enable them to be identified and permit the position of the comet to be deduced with reasonable accuracy. The observer should also estimate the integrated apparent magnitude of the whole comet and of the nucleus separately.

Comets may be photographed with a suitable camera attached to an equatorially mounted telescope and guided during the exposure. Typical comet cameras utilize ex-government $f/4\cdot5$ or $f/5\cdot6$ aero-camera lenses. Exposures required may range from a few minutes to an hour or so, depending upon the instrument used and the brightness of the comet.

Meteors

With the exception of very small dust particles, all objects entering the Earth's atmosphere at high speed will be subjected to very high temperatures, generated by frictional heating. The light emitted enables the path of the object to be seen quite easily. *Meteors* (or 'shooting stars') occur in all degrees of brightness, from faint telescopic objects, lasting a fraction of a second, to bright *fireballs* lasting several seconds. They can be seen on almost any night at a rate of five to seven per hour. These 'sporadic' meteors have no preferred direction nor do they seem to originate from any preferred position in the sky. At certain times in the year, one may see 'shower' meteors, i.e. those which seem to originate from a fixed point in the sky, known as a *radiant*. Showers from radiants within or near to the area of the sky containing the circumpolar stars may be seen all night, but the observing interval shortens as the radiant declination decreases. Shower meteors from a radiant just below the horizon may be visible, however.

The meteors associated with any particular radiant exhibit basically the same general characteristics year after year. There are, however, considerable differences between various showers. In some, the meteors move very swiftly, in others, they move comparatively slowly; in some, the average meteor is faint, in others, a proportion of fireballs may be expected. Trails are characteristic of some showers, while occasionally a bright slow-moving meteor seems to travel in a wavy path. The intensity of a shower may vary considerably with time, the peak period in some cases being very well defined, but in others activity may be spread over a considerable number of days. Activity can vary considerably from year to year. The Leonid shower, for example, gives a reasonably constant display each year except at 33-year intervals, when extraordinary displays involving rates of many thousands per hour are seen for short periods.

Meteors usually appear in the upper region of the atmosphere, about 80–120 km above the Earth's surface and on average disappear at a height of 60–80 km. Whilst it is unlikely that any single observer can record accurately all the information which may be of use, the following points will give general guidance as to what is required.

Date; Time (U.T.).	Duration of train if present.
R.A. and Dec. of beginning and end of flight.	Variation of light or behaviour of meteor
Duration in tenths of a second.	(e.g. sparks, explosions, etc.).
Colour and stellar magnitude.	Behaviour of trail with time.

All observations should be sent to the Meteor Sections of national organizations, some of which are listed on page 116.

If the object entering the atmosphere is large enough, it will produce an extraordinarily bright fireball or *bolide*, with an apparent diameter similar to that of the Sun or Moon. The object itself may not be completely vaporized before reaching the ground. These surviving rocks, called *meteorites*, are of great importance and it is advantageous to examine them as quickly as possible after the fall. Organizations exist to receive reports of these bolides so that the fall area can be located quickly. Only a small percentage of these major fireballs are meteorite-producing, but if sonic phenomena are recorded, this probability is much larger.

There is, however, a very close similarity between natural bolides and fireballs produced by the re-entry of artificial satellites, although generally, the latter move much slower than the natural objects and may take as long as one minute to cross the sky.

Because no-one can predict the arrival of a bolide, the witnessing of such an event is a matter of luck and reports tend to come from inexperienced observers. Any observer of such an event should contact, as soon as possible, the Centre for Short Lived Phenomena, Smithsonian Institution, or, if the bolide is seen over the British Isles, The Director, Artificial Satellite Section, B.A.A. (see page 116).

Information on the following aspects are required:

(i) Name and address of observer; observing position; date; time (U.T.).

(ii) Track—If possible, the track through its star background. If this is not possible, the direction and altitude when first seen, when highest in the sky, and when last seen. If the object passes virtually overhead, whether to the left-hand side or right-hand side as the observer faces the direction from which the bolide came.

(iii) Fireball—size, shape, colour, details of tail; presence of dust trail; fragmentation, extinction.

(iv) Sonic Effects—estimate of time interval between passage of bolide and the recording of the 'sonic boom'.

Principal Meteor Showers. The data given in Table 40 refer to the major night-time streams. Some give a reasonable display annually, others give exceptional displays periodically.

The radiant position may change a degree or two on successive days and a watch should be kept a few days before and after the dates given, as leap-year adjustments cause small variations. Some showers are active over several days but others have peak activity for just a few hours or even less. It is therefore advisable to refer to a reference book for the appropriate year for precise details of the showers listed and also for others that may be particularly active during that year.

TABLE 40. PRINCIPAL METEOR SHOWERS

Shower	Epoch		Radiant		Notes
	Normal limits	Max.	R.A.	Dec.	
			h m °	°	
Quandrantids	Jan 1–5	Jan 4	15 28 (232)	+50	Medium speed. Blue. Many faint meteors.
*Corona Australids	Mar. 14–18	Mar. 16	16 20 (245)	−48	
Lyrids (April)	Apr. 19–24	Apr. 21	18 08 (272)	+32	Fast moving. Brilliant.
η-Aquarids	May 1–8	May 5	22 24 (336)	0	Very fast. Persistent trains.
Lyrids (June)	Jun. 10–21	Jun. 15	18 32 (278)	+35	Blue.
*Ophiuchids	Jun. 17–26	Jun. 20	17 20 (260)	−20	
Capricornids	Jly 10–Aug. 15	Jly 25	21 00 (315)	−15	Yellow. Very slow.
δ-Aquarids	Jly 15–Aug. 15	Jly 28	22 36 (339)	−17	Slow. Long paths.
			22 36 (339)	0	
*Piscis Australids	Jly 15–Aug. 20	Jly 30	22 40 (340)	−30	
α-Capricornids	Jly 15–Aug. 25	Aug. 1	20 36 (309)	−10	Yellow.
ι-Aquarids	Jly 15–Aug. 25	Aug. 6	22 32 (338)	−15	
			22 04 (331)	−6	
Perseids	Jly 25–Aug. 18	Aug. 12	03 04 (046)	+58	Very fast. Fragmenting.
κ-Cygnids	Aug. 18–22	Aug. 20	19 20 (290)	+55	Bright. Exploding.
Orionids	Oct. 16–27	Oct. 21	06 24 (096)	+15	Very fast. Persistent trains.
Taurids	Oct. 10–Dec. 3	Nov. 1	03 28 (052)	+14	Slow. Brilliant.
			03 36 (054)	+21	
Leonids	Nov. 15–19	Nov. 17	10 08 (152)	+22	Very fast. Persistent trains.
*Phœnicids	—	Dec. 4	01 00 (015)	−55	
Geminids	Dec. 7–15	Dec. 14	07 28 (112)	+32	White.
Ursids	Dec. 17–24	Dec. 22	14 28 (217)	+78	

*Visible in southern hemisphere only.

The hourly rate observed depends critically on the altitude of the radiant at the time of the observation. To compute the Zenithal Hourly Rate (ZHR), the observed rate should be multiplied by a factor F corresponding to the altitude of the radiant:

Altitude	Factor	Altitude	Factor
0°		27·4°	
	10·0		1·7
2·6		34·5	
	5·0		1·4
8·6		42·5	
	3·3		1·3
14·5		52·2	
	2·5		1·1
20·7		65·8	
	2·0		1·0
27·4		90·0	

In critical cases ascend.

Moonlight has an adverse effect on observed rates, and during the period of about 10 days centred on Full Moon only the brighter meteors will be seen.

ECLIPSES AND OCCULTATIONS

Eclipses

Lunar eclipses occur when the Moon passes into the shadow-cone of the Earth—always at Full Moon. Solar 'eclipses' are strictly speaking occultations of the Sun by the Moon and always occur at New Moon.

Other examples of eclipses are those of planetary satellites when they pass through the shadow-cone of their primary, or of another satellite of the planet, and those of the components of an eclipsing binary star system.

Solar Eclipses may be total, partial or annular, depending upon the relative positions of the Sun, Moon and Earth at the time. As much as four hours may elapse between first and last contact, but totality never exceeds 7 m 40 s, and annularity $12\frac{1}{2}$ minutes; both are usually much less. At the equator, both totality and contact-interval last for longer than at higher latitudes. The width of the zone of totality averages less than 160 km (100 miles), but may amount to 254 km (167 miles). Total eclipses are rare as seen from any particular point on the Earth's surface; thus in England none occur between 1927 and 1999. Partial and annular eclipses are of little real importance, but a total eclipse provides the only opportunities of seeing the chromosphere, prominences and corona with the naked eye. Moreover, certain investigations can be carried out only during totality. When the Sun is completely hidden the sky becomes dark; the bright planets and stars may then be seen with the naked eye.

Baily's Beads are sometimes seen for an instant before totality: the thin disappearing crescent of the Sun seems to break up into a series of bright moving points, giving the appearance of a string of shining beads. They are caused by the irregularities of the Moon's limb. They may also be seen as totality ends. The name derives from Francis Baily, who first described and discussed the phenomenon following the eclipse of 1836.

Shadow Bands, or fringes, may also occur for an instant as totality begins. They are seen as bands of shadow 10–15 cm wide and up to a metre apart, crossing any light surface. They are probably caused by irregular refraction of the Sun's light.

Lunar Eclipses, when total and central, may last as long as 3 h 48 m from first to last contact of the umbra, or up to 6 h including the penumbral stage; the maximum duration of totality is 1 h 42 m. Usually the Moon does not vanish completely, as light is refracted on to its surface by way of the Earth's atmosphere; the colour and brightness of the eclipsed Moon depend upon the conditions prevailing in the Earth's atmosphere at the time. During a lunar eclipse, a 'wave of cold' sweeps across the lunar surface, and detailed measurements have been made of the cooling of various areas. It has been found that certain so-called 'hot spots', such as the crater Tycho, cool less quickly than their surroundings. Lunar eclipses are interesting to watch, though from the observer's viewpoint they are more spectacular than important.

Occultations

Although, technically, an occultation takes place whenever one body passes in front of another, the term is normally used to refer to the condition when the Moon or a planet passes in front of a star. In the case of the Moon the disappearance or *immersion* is always on the east side of the Moon and re-appearance or *emersion* on the west side. When the star is bright, the instantaneous disappearance and re-appearance are almost startling.

Lunar Occultations. Occultation of stars by the Moon have been observed for over 300 years; the first recorded timed observation is thought to have been made by Bullialdus in 1623 when the Moon occulted the star α Virginis (*Spica*). The Nautical Almanac first published a list of occulted stars in 1824, and by 1834 predictions for occultations visible at Greenwich were published.

Since the Moon moves through about 1 second of arc in 2 seconds of time, a timing accuracy of only 0·2 seconds is required to give the Moon's position to $0''\cdot1$ (corresponding to about 200 metres in the Moon's orbit). It is therefore obvious that useful observations can be made by amateurs using modest equipment.

By agreement with the International Astronomical Union, the prediction and reduction of occultations of stars by the Moon is undertaken by H.M. Nautical Almanac Office, Royal Greenwich Observatory.

Of great interest in recent years have been grazing occultations, information on which provides a much more accurate value for the latitude of the Moon than is possible with ordinary occultations.

Observing Lunar Occultations. An observation of an occultation consists of the time of disappearance or reappearance of a star, referred to a known time signal. It is also necessary to know accurately the position of the observer and of course, the identity of the star.

Beginners may be rather puzzled to know the direction in which the Moon will approach the star, owing to the varying position of the Moon's axis with respect to the horizon: the direction is approximately at right angles to the line joining the cusps, or horns, of the Moon.

The Moon's mean hourly motion being fully $\frac{1}{2}°$, the rate of approach is about a quarter of the Moon's diameter in 14 minutes, or the apparent diameter of Hipparchus in about $2\frac{3}{4}$ minutes, or of Copernicus in about $1\frac{1}{2}$ minutes. This time, however, is modified by the latitude of the observer, etc.

Other Occultations. Occultation of a star by Neptune in 1968 gave a very accurate position for the planet and information on its atmosphere although the major result was the accurate determination of the planet's diameter, about 10% greater than the previously accepted value.

The occultation of radio sources by the Moon have enabled the positions of the radio sources to be found to one or two seconds of arc, a far more precise value than is possible by normal use of a radio telescope.

AURORÆ AND ZODIACAL LIGHT

The Aurora

Auroral displays are known to be due to the gases in the upper atmosphere being stimulated by bombardment from charged particles, protons and electrons, which have originated in the Sun. Auroræ observed in the northern and southern hemispheres are termed *Aurora Borealis* and *Aurora Australis* respectively.

The colours of auroral displays are characteristic of atomic and molecular oxygen and nitrogen.

The auroral spectrum is complex, but the two predominant lines are at 5577 Å (the so-called auroral green line of atomic oxygen) and at 3914 Å (molecular nitrogen).

If the brightness of the emitted light is below the colour perception threshold of the eye, the aurora appears dull white; but with strong displays, involving all the above colours, the overall colour may be a brilliant white.

It is possible to observe some form of display on most clear nights in two regions, one in each hemisphere, at latitudes between 60° and 75° magnetic. Within these regions the aurora appears more or less overhead at heights in excess of 100 km. In the *cis*-auroral regions (regions on the equator side of the auroral zone), the display often takes the form of a glow, resembling dawn, just above the northern [southern] horizon, but at times of great solar activity, the auroral zone moves to lower latitudes and consequently it is possible to see details in the display normally seen only in the more northerly [southerly] latitudes.

Although the way in which an auroral display develops cannot be predicted, there are certain sequences which frequently occur. The display may begin with a *glow* along the northern horizon (southern horizon if in the southern hemisphere). The glow then ascends from the horizon to form a quiet *arc* extending like a rainbow in an approximately E–W direction. The lower border of the arc is usually much more sharply defined than the upper. Although the arc may remain quiescent for hours, drifting north-wards or southwards, it may suddenly brighten with *rays* shooting upwards from the upper edge. Sometimes the arc folds, loosing its regular bow shape to form an irregular *band*. In addition diffuse *patches* of light, resembling clouds, may appear in parts of the sky, completely separated from the ray structure. As the display dies down, waves of light surge upwards in rapid succession giving the impression of fire (*flaming*).

It is difficult to estimate the brightness of the display, but the following scale is used for such estimations:

    (i) weak, comparable with the Milky Way;
    (ii) comparable with moonlit cirrus cloud;
    (iii) comparable with moonlit cumulus cloud;
    (iv) much brighter than (iii), possibly strong enough to cast shadows.

Observing Auroræ. This is one of the few kinds of astronomical observation which can be made with the unaided eye; the only instrument which would help in visual observation of auroræ would be a simple device for measuring the angular height of parts of the aurora above the horizon. Observers situated in higher latitudes, particularly, should observe during the more active part of the sunspot cycle, especially around the equinoxes. A regular series of observations can be very valuable. Photographic observation of auroræ can be carried out with fairly simple equipment and is also useful.

Much importance is attached by auroral investigators to the positions where the auroral feature is overhead. It is therefore important to determine the angle of elevation of the highest point of the *lower* border of an arc or band. This can be carried out using an alidade or similar instrument, but if none is available, the following approximate method may be of use:

30 cm rule (1 foot) held at arm's length subtends an angle of about 25° at the eye, so 6 cm is equivalent to 5°.

Full details of the methods of observation and reporting of auroral displays can be obtained from the Director of the Aurora Section, B.A.A. (see page 116).

The Zodiacal Light

This phenomenon is not well seen from temperate latitudes. It is a faint, hazy, conical beam of light, about 15–20° wide at the base, seen in the west after sunset and in the east before sunrise. The main axis of this lies approximately along the Ecliptic for 90° or more from the horizon, a little south [in southern latitudes, north] of where the Sun is below the horizon. In its brightest parts, it is two or three times as luminous as the Milky Way, but towards its extreme limits, it is always exceedingly faint. Its brightness seems to vary from time to time and it is brighter when observed within the tropics than in temperate latitudes, partly due to the main axis of the cone being more or less at right angles to the horizon and partly due to the short twilight periods.

From the middle northern latitudes, it is best seen near the vernal equinox in the evening and near the autumnal equinox in the morning sky (vice versa in the southern hemisphere). The Zodiacal Light owes its name to the fact that the light is more or less confined to the region of the Zodiac.

It is now generally accepted that this light is actually sunlight that has been scattered by dust particles (micrometeoroids) lying in the plane of the ecliptic and orbiting the Sun. The spectrum of the Zodiacal Light is essentially the same as normal sunlight. It is partly polarized but the degree of polarization is too small to permit an 'electron' origin for the light. The small amount of broadening due to the Doppler effect caused by random motion is also evidence against an electron theory. Observations suggest particle sizes within the range of 1–350 microns and there is much evidence to suppose that the Zodiacal Light is an extension of the F-corona (or dust corona) of the Sun.

The table below gives the approximate dates and hours when the Ecliptic is most nearly vertical during the short observing season. The dates at the top are for the northern hemisphere; those at the foot (in italic) for the southern hemisphere. The position of the foot of the Zodiacal Light on the horizon for three or four hours after (or before) the hours mentioned is easily found, as its movement in azimuth westwards may be taken as about 6° per hour over that period; similarly, the decrease per hour in inclination after (or before) greatest verticality is, roughly, 2°.

Feb. 5	Feb. 12	Feb. 20	Feb. 27	Mar. 7	Mar. 14	Mar. 22	Sept. 22	Sept. 29	Oct. 7	Oct. 14	Oct. 22	Oct. 30	Nov. 7
9 p.m.	8·30	8 p.m.	7·30	7 p.m.	6·30	6 p.m.	6 a.m.	5·30	5 a.m.	4·30	4 a.m.	3·30	3 a.m.
Aug. 6	*Aug. 13*	*Aug. 21*	*Aug. 29*	*Sept. 6*	*Sept. 13*	*Sept. 21*	*Mar. 23*	*Mar. 31*	*Apr. 8*	*Apr. 15*	*Apr. 23*	*Apr. 30*	*May 8*

The Gegenschein

This phenomenon—also known as the Counterglow—is a very faint patch of light situated at or near to the anti-solar point, i.e. a point on the ecliptic diametrically opposite to the position of the Sun at the time of the observation. It is normally elliptical in shape, typically 10° × 20°, although in the tropics it may be seen to extend over 30°. It can normally be seen only on very clear moonless nights, the best times being when the ecliptic is highest above the horizon, viz. December and January for northern observers.

It is thought that the origin of this light is due to scattering of sunlight by dust particles orbiting the Sun, although recently a suggestion has been put forward that it is due to a tail of dust (similar to a comet's tail) following the Earth as it moves round the Sun.

The Gegenschein is sometimes seen joined to the Zodiacal Light by a parallel beam of light called the *Zodiacal Band*. At times this Band may be seen just as an extension of the Zodiacal Light and at others just as an extension on either side of the Gegenschein.

ARTIFICIAL SATELLITES

Artificial satellites appear as star-like points of light travelling slowly against the star background. The brightness of satellites varies considerably, due mainly to the distance of the object from the observer, the phase angle—i.e. the angle between the directions of the Sun and observer as seen from the satellite—and the clarity of the atmosphere. Further, because most satellites are seen solely by reflected sunlight, the magnitude depends on the shape of the object. Some satellites, such as the spherical balloons, have reasonably constant absolute magnitudes, but others may appear to flash at regular or irregular intervals or just fade and brighten with regularity or irregularity. This variability is due mainly to controlled motion of the satellite or uncontrolled tumbling as in the case with many discarded rockets. These motions cause the sunlight to be reflected from varying surfaces.

The rate of travel across the sky depends on the height of the object above the Earth's surface. For a satellite in a circular equatorial orbit, i.e. where the inclination of the orbital plane = 0°, and at a height of 36,000 km, the eastward motion is $\frac{1}{4}$° per minute. This just balances the westward motion of the stars due to the Earth's rotation and hence the satellite appears stationary in the sky relative to an observer on the Earth's surface. This is called a synchronous orbit.

The minimum height for a stable orbit is about 160 km, corresponding to an orbital period of just under 88 minutes. Below this height, atmospheric drag becomes so great that the object rapidly loses height and enters the denser regions of the atmosphere and then suffers the same fate as a natural body entering the atmosphere (see section on **Meteors**).

The principal perturbing forces which cause the track of a satellite to deviate from the simple Keplerian ellipse are:

(1) *Non-spherical Earth*. The equatorial bulge has two effects, the magnitude of each depending on the average height of the satellite and the orbital inclination to the equator.

(*a*) The orbital plane rotates about the spin axis of the Earth, the rate of regression (X) being given by

$$X = 9\text{·}97\left(\frac{R}{R+h}\right)^{3\text{·}5}\cos i \text{ degrees/day}$$

where

R = radius of Earth;
h = average height of satellite above Earth's surface;
i = inclination of orbit.

(*b*) The major axis of the ellipse rotates within the plane of the ellipse, the daily rotation being given by

$$4\text{·}98\left(\frac{R}{R+h}\right)^{3\text{·}5}(5\cos^2 i - 1)\text{ degrees/day}.$$

(2) *Atmospheric drag*. This has the effect of decreasing the apogee height whilst keeping the perigee height roughly the same. The rate of change of eccentricity of the orbit depends on the initial eccentricity and the average height of the orbit.

(3) *Solar Radiation Pressure*. This is very pronounced in the case of satellites having a large area/mass ratio, e.g. the balloon satellites. The effect is complex, depending on the orbital inclination and the time spent by the satellite in the Earth's shadow.

(4) *Changes in upper atmosphere caused by solar activity*, e.g. solar flares. Solar activity can alter by a high factor the density of the atmosphere at a given height, thus modifying the drag factor. Unfortunately this effect cannot be predicted in advance and hence an element of uncertainty is introduced into predictions for the position of a satellite at a given time.

Artificial satellites can normally be observed when the following conditions are satisfied:

(*a*) The satellite is above the observer's horizon and is illuminated by the Sun.

(*b*) The observer is located at a position where it is night-time, i.e. the sky is dark.

The above conditions will generally lead to two observing periods, just after sunset and just before sunrise, the length of these periods depending on the height of the satellite, the location of the observer and the time of the year. In the summer months in the middle latitudes, the two visibility periods merge together and satellites can be seen throughout the whole night. Conversely, during the winter months, the visibility period may be as little as half an hour. The number of days in which a satellite can be seen during a visibility period depends on the orbital elements.

In general, a satellite will not pass over a given point on the Earth's surface at the same time on consecutive days. The daily westward movement of the orbital plane is given by

$$X + 1 + \frac{n}{4}$$

where X = regression angle (see above);

1 = average value for the westward movement of the stars, due to the Earth's motion round Sun;

n = difference in time in minutes between 24 hours and the time for an integral number of revolutions of the satellite in 24 hours, since it is not usual for a satellite to make an exact number of revolutions in 1 day.

Predictions for artificial satellites are of two types. The first are of a general form, called 'Equator Crossing' predictions, from which it is possible to locate the position of a satellite at any required time. The information provided gives the time and longitude for each north-bound crossing of the equator. A subsidiary table gives, relative to this point, the latitude, longitude, height and whether it is in the Earth's shadow for other points along its orbit. The second type of prediction, referred to as 'Look Data' predictions, give the co-ordinates of the predicted positions in the sky as seen from a particular position. The latter type is used by experienced observers.

Observing Artificial Satellites

The basic equipment required for making observations of satellites is:

(1) *Optical aid.* The main requirements are light grasp, wide field of view and manœuvrability. Normally, 7×50 binoculars or 'elbow' predictor-type telescopes are used. The traditional astronomical telescope, with its small field of view, is unsuitable.

(2) *Timing device.* The normal practice is to use a stop watch (reading to $\frac{1}{10}$ s) in conjunction with a standard time signal, e.g. MSF (Rugby), DIZ (Nauen, East Germany) or WWV (Fort Collins, Colorado, U.S.A.), or for the British Isles, the Post Office Speaking Clock.

An observation of a satellite is obtained by noting the time and position as accurately as possible when the satellite crosses a line joining two relatively close stars. The distance to the nearest star is normally given as a fraction of the distance separating the two reference stars. To convert this position to celestial co-ordinates, it is necessary to use a star catalogue or accurate star maps. The star maps included in this reference book should *only* be used for identification purposes.

Detailed instructions for satellite observing can be obtained from the Director of the Artificial Satellite Section, B.A.A. (see p. 116).

IV. STARS, NEBULÆ AND GALAXIES

RADIATION, MAGNITUDE AND LUMINOSITY

Radiation

Virtually all information about celestial objects is conveyed to the observer by means of electro-magnetic radiation. It is the analysis of this radiation by the photometer, spectrometer, polarimeter, etc., which enables hypotheses to be verified (or in some cases discredited).

Electromagnetic Spectrum. This is a way of classifying the radiation by separating it into groups of frequencies or wavelength intervals. The division is somewhat arbitrary but Fig. 15 shows a generally accepted scale.

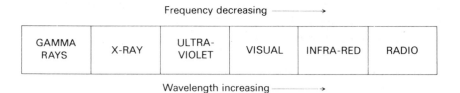

FIGURE 15. Schematic representation of the electromagnetic spectrum

The visual part of the spectrum is further expanded in Fig. 16.

Colour	Blue	Green	Yellow	Red
Wavelength (Å)	4400	5200	5700	6000

FIGURE 16. The visible spectrum

Brightness and Magnitude

The apparent brightness of a star is an estimate of how much radiation from the star is received by the eye (or the measuring instrument); the estimation of the value of this brightness is based on a system of comparisons in which certain stars are used as standards. These comparisons have largely been super-seded by photo-electric photometers, instruments which measure precisely the intensity of the radiation received from the star. Consequently it is possible to attribute an intensity of radiation to a particular stellar magnitude, i.e., a range of brightnesses corresponds to a scale of magnitudes such that a star one magnitude brighter than another is 2·512 times as bright—i.e., it is approximately $2\frac{1}{2}$ times as bright.

Star Magnitudes. The brightest stars are said to be 1st magnitude; those less bright 2nd magnitude, and so on, a standard 1st magnitude star (e.g. *Aldebaran, Altair*) being 100 times as bright as a standard 6th magnitude star, which is about the faintest star that can be seen with the naked eye. Some stars, however, are brighter than first magnitude, so the range of magnitudes extends in the other direction, a star of magnitude 'o' being approximately $2\frac{1}{2}$ times as bright as one of magnitude 1, and a star of magnitude −1 about $2\frac{1}{2}$ times brighter than one of magnitude 0, and so on. Below magnitude 6 the magnitudes run on—7th, 8th, etc., for the telescopic stars. Typically an 11th magnitude star is visible in a refractor of 7·5 cm (3 in.) aperture.

Intermediate magnitudes are denoted in tenths or even hundredths of a magnitude, thus magnitude 3·00 is very slightly brighter than 3·01 but slightly less bright than 2·99. On the minus side of 0·00, however, the magnitude figure increases with brightness. Thus magnitude −0·10 is brighter than 0·00, −1·90 is brighter than −1·89, and so on. Where there is no sign magnitudes are always understood to be positive.

The magnitudes in modern catalogues are always calculated for the zenith: at lower altitudes atmospheric effects diminish the brightness and must be allowed for when comparing stars at different altitudes.

The magnitude scale essentially describes *ratios* of brightness and in order to use it as an absolute scale (not to be confused with absolute magnitude) a convention has to be adopted which is as follows:

The amount of energy received outside the earth's atmosphere from a star of bolometric magnitude 0·00 is equal to $2·48 \times 10^{-8}$ watts per square metre.

This then defines the actual magnitude of any star whose brightness is known.

Relationships for Calculating Magnitude Differences. The magnitude scale is defined exactly by specifying that two stars which have brightnesses in the ratio of 1:100 have a magnitude difference of precisely 5. Hence if two stars have brightnesses B_1 and B_2 then it follows that

$$B_1/B_2 = 2·512^{(m_2 - m_1)}$$

$$\text{or } m_2 - m_1 = 2·500 \log (B_1/B_2)$$

The data in Table 7 are calculated using these relationships.

Apparent Magnitude. This is the magnitude of a celestial object as directly estimated by the human eye, or measured instrumentally by a photometer, without any corrections being made for the object's distance. It is denoted by the symbol *m*.

In astronomical photometry, measurements of apparent magnitude are made at different wavelengths. This is generally called *UBV* photometry, *U* standing for ultra-violet, *B* for blue and *V* for visual, and the resulting apparent magnitudes are thus designated $U, B, V = m_U, m_B, m_V = $ apparent magnitudes in the resultant ultra-violet, blue and visual systems.

In some photometers the wavelength range is extended to include red, infra-red and bolometric. The subscripts in these cases are r, ir, and bol.

The wavelength (in Ångström Units, Å) corresponding to these colours is given in Table 41:

TABLE 41

Colour	U	B	V	R	IR
Wavelength	3600	4400	5500	7000	10,000

The infra-red wavelengths are again sub-divided as in Table 42.

TABLE 42

Colour	I	J	K	L	M	N	Q
Wavelength (microns = 10^3 Å)	0·9	1·25	2·2	3·4	5·0	10·0	22·0

Colour Index. This is the difference between the magnitude of a star measured at one wavelength and its magnitude at another wavelength, the wavelength intervals corresponding to those given in Table 41. Hence, commonly, colour index $= B - V = m_B - m_V$. Various other colour indices can be formed, e.g., $U - B = m_U - m_B$. The *U, B, V* system has replaced the international photographic and photovisual systems. Data on several well known stars are given in Table 43.

TABLE 43

Star	m_V	Colour Index	M_V	Spectral Class
Aldebaran (α Tau)	0·8	+1·55	−0·8	K 5
Betelgeuse (α Ori)	0·4 (var.)	+1·85	−5·9	M 2
Rigel (β Ori)	0·1	−0·05	−7·0	B 8
Capella (α Aur)	0·1	+0·81	−0·6	G 8

Bolometric Magnitude. This gives the total radiation received from the star . . . ultra-violet, light, radio, heat, etc. Measurement is made by a bolometer, a detecting device which produces an output signal which depends on the total incident radiation irrespective of wavelength.

Intrinsic Colour Index. This is obtained by applying extinction terms to the observed quantities V, $B - V$, and $U - B$. They are denoted by the subscript 'o', i.e., intrinsic colour index $= (B - V)_0$. From this the colour excess may be obtained: Colour Excess $E = B - V - (B - V)_0$.

Bolometric Correction. This is the difference between the apparent visual magnitude m_V and the bolometric magnitude m_{bol}. Hence bolometric correction B.C. $= m_V - m_{bol}$. Consequently bolometric correction is always positive.

Absolute Magnitude. Visual magnitude is no criterion of intrinsic luminosity, as many distant stars appear far brighter than some very near stars. Absolute magnitude is the brightness a star would have if all the stars were at the same distance from us: it is found by calculating what the observed visual magnitude would be if each were placed at a distance of 10 parsecs or about 33 light years—equivalent to a parallax of 0·1 seconds of arc. This calculation requires a knowledge of the star's distance. Conversely, if the absolute magnitude can be found by some other means, the distance of the star can be found.

Absolute magnitude is of great importance in stellar research as it enables luminosities to be compared. The integrated magnitude of a nebula or star cluster is that of the total light received from the object. The Sun's visual absolute magnitude is $+4·9$ and Table 43 gives absolute and apparent magnitudes of a few well known stars. The absolute magnitudes of giant stars vary only one or two magnitudes (from about $+1·0$ to $-1·0$) in their progression from spectral types M to B. Those of the dwarfs fall off a magnitude or two as each successive class below is reached, reaching about $+15$ in *Proxima Centauri*. At the other end of the scale Rigel has an absolute magnitude of $-7·0$ and supernovæ range from about $-13·6$ to -16. The most luminous star known is S Doradûs at about $-8·9$, and the least luminous is BD $+4°$ 4048(B) at $+21·2$.

Absolute magnitude can be calculated from:

$$M = m + 5 + 5 \log \pi, \quad \text{where} \quad \pi = \text{parallax in seconds of arc.}$$

Space Absorption and Distance Modulus. Absolute magnitude is apparent magnitude standardized to 10 parsecs without absorption. Space absorption, denoted by A, allows the intrinsic apparent magnitude to be found from $m_0 = m - A$. The distance modulus $m - M$ is calculated from $5 \log$ (distance in parsecs) $- 5 + A$, and the corrected distance modulus $m_0 - M = 5 \log$ (distance in parsecs) $- 5$.

Combined Magnitude. This is used in the case of two or more stars so close together that they appear to the eye as a single star, or for other reasons are to be treated as such. It is in fact the sum of the individual brightnesses of the component stars, expressed relative to that of a star of magnitude 0·0. It cannot be obtained by simply adding the magnitudes of the component stars as this would give a higher figure, whereas being brighter the combined magnitude must be a lower number than any of the component magnitudes. The combined magnitude is usually calculated with the aid of conversion tables.

Limiting Magnitude. The limiting magnitude of a star catalogue—the index of its completeness, as omissions become inevitable at a certain stage—is that magnitude on the brighter side of which stars omitted from the catalogue about equal in number the stars on the fainter side that are included in the catalogue.

Luminosity

The luminosity of a star is its intrinsic or absolute brightness. It is a measure of the total outflow of radiation emitted by the star and is denoted by the symbol $\mathscr{L}$. Units are erg sec^{-1} and an example is the luminosity of the Sun which is given (Allen, *Astrophysical Quantities*, 1963) as $(3·90 \pm 0·04) \times 10^{33}$ erg sec^{-1}. This corresponds to radiation emitted at the surface as $6·41 \times 10^{10}$ erg cm^{-2} sec^{-1}. This luminosity corresponds to an apparent bolometric magnitude $m_{bol} = -26·85$ and an absolute bolometric magnitude $M_{bol} = +4·72$.

The relationship between the luminosity and the absolute magnitude of the Sun and those of a star is given by:

$$\log\left(\frac{\mathscr{L}}{\mathscr{L}_\odot}\right) = 0{\cdot}4(M_\odot - M)$$

hence, if the absolute magnitude of a star can be determined, a rearrangement of the above equation will enable its luminosity to be found. Applying the above relationship to the star α Canis Majoris (*Sirius*) its apparent magnitude is −1·44, the parallax is 0·375 seconds of arc, yielding an absolute magnitude of +1·4. Thus *Sirius* is 3·32 magnitudes intrinsically brighter than the Sun, i.e. its luminosity is over twenty times that of the Sun.

Mass–Luminosity Relationship. The more massive a star is, the more luminous it is. A graph of absolute magnitudes plotted against solar masses yields a curve which is represented conveniently by the approximation

$$\log\left(\frac{\mathscr{L}}{\mathscr{L}_\odot}\right) = 3{\cdot}3 \log\left(\frac{\mathscr{M}}{\mathscr{M}_\odot}\right).$$

This relationship may be used to determine the masses of single stars, i.e. stars not forming part of a binary or multiple system.

The ratio $\log(\mathscr{M}/\mathscr{M}_\odot)$ varies significantly with spectral class, and also depends on whether the star under consideration is a supergiant, giant or dwarf.

THE STARS—NOMENCLATURE AND CONSTELLATIONS

The Constellations

The origin of most of the constellation names is lost in antiquity. Coma Berenices was added to the old list about 200 B.C., though not definitely fixed till the time of Tycho Brahe. No further addition was made till the 17th century, when Bayer, Hevelius and other astronomers formed many constellations in the hitherto uncharted regions of the southern heavens, and marked off portions of some of the large or ill-defined ancient constellations into new constellations. Many of these, however, were never generally recognized, and are now either obsolete or have had their rather clumsy names abbreviated into more convenient forms. Since the middle of the 18th century, when Lacaille added thirteen names in the southern hemisphere, and sub-divided the unwieldy Argo into Carina, Malus (now Pyxis), Puppis, and Vela, no new constellations have been recognized. Originally, constellations had no boundaries, the position of a star in the 'head', 'foot', etc., of the figure answering the needs of the time; the first boundaries were drawn by Bode in 1801. For List of Constellations, see Table 44.

Constellation Boundaries. Bode's boundaries were not treated as standard, and charts and catalogues issued before 1930 may differ as to which of two adjacent constellations a star belongs. Thus Flamsteed numbered in Camelopardus several stars now allocated to Auriga, and by error he sometimes numbered a star in two constellations. Bayer, also, sometimes assigned to the same star a Greek letter in two constellations, ancient astronomers having stated that it belonged to both constellation figures: thus β Tauri = γ Aurigæ, and α Andromedæ = δ Pegasi.

To remedy this inconvenience, in 1930 the International Astronomical Union standardized the boundaries along arcs of Right Ascension and Declination for the Epoch 1875 January 1, having regard as far as possible to the boundaries of the best star atlases. The work had already been done by Gould on that basis for most of the southern hemisphere constellations.

The I.A.U. Boundaries. These do not change their positions among the stars, thus objects can always be correctly located, though owing to precession the arcs of Right Ascension and Declination of to-day no longer follow the boundaries, and are steadily departing from them. After some 12,900 years, however, these arcs will begin to return towards the boundaries, and 12,900 years after this, on completing the 25,800-year precessional period they will once again approximate to them, but not exactly coincide.

Standard Names and Abbreviations for the Constellations. Several of the constellation names currently in use are reduced forms of names used in earlier times, thus Antlia was formerly known as Antlia Pneumatica; Cælum as Cæla Sculptoris; Columba as Columba Noachii; Fornax as Fornax Chemica; Mensa as Mons Mensæ; Musca as Musca Australis; Octans as Octans Hadleianus; Pictor as Equuleus Pictoris; Reticulum as Reticulum Rhomboidalis; Sculptor as Apparatus Sculptoris; Scutum as Scutum Sobieskii; Sextans as Sextans Uraniæ; Volans as Piscis Volans; Vulpecula as Vulpecula et Anser. These older versions will often be found in early atlases and charts.

The old constellation Argo, sometimes termed Argo Navis, was sub-divided into Carina, Malus and Puppis; Malus was later re-named Pyxis Nautica, now shortened to Pyxis. The original Bayer Letters are still used, however, a single set being shared by these three modern constellations.

The constellation Serpens is in fact in two parts separated by Ophiuchus; they were formerly known as Serpens Caput and Serpens Cauda, and they also share a single set of Bayer Letters.

It should be noted that Scorpius is sometimes encountered in the form Scorpio, and Camelopardalis is sometimes referred to as Camelopardus (genitive Camelopardi).

The genitive form of the constellation name is used with the Bayer Letter for the brighter stars, and often with catalogue designations. For practical purposes, however, it is more usual to use the 3-letter abbreviations for the constellations adopted by the I.A.U. in 1922. The I.A.U. abbreviations are listed in Table 44.

TABLE 44. NAMES AND ABBREVIATIONS FOR THE CONSTELLATIONS

Constellation name	Genitive	I.A.U. Abbreviation	Constellation name	Genitive	I.A.U. Abbreviation
Andromeda	Andromedæ	And	Lacerta	Lacertæ	Lac
Antlia	Antliæ	Ant	Leo	Leonis	Leo
Apus	Apodis	Aps	Leo Minor	Leonis Minoris	LMi
Aquarius	Aquarii	Aqr	Lepus	Leporis	Lep
Aquila	Aquilæ	Aql	Libra	Libræ	Lib
Ara	Aræ	Ara	Lupus	Lupi	Lup
Aries	Arietis	Ari	Lynx	Lyncis	Lyn
Auriga	Aurigæ	Aur	Lyra	Lyræ	Lyr
Boötes	Boötis	Boo	Mensa	Mensæ	Men
Cælum	Cæli	Cae	Microscopium	Microscopii	Mic
Camelopardalis	Camelopardalis	Cam	Monoceros	Monocerotis	Mon
Cancer	Cancri	Cnc	Musca	Muscæ	Mus
Canes Venatici	Canum Venaticorum	CVn	Norma	Normæ	Nor
Canis Major	Canis Majoris	CMa	Octans	Octantis	Oct
Canis Minor	Canis Minoris	CMi	Ophiuchus	Ophiuchi	Oph
Capricornus	Capricorni	Cap	Orion	Orionis	Ori
Carina	Carinæ	Car	Pavo	Pavonis	Pav
Cassiopeia	Cassiopeiæ	Cas	Pegasus	Pegasi	Peg
Centaurus	Centauri	Cen	Perseus	Persei	Per
Cepheus	Cephei	Cep	Phœnix	Phœnicis	Phe
Cetus	Ceti	Cet	Pictor	Pictoris	Pic
Chamæleon	Chamæleontis	Cha	Pisces	Piscium	Psc
Circinus	Circini	Cir	Piscis Austrinus	Piscis Austrini	PsA
Columba	Columbæ	Col	Puppis	Puppis	Pup
Coma Berenices	Comæ Berenices	Com	Pyxis	Pyxidis	Pyx
Corona Austrinus	Coronæ Austrini	CrA	Reticulum	Reticuli	Ret
Corona Borealis	Coronæ Borealis	CrB	Sagitta	Sagittæ	Sge
Corvus	Corvi	Crv	Sagittarius	Sagittarii	Sgr
Crater	Crateris	Crt	Scorpius	Scorpii	Sco
Crux	Crucis	Cru	Sculptor	Sculptoris	Scl
Cygnus	Cygni	Cyg	Scutum	Scuti	Sct
Delphinus	Delphini	Del	Serpens	Serpentis	Ser
Dorado	Doradûs	Dor	Sextans	Sextantis	Sex
Draco	Draconis	Dra	Taurus	Tauri	Tau
Equuleus	Equulei	Equ	Telescopium	Telescopii	Tel
Eridanus	Eridani	Eri	Triangulum	Trianguli	Tri
Fornax	Fornacis	For	Triangulum Australe	Trianguli Australe	TrA
Gemini	Geminorum	Gem	Tucana	Tucanæ	Tuc
Grus	Gruis	Gru	Ursa Major	Ursæ Majoris	UMa
Hercules	Herculis	Her	Ursa Minor	Ursæ Minoris	UMi
Horologium	Horologii	Hor	Vela	Velorum	Vel
Hydra	Hydræ	Hya	Virgo	Virginis	Vir
Hydrus	Hydri	Hyi	Volans	Volantis	Vol
Indus	Indi	Ind	Vulpecula	Vulpeculæ	Vul

Star Nomenclature

The star names tabulated below have, for the most part, been handed down from classical or early mediæval times, but only a few of them are now in use. A system devised by Bayer in 1603 has been found more convenient, i.e. the designation of the bright stars of each constellation by the small letters of the Greek alphabet, the brightest star being usually made α, the second brightest β, etc.—although sometimes, as in Ursa Major, sequence or position in the constellation figure was preferred. When the Greek letters were exhausted, the small Roman letters—a, b, c, etc.—were employed, and after these the capitals, A, B, etc. (mostly in the Southern constellations). The capitals after Q were not required, so Argelander utilized R, S, T, etc., to denote *variable* stars in each constellation, a convenient index to their peculiarity (see also p. 99).

The fainter stars are most conveniently designated by their numbers in some star catalogue. By universal consent, the numbers of Flamsteed's *Historia Cælestis Britannica* (published 1725) are adopted for stars to which no Greek letter has been assigned, while for stars not appearing in that catalogue, the numbers of some other catalogue are utilized. The usual method of denoting any lettered or numbered star in a constellation is to give the letter or Flamsteed number, followed by the genitive case of the Latin name of the constellation: thus α of Canes Venatici is described as α Canum Venaticorum.

Flamsteed catalogued his stars by constellations, numbering them in the order of their 'Right Ascension'—that is, the number of hours and minutes they southed after the southing of a certain zero point among the stars. Most modern catalogues are on this convenient basis (ignoring constellations), as the stars follow a regular sequence. But when Right Ascensions are nearly the same, especially if the Declinations differ much, in time 'precession' may change the order: Flamsteed's 20, 21, 22, 23 Herculis, numbered 200 years ago, now south in the order 22, 20, 23, 21.

For convenience of reference, the more important star catalogues are designated by recognized contractions: thus 'B.A.C. 2130' is at once known by astronomers to denote the star numbered 2130 in the British Association Star Catalogue of 1845. In most star catalogues a number is assigned to each star included in them, whether it has a Greek or other letter or not. Thus, *Vega* is α Lyræ, 3 Lyræ (Flamsteed's number), and (constellations ignored) Groombridge 2616. A list of some of the best-known catalogues, and their contractions, is given in Table 26 on page 40.

Proper Names of Stars. The proper names of stars are falling into general disuse, except for stars of the first magnitude and a few exceptional cases such as *Polaris* and *Mizar*. The following list is by no means exhaustive, but includes all the names still commonly encountered. In some cases there are alternative forms or spellings; thus *Alkaid* is also known as *Benetnasch*, while *Betelgeuse* may be spelled *Betelgeux* or *Betelgeuze*.

α Andromedæ	Alpheratz	α Draconis	Thuban	γ Pegasi	Algenib
β Andromedæ	Mirach	γ Draconis	Etamin	ε Pegasi	Enif
γ Andromedæ	Almaak	α Eridani	Achernar	α Persei	Mirphak
α Aquarii	Sadalmelik	θ Eridani	Acamar	β Persei	Algol
α Aquilæ	Altair	α Geminorum	Castor	α Phœnicis	Ankaa
β Aquilæ	Alshain	β Geminorum	Pollux	α Piscis Austrini	Fomalhaut
γ Aquilæ	Tarazed	γ Geminorum	Alhena	ε Sagittarii	Kaus Australis
α Argûs (Carinæ)	Canopus	α Gruis	Alnair	σ Sagittarii	Nunki
α Arietis	Hamal	α Herculis	Rasalgethi	α Scorpii	Antares
α Aurigæ	Capella	α Hydræ	Alphard	λ Scorpii	Shaula
α Boötis	Arcturus	α Leonis	Regulus	α Serpentis	Unukalhai
ε Boötis	Izar	β Leonis	Denebola	α Tauri	Aldebaran
α Canum Venaticorum	Cor Caroli	γ Leonis	Algieba	β Tauri	Alnath
α Canis Majoris	Sirius	α Leporis	Arneb	η Tauri	Alcyone
ε Canis Majoris	Adara	β Leporis	Nihal	α Ursæ Majoris	Dubhe
α Canis Minoris	Procyon	α Lyræ	Vega	β Ursæ Majoris	Merak
α Cassiopeiæ	Shedir	α Ophiuchi	Rasalhague	γ Ursæ Majoris	Phad
β Centauri	Agena	α Orionis	Betelgeuse	δ Ursæ Majoris	Megrez
α Cephei	Alderamin	β Orionis	Rigel	ε Ursæ Majoris	Alioth
α Ceti	Menkar	γ Orionis	Bellatrix	ζ Ursæ Majoris	Mizar
β Ceti	Diphda	δ Orionis	Mintaka	η Ursæ Majoris	Alkaid
o Ceti	Mira	ε Orionis	Alnilam	80 Ursæ Majoris	Alcor
α Coronæ Borealis	Alphekka	ζ Orionis	Alnitak	α Ursæ Minoris	Polaris
α Crucis	Acrux	κ Orionis	Saiph	β Ursæ Minoris	Kocab
α Cygni	Deneb	α Pegasi	Markab	α Virginis	Spica
β Cygni	Albireo	β Pegasi	Scheat	ε Virginis	Vindemiatrix

THE STARS—PHYSICAL DATA

The Nearest and Brightest Stars

The twenty-five nearest stars (excluding the Sun) are listed in Table 45, and the twenty-five stars having the greatest visual apparent magnitude in Table 46. For each star the position, apparent and absolute magnitude, distance, trigonometrical parallax and spectral classification are given.

TABLE 45. THE NEAREST STARS

	Star	Position 1950·0 R.A. h m	Dec. ° ′	Parallax ″	Distance l.y.	Spectral type	Apparent magnitude	Absolute magnitude
1	*Proxima* Cen	14 26·3	− 62 28	0·762	4·3	M5*e*	+ 10·7	+ 15·1
2	α Cen A	14 36·2	− 60 38	0·751	4·3	G2	0·0	4·4
3	α Cen B	14 36·2	− 60 38	0·751	4·3	K1	1·4	5·8
4	Barnard's star	17 55·4	+ 04 24	0·545	6·0	M5	9·5	13·2
5	Wolf 359	10 54·1	+ 07 20	0·402	8·1	M8	13·5	16·5
6	Lal 21185	11 00·7	+ 36 18	0·398	8·2	M2	7·5	10·5
7	*Sirius* A	06 42·9	− 16 39	0·375	8·7	A1	− 1·5	1·4
8	*Sirius* B	06 42·9	− 16 39	0·375	8·7	wA5	+ 8·5	11·4
9	UV Cet A	01 36·4	− 18 13	0·369	9·0	M6*e*	12·5	15·3
10	UV Cet B	01 36·4	− 18 13	0·369	9·0	M6*e*	13·0	15·8
11	Ross 154	18 46·7	− 23 53	0·351	9·3	M6	10·6	13·3
12	Ross 248	23 39·5	+ 43 56	0·316	10·3	M6	12·2	14·7
13	ε Eri	03 30·6	− 09 38	0·303	10·8	K2	3·7	6·1
14	L 789–6	22 35·7	− 15 36	0·295	11·1	M7	12·2	14·6
15	Ross 128	11 45·3	+ 01 06	0·294	11·1	M5	11·1	13·5
16	61 Cyg A	21 04·7	+ 38 30	0·292	11·2	K5	5·2	7·5
17	61 Cyg B	21 04·7	+ 38 30	0·292	11·2	K7	6·0	8·4
18	*Procyon* A	07 36·7	+ 05 21	0·288	11·3	F5	0·3	2·6
19	*Procyon* B	07 36·7	+ 05 21	0·288	11·3	wF	10·8	13·1
20	ε Ind	21 59·6	− 57 00	0·285	11·4	K3	4·7	7·0
21	Σ 2398 A	18 42·2	+ 59 33	0·280	11·6	M4	8·9	11·1
22	Σ 2398 B	18 42·2	+ 59 33	0·280	11·6	M5	9·7	11·9
23	Grb 34 A	00 15·5	+ 43 44	0·278	11·7	M1	8·1	10·3
24	Grb 34 B	00 15·6	+ 43 44	0·278	11·7	M6	11·0	13·3
25	Lac 9352	23 02·6	− 36 09	0·273	11·9	M2	7·4	9·6

TABLE 46. THE BRIGHTEST STARS

	Star	Proper name	Position 1950·0 R.A. h m	Dec. ° ′	Apparent magnitude	Spectral type	Parallax ″	Distance l.y.	Absolute magnitude
1	α CMa	*Sirius*	06 42·9	− 16 39	− 1·47	A1 v	0·375	8·7	+ 1·41
2	α Car	*Canopus*	06 22·8	− 52 40	− 0·71	F0 Ib	0·018	180	− 4·7
3	α Cen	*Rigil Kent*	14 36·2	− 60 38	− 0·1	G2 v	0·751	4·3	+ 4·3
4	α Boo	*Arcturus*	14 13·4	+ 19 26	− 0·06	K2 IIIp	0·090	36	− 0·2
5	α Lyr	*Vega*	18 35·2	+ 38 44	+ 0·03	A0 v	0·123	26	+ 0·5
6	β Ori	*Rigel*	05 12·2	− 08 15	0·08	B8 Ia	0·004	815	− 7·0
7	α Aur	*Capella* (binary)	05 13·0	+ 45 57	0·09	{G8 III}{G0 III}	0·073	45	{+ 0·12}{+ 0·37}
8	α CMi	*Procyon*	07 36·7	+ 05 21	0·34	F5 IV–v	0·288	11	+ 2·65
9	α Eri	*Achernar*	01 35·9	− 57 29	0·49	B5 v	0·023	142	− 2·2
10	β Cen	*Hadar*	14 00·3	− 60 08	0·61	B1 II	0·008	400	− 5·0
11	α Aql	*Altair*	19 48·3	+ 08 44	0·75	A7 IV–v	0·198	16	+ 2·3
12	α Tau	*Aldebaran*	04 33·0	+ 16 25	0·78	K5 III	0·048	68	− 0·7
13	α Cru	*Acrux*	12 23·8	− 62 49	0·80	B2 IV	0·012	270	− 3·5
14	α Ori	*Betelgeuse* (var.)	05 52·5	+ 07 24	(mean) 0·85	M2 Ib	0·005	650	− 6·0
15	α Sco	*Antares*	16 26·4	− 26 19	0·92	M1 Ib	0·008	400	− 4·7
16	α Vir	*Spica*	13 22·6	− 10 54	0·98	B1 v	0·012	270	− 3·4
17	β Gem	*Pollux*	07 42·3	+ 28 09	1·15	K0 III	0·093	35	+ 0·95
18	α PsA	*Fomalhaut*	22 54·9	− 29 53	1·16	A3 v	0·144	23	+ 1·9
19	α Cyg	*Deneb*	20 39·7	+ 45 06	1·26	A2 Ia	0·002	1600	− 7·3
20	β Cru	*Mimosa*	12 44·8	− 59 25	1·28	B0 IV	0·007	460	− 4·7
21	α Leo	*Regulus*	10 05·7	+ 12 14	1·33	B7 v	0·039	85	− 0·6
22	ε CMa	*Adhara*	06 56·7	− 28 54	1·42	B2 II	0·005	650	− 5·0
23	γ Ori	*Bellatrix*	05 22·5	+ 06 18	1·61	B2 III	0·011	300	− 3·3
24	λ Sco	*Shaula*	17 30·2	− 37 04	1·61	B1 v	0·010	300	− 3·4
25	β Tau	*El Nath*	05 23·1	+ 28 34	1·64	B7 III	0·018	180	− 2·0

Stellar Distances

The first measurement of the distance of a star, 61 Cygni, was achieved by Bessel in 1838 using the method of *parallax*.

Trigonometrical Parallax is the angular difference in position of an object when seen from two different viewpoints. In Fig. 17 below a relatively nearby star is seen against a background of distant

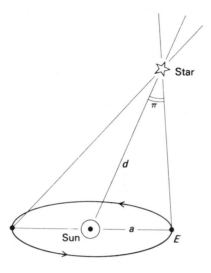

FIGURE 17. Stellar parallax

stars: the difference in position of the star when seen by an observer located on the Sun and an observer on the Earth at E is the instantaneous value of parallax, π. The value of π can be determined in principle by making observations of the star when the Earth is at E and again six months later when the Earth is at the opposite side of its orbit. In practice, during the period of one year, because of the motion of the Earth around the Sun, the star will appear to trace out an ellipse on the celestial sphere, and the value of the semi-major axis of this ellipse is known as the *Annual Parallax* (Π) of the star. This is the maximum displacement of the star away from its mean position (due to parallax) and corresponds to the situation where the angle star–Sun–Earth = 90°. If a is the Sun–Earth distance, and d is the distance of the star, then if Π is expressed in radians, we have $\Pi = a/d$. If a is known and Π is measured, then d can be obtained.

The value of a is known as the *astronomical unit* and is equal to 1.5×10^8 km. In principle this can be measured by means of *planetary parallax*, the displacement in position of the Sun or other object in the solar system when seen from the point of view of observers located on opposite sides of the Earth. The *solar parallax* is 8·80 seconds of arc. The effect of planetary parallax is greatest on an object which is located on the horizon. It is then known as *horizontal parallax*.

If a star has a parallax of exactly 1 second of arc it is said to lie at a distance of one *parsec* (abbreviated pc), where one parsec = 206,265 A.U. The parsec is equivalent to 3·26 light years, where the *light year* (abbreviated l.y.) is the distance travelled by a ray of light, moving at a velocity of 3×10^5 km/s, in one year. It is approximately equal to 10^{13} km. The parsec is a convenient unit since parallax measurements in arcsecs can be directly converted to distance in parsecs. Common multiples of the parsec are the *kiloparsec* (1000 pc, abbreviated kpc) and *megaparsec* (1,000,000 pc, abbreviated Mpc). No star is known with a parallax as large as 1 second of arc, the greatest measured parallax being that of *Proxima Centauri*, 0·76 second of arc, corresponding to a distance of 1·32 pc or 4·25 l.y.

Trigonometric parallax, measured directly or photographically, can only be employed to a range of a few hundred light years at most because of the difficulties of measuring very small angles. Other forms of parallax can be obtained, several of them utilizing the *distance modulus* (see page 85), for stars at large distances. Some of these are described below.

Spectroscopic Parallax. A good estimate of the true absolute magnitudes of many stars can be obtained from an examination of their spectra (see *Spectral Classification*, below). This can be compared with the observed apparent magnitudes, and, after corrections for interstellar extinction, a distance or parallax derived.

Absolute magnitude can be estimated in other ways for certain types of stars. In particular the Cepheid Variables (see *Variable Stars*, below) show a well defined relationship between absolute magnitude and period of light variation (the *Period–Luminosity Law*), and so measurement of the period provides a value of absolute magnitude for the distance modulus. Because of their great luminosity, Cepheids can be used as 'standard candles' for stellar distance measurements out to very large ranges.

Dynamical Parallax. With binary pairs (see *Double Stars*) an estimate of the distance can be made by assuming that the combined mass of the pair of stars is two solar masses (see *Stellar Masses*), measuring the period of revolution of the pair of stars and obtaining the linear dimensions of the orbit by means of Kepler's Laws. These dimensions are then compared with the observed angular dimensions of the stars' orbit, and a value of the distance obtained. Fortunately an error in the estimated mass of the system does not introduce a large error in the value of the dynamical parallax.

Secular Parallax. The Sun's motion through space with respect to the background framework of stars in the Sun's neighbourhood provides a baseline for parallax measurements which is continually increasing. The average distance of a group of stars can be estimated from this *parallactic motion*, knowing the value of the solar motion (about 19·5 km per sec). If H is the secular parallax in arcsecs, and U the Sun's velocity in km/s, then $\pi = 0.243H$ where $H = \pi U/4.74$.

Stellar Motions

The motion of a star relative to the Sun can be considered to consist of two components, a radial component R (*radial velocity*), i.e. motion in the line of sight, and a transverse component (transverse velocity), T. If both R and T can be determined, then the magnitude of the star's velocity V is obtained from $V = \sqrt{(R^2 + T^2)}$, and the direction, θ, of its motion relative to the radial direction from the Sun from $\tan \theta = T/V$.

Radial Velocity can be obtained from the displacement of the spectral lines (see *Spectroscopy*) of the star's spectrum due to the *Doppler Effect* (see page 18). The velocity is obtained directly, and it is not necessary to know the distance of the star. Positive radial velocity means the star is receding, a negative value means the star is approaching. Radial velocities in excess of 100 km/s are rarely found in stars, and, typically, values lie in the range 10 to 40 km/s. Periodic variations in radial velocity are often indicative of orbital motion as found in spectroscopic binaries, i.e. double stars which are too close together to be separated visually. It is noticed that radial velocities tend to increase with advancing spectral type (see *Spectral Classification*).

Proper Motion. The transverse component of stellar motion shows up as secular change in the position of a star. The transverse component of a star's motion which takes place in one year is known as *annual proper motion* and is generally expressed in seconds of arc. The largest known value of proper motion, μ, is that of Barnard's Star where $\mu = 10.2$ seconds of arc per annum. To convert proper motion to transverse velocity it is necessary to know the parallax of the star. Transverse velocity, V_μ, is then given by $V_\mu = 4.74\mu/\pi$ km/s. Proper motion so obtained, after allowing for parallax, aberration, etc., gives the transverse component of velocity relative to the Sun; to obtain the star's motion relative to the frame of the local stars it is necessary to allow for *Solar Motion* (see page 41).

Star Streaming. In 1904 Kapteyn discovered, from studies of the proper motions of the brighter stars, that the stars, in general, are moving in two preferred directions—towards the *apparent vertices*. These points are situated in Lepus, at R.A. 6 h, Dec. − 15°, and in Pavo at R.A. 19 h, Dec. − 64°.

About 60% of the stars belong to Stream I, moving towards the Lepus vertex, and 40% belong to Stream II, moving towards the Pavo vertex at a velocity about half that of Stream I.

Not all stars share in the streaming, however; type A stars are very prone to do so, and type F and later classes in the spectral sequence (see page 93) show the same tendency, though less strongly. Most type B stars are not members of either stream, but seem to be practically stationary: they are presumably members of the Local System (see *Gould Belt*, page 99).

If the apparent streaming is corrected for the effect of *solar motion*, the streams are found to be moving towards diametrically opposite points in the galactic plane—the *true vertices*, at R.A. 6 h 20 m, Dec. + 12° in Orion, and R.A. 18 h 20 m, Dec. − 12° in Scutum.

High-Velocity Stars. There are a number of stars in the neighbourhood of the Sun whose velocities relative to the Sun are extremely high, greater than 200 km/s. It is now known that these apparently high velocities are due to the fact that most of the Stars in the Sun's neighbourhood, including the Sun itself, are moving around the centre of our Galaxy in approximately circular orbits with velocities of the order of 250 km/s. The high-velocity stars do not share this common motion, and are being overtaken by stars such as the Sun and so left behind.

Stellar Masses

The masses of stars can only be obtained directly in the case of binary pairs (see *Double Stars*). If the orbital period of the pair in years, P, the mean angular separation, a, and the parallax, π, are known, then the combined mass of the pair can be obtained in terms of solar masses from

$$\frac{\mathcal{M}_1 + \mathcal{M}_2}{\mathcal{M}_\odot} = \frac{a^3}{\pi^3 P^2}.$$

If the position of the centre of mass of the system can be obtained, then the ratio of the distances of the two stars from the centre of mass will yield the ratio of the masses. The individual masses can then be obtained.

The masses of stars can be estimated from the mass-luminosity relationship if their absolute magnitudes are known. Stars with masses less than one tenth of that of the Sun are rarely found, and likewise stars with masses greater than ten times that of the Sun are rare, but only a few tens of stars have accurately known masses.

Stellar Temperatures

It is difficult to assign an unambiguous value to the 'temperature' of a star, and several definitions of temperature are used, some of which are listed below.

Effective Temperature. For a star, the effective temperature is the temperature of a black body (see page 16)—i.e. a perfect radiator of the same radius as the star, and which radiates the same total amount of radiation—that is, which has the same luminosity as the star. For the Sun, the effective temperature—the temperature of the photosphere—is about 5800°K (Kelvin). The *Kelvin* or *Absolute* temperature scale has its origin at $-273°$ Centigrade, this being the temperature at which all atomic motion ceases (according to kinetic theory). The Kelvin temperature of a body is thus its Centigrade temperature plus 273 degrees.

Colour Temperature. This temperature is obtained from the distribution of energy in the continuous spectrum (see *Spectroscopy*) of the star, and can thus be related to colour index. If the $B - V$ colour index is denoted by I, then the colour temperature, $T_c = 7200°\text{K}/(I + 0.64)$. The value of colour temperature is always greater than the effective temperature, the difference being most pronounced in the hot early-type stars (see *Spectral Classification*). For the Sun, the colour temperature is 6500°K.

The central temperatures of stars are much higher than the surface temperatures: in the case of the Sun, the temperature at the centre is reckoned to be of the order of 14,000,000°K. In the tenuous outer atmosphere of the Sun, the Corona, the *kinetic temperature* (i.e. the temperature corresponding to the velocities of atomic particles) is of the order of millions of degrees Kelvin.

Stellar Diameters

Direct measurements of stellar diameters have been accomplished in only a few cases. Although no telescope at ground level will show a star as a measurable disk, application of the phenomenon of the interference of light from an object of finite size by means of the *stellar interferometer* has yielded values for the angular diameters of a few giant stars such as *Betelgeuse*. In the case of *Betelgeuse* a value of 0.047 seconds of arc (variable, since *Betelgeuse* pulsates) combined with a knowledge of its parallax yielded a diameter of 360 million km, rather greater than the orbit of the Earth. Where interferometric observations are not possible, diameters can be estimated by observations of occultations of stars by the Moon. In general, however, diameters are inferred from a consideration of effective temperature and luminosity, using the relationship $\mathscr{L} = 4\pi\mathscr{R}^2\sigma T_e{}^4$, where $\mathscr{R}$ is the radius of the star. Thus if two stars have the same effective temperature, but differing luminosities, then it follows that the radius of the one with the higher luminosity must be greater than that of the other (see giants, dwarfs, etc., under *Spectral Classification*). Typical stellar diameters range from several hundred million kilometers (supergiants), through 1·4 million km for the Sun, down to a few thousand km in the case of some white dwarfs. Neutron stars (see *Stellar Evolution*) are thought to have diameters of only tens of km.

Stellar Densities. Although stellar radii vary enormously, stellar masses do not vary by such large amounts. Consequently there are large variations in star densities. The Sun has a density of 1·4 gm/cm³; supergiants have densities of the order 10^{-5} g/cm³; white dwarfs are typically of the order 10^5 g/cm³.

Stellar Rotation. With certain stars, a broadening of the spectral lines (see *Spectroscopy*) can be interpreted in terms of the rotational velocity of the star on its axis. This effect is only detectable for rapidly rotating stars. For example, *Altair* is thought to rotate at 260 km/s (at its equator), thus rotating on its axis in 7 hours. Rapid rotation is a characteristic normally associated with early-type stars. The Sun rotates, at its equator, in some 25 days.

SPECTRAL CLASSIFICATION

Spectral classification is the sub-division of stars into various types on the basis of features in their spectra. Secchi, in 1863–67, made the first attempt to so classify the stars by visually observing their spectra. He divided the stars into four groups. Later classifications were based on photographs of spectra and were much more finely divided. The *Harvard* classification system, first introduced by E. C. Pickering in 1890 and later developed by Cannon and Fleming, was the immediate precursor of the system currently in use. The current system is the *MKK* (after Morgan, Keenan and Kellman) or *Yerkes* system.

The MKK system divides the stars into thirteen main classes, of which ten are each then further sub-divided into ten equal sub-classes. The main divisions are denoted by letters, which are, in the order of decreasing temperature:

O   B   A   F   G   K   M   R   N   S

plus the types W, P and Q. A useful mnemonic for the first ten classes is 'Oh **B**e **A** **F**ine **G**irl **K**iss **M**e **R**ight **N**ow **S**mack!' The division into ten sub-classes is denoted by a numeral between 0 and 9 placed after the letter. Thus A5 is a star whose spectrum is half way between those of stars of types A0 and F0 etc.

The criteria used to place a star accurately into its spectral class are exceedingly complex. Nevertheless, the principal features in the spectra of each of the main classes, indicated by absorption lines, may be quite simply itemized:

Class O: Ionized and neutral helium, ionized metals, weak hydrogen;
    B: neutral helium, ionized metals, hydrogen stronger;
    A: hydrogen dominant, plus singly ionized metals;
    F: hydrogen weaker, neutral and singly ionized metals;
    G: Ca II prominent, hydrogen weaker, neutral metals;
    K: neutral metals, some molecular bands;
    M: neutral metals, Ti O bands dominant;
    R and N: neutral metals, C_2, CN and CH bands;
    S: neutral metals, Zr O and Ti O bands.

The three remaining classes are: Q—Novæ (see *Variable Stars*); P—Gaseous Nebulæ (see *Nebulæ*) and W—Wolf–Rayet stars. The Wolf–Rayet stars are very peculiar objects whose spectra are characterized by bright emission bands of hydrogen and helium. They are divided into two sub-classes: the WC stars, which in addition to hydrogen and helium emission, also contain emission lines of carbon and oxygen, and the WN stars, in which emission lines of nitrogen replace those of carbon and oxygen. The difference between the two sub-classes may reflect a real abundance difference. Their excitation temperature is about 100,000°K, while their colour temperature is about 13,000°K. They may be ejecting material at velocities of some hundreds or thousands of km/s. Some of these objects appear to be allied to the recurrent

94

novæ. It is not possible to relate these three classes (Q, P and W) to the others by a simple temperature difference, and they are hence considered as separate objects.

TABLE 47. SOME PHYSICAL PARAMETERS OF STARS
FOR VARIOUS SPECTRAL CLASSES

Spectral Type	M_V	T_C (°K)	$\mathcal{M}/\mathcal{M}_\odot$	$\mathcal{R}/\mathcal{R}_\odot$	$\mathcal{L}/\mathcal{L}_\odot$	Density (g/cm³)
MAIN SEQUENCE (v)						
O5	−6	70,000	40	18	300,000	0·01
B0	−3·7	38,000	17	7·6	13,000	0·05
B5	−0·9	23,000	7·1	4·0	600	0·16
A0	+0·7	15,400	3·5	2·6	80	0·25
A5	+2·0	11,100	2·2	1·8	20	0·50
F0	+2·8	9000	1·8	1·35	6·3	1·00
F5	+3·8	7600	1·30	1·20	2·5	1·2
G0	+4·6	6700	1·07	1·05	1·26	1·3
G5	+5·2	6000	0·93	0·93	0·79	1·6
K0	+6·0	5400	0·81	0·85	0·40	2·0
K5	+7·4	4500	0·69	0·74	0·16	2·5
M0	+8·9	3800	0·48	0·63	0·063	3·2
M5	+12·0	3000	0·22	0·31	0·008	13
GIANTS (III)						
G0	+1·8	6000	2·5	6·3	32	0·016
G5	+1·5	5000	3·2	10	50	0·004
K0	+0·8	4400	4·0	16	100	0·0013
K5	0·0	3700	5·0	25	200	0·0004
M0	−0·3	3400	6·3	43	400	0·0001
M5	−0·5	3000	—	—	1000	—
SUPERGIANTS (I)						
O5	−6·6	—	160	—	—	—
B0	−6·4	—	50	20	300,000	0·008
B5	−6·2	—	25	32	80,000	0·0013
A0	−6·0	—	16	40	25,000	0·0003
A5	−5·8	—	13	50	13,000	0·00016
F0	−5·6	—	12	63	8000	0·00006
F5	−5·0	—	10	79	6300	0·00003
G0	−4·4	6200	10	100	6300	0·000013
G5	−4·4	5300	12	130	6300	0·000006
K0	−4·4	4600	13	200	10,000	0·000002
K5	−4·4	—	14	400	20,000	0·0000004
M0	−4·4	—	16	500	32,000	0·0000002

The principal difference between the ten main classes is one of temperature (for historical reasons, the hot stars—O, B, A, etc.—are often referred to as *early* stars, while the cool stars—K, M, N, R, S, etc.—are referred to as *late* stars). In addition there are differences due to the luminosity of the star: in a given spectral sub-class, a bright star will be larger, and its outer regions will be more rarefied than in a faint star. Hence the more luminous a star, the narrower will be its spectrum lines, since pressure is often one of the principal line-broadening mechanisms. Thus on the basis of the quality of the spectrum lines (together with, in some cases, intensity differences) the stars in a given spectral sub-class may be further sub-divided into their *luminosity classes*. The luminosity class is denoted by a roman numeral between I and V, placed after the spectral type, e.g. F2 III. On the MKK system, the luminosity classes are:

I: Supergiants;
II: Bright Giants;
III: Giants;
IV: Sub-Giants;
V: Main Sequence, Dwarfs.

If necessary the luminosity classes may be further sub-divided by using the suffixes a, ab and b.

Thus the full spectral class of a normal star consists of three items: a letter and an arabic numeral to denote the temperature class and a roman numeral to denote the luminosity class. The spectral types of some of the brighter stars are:

δ Ori, O9·5 II $\qquad$ β Per (*Algol*), B8 v

α CMa (*Sirius*), A1 v $\qquad$ α CrB, Ao III

β Cas, F2 IV $\qquad$ Sun, G2 v

β Cet, Ko III $\qquad$ α Ori (*Betelgeuse*), M2 I

In addition to the standard spectral class notation, lower case letters may be added after the temperature class to show certain non-standard features in the spectrum. These are:

e emission lines (f in some O-type stars);
n nebulous lines;
s sharp lines;
k interstellar lines;
m metallic lines;
p peculiar spectrum;
v variable.

Examples of the use of this notation are:

HD 20336, B2 ep v $\qquad$ ψ Per, B5 ne III

17 Lep, A2 ?pe $\qquad$ 48 Lib, A3 ?se

Ross 986, M5 e $\qquad$ Kruger 60B, M4 e

Using the full system of classification, 90 to 95% of all stellar spectra may be dealt with. The remainder are composite spectra of unresolved double or multiple stars, or stars with major individual peculiarities.

In Table 47 the absolute magnitude, colour temperature, mass, radius, luminosity, and mean density are listed with spectral class. The data are taken from Allen, C. W.: *Astrophysical Quantities*, Athlone Press, 1963.

Colour Index and Spectral Type (see *Magnitude*)

These are closely related, and often the spectral type may be replaced by the $B - V$ colour index. Table 48 below relates the spectral type for various luminosity classes to the $B - V$ and also the $U - B$ colour indices. The data are taken from Allen, C. W.: *Astrophysical Quantities*, 1963.

TABLE 48. RELATIONSHIP BETWEEN SPECTRAL TYPE
AND COLOUR INDEX

Spectral Type	Main Sequence (v)		Colour Index Giants (III)		Supergiants (I)	
	$B - V$	$U - B$	$B - V$	$U - B$	$B - V$	$U - B$
O5	− 0·45	− 1·2	—	—	− 0·33	—
Bo	− 0·31	− 1·07	—	—	− 0·21	− 1·20
B5	− 0·17	− 0·56	—	—	− 0·10	− 0·75
Ao	0·00	0·00	—	—	0·00	− 0·30
A5	+ 0·16	+ 0·09	—	—	+ 0·15	− 0·02
Fo	+ 0·30	+ 0·20	—	—	+ 0·30	+ 0·26
F5	+ 0·45	− 0·01	—	—	+ 0·53	+ 0·44
Go	+ 0·57	+ 0·04	+ 0·65	+ 0·30	+ 0·76	+ 0·62
G5	+ 0·70	+ 0·20	+ 0·84	+ 0·52	+ 1·06	+ 0·86
Ko	+ 0·84	+ 0·46	+ 1·06	+ 0·90	+ 1·42	+ 1·35
K5	+ 1·11	+ 1·06	+ 1·40	+ 1·6	+ 1·71	+ 1·73
Mo	+ 1·39	+ 1·24	+ 1·65	+ 1·9	+ 1·94	+ 1·75
M5	+ 1·61	+ 1·19	+ 1·85	—	+ 2·15	—

Hertzsprung–Russell Diagram

This colour/magnitude diagram is a very convenient way in which to display the relationship between spectral type (colour index, temperature) and luminosity (magnitude). In it, the spectral type (or colour index, or temperature) is plotted along the horizontal axis with cool stars to the right and hot stars to the left. The luminosity (or absolute magnitude) is plotted vertically. Some 90% of the stars are found to lie on a line from top left to bottom right. This is called the *Main Sequence* of stars. The remainder are distributed in groups, which are given individual names (e.g. Supergiants, Giants, Dwarfs, White Dwarfs, etc.). The main features of the Hertzsprung–Russell diagram are reproduced in Fig. 18.

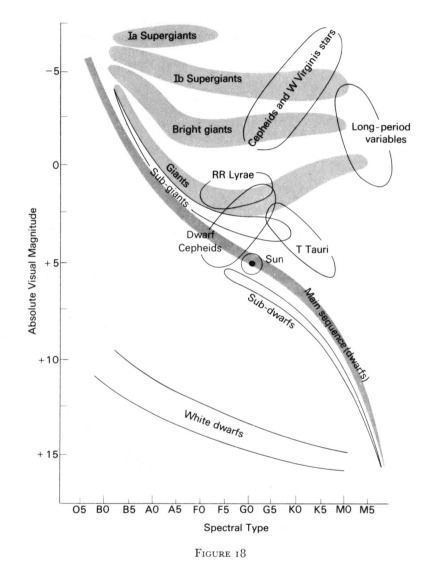

FIGURE 18

Population Types

It is found that stars in the spiral arms of galaxies are, in general, bluer and richer in heavy elements than stars in the galactic nuclei or in elliptical galaxies. The stars in the spiral arms are called *Population I stars* and are thought to be younger than stars in the nuclei of galaxies and elliptical galaxies, which are called *Population II stars*.

STELLAR EVOLUTION

The Hertzsprung–Russell Diagram provides a very useful visual aid to the understanding of the evolution of the stars. Early ideas suggested that stars began life as diffuse, low-temperature red giants and, as they contracted as a result of gravitational forces, so they increased in temperature (Lane's Law). Consequently they moved from right to left on the H–R diagram. Eventually, the star was thought to reach a maximum possible temperature and then to cool down and decrease in luminosity, passing back to later and later spectral types until it cooled to invisibility. Although superficially attractive, the theory was unsatisfactory on several counts, and in particular it led to stellar lifetimes which were far shorter than the estimated lifetime of the Sun.

The presently accepted view suggests that stars condense out of clouds of gas—principally hydrogen— heating up as a result of contraction, and so moving from right to left on the H–R diagram. When conditions in the central regions of the *proto-star* are suitable, i.e. when central temperatures are of the order 10^7 °K, nuclear reactions can take place whereby helium is produced by fusion from hydrogen, with the release of large amounts of energy. At this stage the star reaches a stable state corresponding to a point on the Main Sequence, the position of the star on the Main Sequence being determined principally by its mass. The more massive the star, the greater its luminosity, and the further up the Main Sequence it will lie.

Stars spend the major part of their lifetimes on the Main Sequence. However, the time spent on the Main Sequence is restricted by the *Schönberg–Chandrasekhar Limit* which states that the amount of helium in the central core of the star cannot exceed about 10% of the mass of the star. An approximate formula for the Main Sequence lifetime of a star, T_{MS}, due to A. R. Sandage, is $T_{MS} = 1.1 \times 10^{10}(\mathscr{M}/\mathscr{M}_\odot)/(\mathscr{L}/\mathscr{L}_\odot)$ years, where $\mathscr{M}$ and $\mathscr{L}$ are the mass and luminosity of the star, and $\mathscr{M}_\odot$ and $\mathscr{L}_\odot$ the mass and luminosity of the Sun. It is apparent that the more massive a star the quicker it evolves and the shorter its lifetime. While the Sun is expected to have a Main Sequence lifetime of about 10^{10} years, a highly luminous B0 star would probably spend only a few tens of millions of years on the Main Sequence.

This stage is followed by the onset of hydrogen burning in a shell surrounding the core, and the star begins to evolve fairly rapidly away from the Main Sequence. The luminosity increases, the surface temperature in general decreases, and the radius of the star increases during this stage of its evolution. This stage concludes when the star becomes a red giant, at which point energy is being produced by helium-fusion reactions.

The post-giant evolution of a star is again dependent on its mass. A relatively low-mass star such as the Sun is thought eventually to evolve to the white dwarf region, when the density of the star becomes of the order of 10^5 g/cm³. Luminosity is then very low, but surface temperature high, so that these stars are found in the lower left region of the H–R diagram. White dwarfs do not produce energy by nuclear processes, and so eventually cool down to non-luminous bodies (*black dwarfs*).

It seems that a star whose mass is greater than $1.4\mathscr{M}_\odot$ cannot become a white dwarf unless it loses sufficient mass in some way to come below this limit. A star or stellar remnant of mass greater than $1.4\mathscr{M}_\odot$ may collapse to a super-dense state, where atoms are broken down and nuclear components combined to form a body composed of neutrons. Such *neutron stars*—with densities of the order of 10^{15} g/cm³—have been identified with the *pulsars* discovered in 1968. The remnants of supernovæ are thought to collapse to the neutron star stage.

Finally, it is possible that very massive objects may enter a state of *gravitational collapse* where no known physical process can halt the contraction. The body will then contract within a critical radius known as the *Schwarzschild radius* at which point its gravitational field becomes so strong that no radiation can escape from the body. Such an object is known as a *black hole*.

DOUBLE STARS

Double stars are stars which to the naked eye appear as a single point of light, but when viewed through a telescope are found to be composed of two stars. The stars may be connected gravitationally, or they may simply happen to lie nearly in the same direction. *Triple stars* have three, *quadruple stars* four, and *multiple stars* many components. The fainter star of the pair is called the *comes* (plural *comites*) or companion. The most interesting 'doubles', etc., are indicated in the notes appended to each star chart. The brightest star of a multiple is designated A, the companion(s) as B, C, etc. Thus *Sirius A*, *Sirius B*, etc.

Binary Stars

These are double or multiple stars which are connected gravitationally and which orbit around a common centre of gravity. A binary star is said to be a *visual binary* if the components may be resolved in the telescope and their orbital motion detected by positional measurement; a *spectroscopic binary* if it is detected from the periodic doubling and displacement of lines in its spectrum; or a *photometric binary* if it is detected by the periodic variations in its magnitude (see *Variable Stars*). A binary star may fall into more than one of these categories. The orbital periods range from a day or two to many centuries—the visual binaries having periods of at least two years and the other two types normally having much shorter periods.

In a visual binary system, the motion of the companion is *direct* when the position angle [$N(0°) \to E(90°) \to S(180°) \to W(270°)$] is increasing, and *retrograde* when it is decreasing. The companion is said to be at *periastron* when its actual distance (as distinct from its apparent distance) from the main star is a minimum, and at *apastron* when it is a maximum. About half the stars in the solar neighbourhood belong to binary or multiple systems.

STAR CLUSTERS

Star clusters are groups of stars with between ten and ten million members, which fall into the distinct categories listed below. Some of the more prominent clusters are noted on the star charts.

Star Clouds are portions of the Milky Way in which the stars are so closely packed as to appear as a continuous irregular bright cloud. They are most conspicuous towards the galactic centre in Sagittarius. They are probably equivalent to the bright 'knots' seen in the spiral arms of nearby galaxies.

Globular Clusters are globe-shaped aggregations of stars with between 10^5 and 10^7 members, packed into a region of space about 100 pc across. The number density in the centre is very great, so that individual stars cannot be resolved, but it thins very rapidly towards the edges. Some 120 globular clusters are known, and it is believed that there are not many more in the Milky Way system. They are distributed spherically about the galactic centre, normally closer than 10 kpc, and hence are seen from the Earth in the direction of the centre of the galaxy—mainly in the Scorpio–Sagittarius direction. They orbit around the galactic centre in elliptical, highly inclined orbits, with periods of hundreds of millions of years. The two brightest globular clusters, NGC 5139 and NGC 104 (ω Cen and 47 Tuc) are in the southern hemisphere. The brightest one in the northern sky is NGC 6205 (M13), which at a distance of 8·2 kpc is still a naked-eye object.

Open Clusters (galactic clusters) contain between a few tens and several hundred members, and have little obvious structure. Their diameter is normally less than 10 pc, although it may be as great as 100 pc. They are concentrated along the galactic equatorial plane and predominate slightly in the direction opposite to the galactic centre. Over 750 of these clusters have been recorded. It is thought that the stars in these clusters are relatively young and have recently (10^6 to 10^9 years) been formed from the interstellar gas clouds. After a few rotations around the galaxy, gravitational fields will have disrupted them and their constituent stars will go to join the general background of stars. Prominent examples of open clusters are the *Pleiades* and *Hyades* clusters in Taurus, *Præsepe* in Cancer, and h and χ Persei (the famous 'Double Cluster').

OB Associations are loose groups of between ten and a thousand O and B stars. They sometimes have an open cluster as a nucleus (e.g., the ζ Persei association which surrounds the h and χ Persei open cluster), but often are so amorphous as to be indistinguishable from the background stars, except by spectroscopic analysis. Over eighty of these objects are known and they are concentrated in and close to the galactic plane. Their distances range from 500 to 3000 pc.

T Associations are similar objects to the OB associations, except that they are constituted from T Tauri and RW Aurigæ stars. About forty of these objects are known, normally with fewer than thirty members, although there may be as many as four hundred. Their distances range from 100 to 800 pc. They are probably much more common than the OB associations, although the intrinsically lower magnitude of their components means that only half as many are actually known.

Moving Clusters (Star Groups) are groups of apparently unrelated stars which have a common velocity. One of the most prominent of these clusters is the Ursa Major cluster which includes the stars, β, γ, δ, ϵ, ζ UMa, ζ Leo, α CMa, β Eri, β Aur, and γ CrB.

Gould Belt (Local System)

This is a group of some 10^8 stars, of which the Sun is a member. The Sun is about 100 pc from the centre of the system and 12 pc north of its equatorial plane. The diameter of the system is about one thousand parsecs, and it extends from Cygnus to Carina. The system is detected from the distribution of hot stars, gaseous nebulæ and dust clouds, and from 21 cm radio observations. It appears that the Gould Belt is a section of the spiral arm of the Milky Way galaxy in which the Sun is situated.

VARIABLE STARS

Variable stars are stars whose brightness changes with time. The variations may be periodic, semi-periodic or irregular, with time-scales between a few minutes and many centuries. Very frequently other aspects of the star—its radial velocity, temperature, spectrum, etc.—are also found to be variable. The *amplitude* of a variable star is the range between its magnitude at maximum and at minimum.

The many types of variable fall into two broad classes: the *extrinsic* and the *intrinsic* variables. The intrinsic variables are due to a change in the nature of the star itself, while the extrinsic variables change because of some process external to the star (e.g. orbital motion, rotation).

Nomenclature of Variable Stars. Argelander designated those not otherwise lettered or numbered, in any constellation, by the Roman capital letters, R, S, T, U, V, W, X, Y, Z. After Z, the double form RR to RZ, SS to SZ, TT to TZ, and so on to ZZ, was used, which provided for 54 variable stars in any constellation. As that number proved insufficient, AA to AZ, BB to BZ, and so on, was employed, J being omitted. The simplest system, which denotes the variables of each constellation by the letter V followed by a number—thus $V1 = R$; $V2 = S$; $V54 = ZZ$, etc., is used from V^{335}, when QZ has been reached. Letters are assigned when the variability is confirmed; provisionally, novæ and ordinary variables are now designated by a number, year, and constellation, Nova Aquilæ 1918 being 7·1918 Aquilæ, in the 'variable' discoveries of 1918.

Extrinsic Variables

Algol-type Eclipsing Variables consist of a binary star in which the components are sufficiently far apart to retain a normal shape and structure, and in which the line of sight is close to the star's orbital plane so that they periodically eclipse each other (see Fig. 19). The deeper of the minima—when the brighter star is eclipsed—is called the *primary eclipse*, and the shallower minimum is called the *secondary eclipse*. If the eclipse is total or annular then the minima will have flat bases.

β **Lyræ-type Eclipsing Variables** differ from *Algol*-type variables in that the stars are so close that tidal and rotational interaction distorts the stars into ellipsoids and causes considerable variation in the light intensity over their surfaces. The shape of the stars and their variable surface intensity means that their light curves show a continuous variation, even outside an eclipse.

W Ursæ Majoris Variables are even closer and more distorted than the β Lyræ stars. They have periods as short as five hours and are close enough for physical interaction between the stars to occur on a large scale. The light curves show continuous variation and are due to a combination of eclipse, surface intensity variation, and the distorted shape of the stars.

Eclipsing variables form about 19% of the total of known variables.

Rotational Variables are stars which show a small regular variation in magnitude with a period of about a day or so. It is possible that this is due to the rotation of the star coupled with a surface disturbance.

Pulsars are normally radio variables, but one—the pulsar in the Crab Nebula—has also shown periodic light variations with a period of 0·0332 seconds. It is believed that this object is a *neutron star* (a star whose gravitational field is so intense that the protons and electrons have been forced to combine with each other to form neutrons) which was left behind when the Crab Nebula was formed. The variations are due to the object's rotation combined with a directional form of light emission.

Intrinsic Variables

The main pulsating variables (Cepheids and Long Period Variables), and to some extent the explosive variables, show a correlation between their amplitude and their period. These stars form the *great sequence of variable stars* and their amplitude (Δm) is approximately related to their period (P) by the equation

$$\Delta m = 0\cdot5 + 1\cdot7 \log P.$$

Cepheid Variables are bright stars whose period and mean magnitude are closely related. They are comprised of the following sub-groups: *Classical Cepheids* (period 2 to 40 days), *RR Lyræ stars* (period 0·2 to 1·2 days), *Dwarf Cepheids* (period less than 0·2 days), δ *Scuti stars* (period 0·08 to 0·19 days), *W Virginis stars* (period 1 to 50 days), and β *Canis Majoris variables* (period less than 0·2 days). The mean period is about $4\frac{1}{2}$ days and the amplitude is normally less than one magnitude. A typical light curve is shown in Fig. 20.

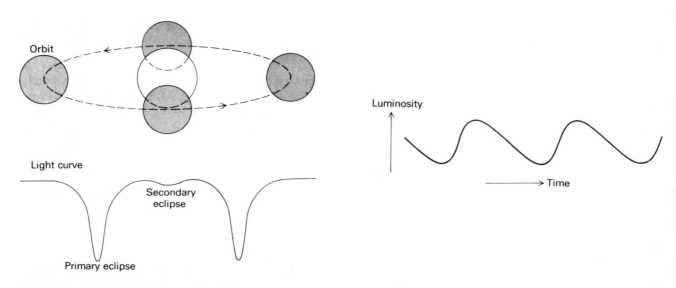

FIGURE 19. An *Algol*-type eclipsing variable   FIGURE 20. Light curve of a typical Cepheid variable

The cause of the Cepheid phenomenon appears to be a self-propagating, periodic ionization and recombination of helium in the star's atmosphere, which causes a periodic variation in the opacity. The changing opacity results in a concomitant change in the stellar radius, and hence in its luminosity.

Long-Period Variables (*Mira*-type variables) are late-type giants, with semi-regular periods of between a hundred and a thousand days and amplitudes of at least $2\frac{1}{2}$ magnitudes. Since it is impossible to predict the times of the minima of these stars to within thirty or forty days, they make useful objects for amateur observers to study.

Irregular and Semi-regular Variables occur in most spectral types, have amplitudes of up to four magnitudes, and have time-scales of between ten and a thousand days. There are a large number of types of stars in this classification, and these are listed below, with brief comments on each. The data are taken from Allen, C. W.: *Astrophysical Quantities*, 1963.

Explosive Variables are objects which undergo an increase in brightness of many magnitudes in a few hours, and then gradually, over a period of months or years, fade away again. They are divided into the sub-classes of *Recurrent Novæ, Novæ* and *Supernovæ, types I and II*. Recurrent novæ have periods from ten to a hundred years and amplitudes of six to eight magnitudes. Novæ are probably very long-period recurrent novæ, only one of whose outbursts has been observed. Their amplitudes can be up to twelve

TABLE 49. SOME IRREGULAR AND SEMI-REGULAR VARIABLES

Type	M	Amplitude (magnitudes)	Mean Period if any (days)	Spectral Type	Comments
RV Tau, UU Her	−2	1·3	75	G to K	Irregular minimum, alternating depth.
μ Cep, δ Ori	−1	1·6	100	G to N	Semi-regular.
Irregular	−0·5	1·3		K to N	
T Tau, RW Aur	+5	3		Fe v, Ge v	Emission lines, associated with nebulæ.
R CrB	−5?	4		G, K, R	Sudden decrease of brightness.
U Gem, SS Cyg	+8±3	3·6	60	B, A	Sudden cyclic increase of brightness.
Z Cam	+10±3	3·2	20	F	Cyclic, but with standstills.
SX Cen		1·2–2·0	30–800	F to M	Superimposed long and short periods.
Flare stars, UV Cet	+15	2		M3 v to M6 v	

magnitudes. About thirty novæ are thought to occur in the Milky Way galaxy every year, although only two or three are actually seen. The type II supernovæ have an amplitude of about seventeen magnitudes, and the type I supernovæ, an amplitude of about twenty magnitudes. On average, three type I and ten type II supernovæ will occur in a galaxy the size of the Milky Way every thousand years. The energy emitted during the outbursts of these stars is 10^{43} ergs for the recurrent novæ, $10^{44·5}$ ergs for novæ, $10^{47·5}$ ergs for type II supernovæ, and $10^{49·5}$ ergs for type I supernovæ. (For comparison, the Sun emits, about 4×10^{33} erg/s, so that for a short period a type I supernovæ may be as bright as an entire galaxy.)

Nomenclature of Novæ. The older novæ are designated by the constellation and year in which they appeared, e.g. Nova Scorpii, 134 B.C.: some having also a 'popular' name, such as *Kepler's Star, Tycho's Star*, etc. Modern novæ were similarly designated until 1925: if more than one appeared in a constellation, they were numbered successively Nova I, Nova II, and so on, of that constellation, in order of discovery, disregarding the novæ before 1572. As many novæ were only discovered years after their appearance, when comparing star photographs of the same region taken at different times, this sometimes resulted in the numbers being out of order as regards date of *appearance*: the nomenclature was therefore altered to constellation and year, with the date in tenths of a year, if more than one in a year.

When a nova has been under observation for a sufficient period, it may be given an ordinary variable star designation; thus Nova Delphini 1967 is now known as HR Delphini.

Modern Novæ. Only the brighter novæ are included in this list. Many so-called 'New Stars' have been recorded in years previous to those given in the list below. Thus the appearance of a new star about the year 150 B.C. is said to have led Hipparchus to make his catalogue of stars, but generally the old records are vague and indefinite, and, in some cases, undoubtedly refer not to novæ but to comets.

Secular Variables are stars which have faded or brightened slowly and steadily over a long period of time. The presence of such a variable in the Pleiades (possibly *Pleione*) could be the reason why they are sometimes called 'The *Seven* Sisters', although there are only six bright naked-eye stars in the cluster.

Observing Variable Stars

For really accurate estimates, photoelectric methods are used; but for useful work in the amateur range, the procedure is to compare the variable with comparison stars which are of constant brightness. Special charts and sequences are required. These are issued by organizations such as the American Association of Variable Star Observers (AAVSO) and the Variable Star Section of the British Astronomical Association. It is essential to use several comparison stars for each estimate. A good observer may expect to be accurate to 0·1 magnitude.

A few variables are bright enough to be followed with the naked eye; when estimating the magnitudes, allowance must be made for atmospheric extinction, and, if possible, comparison stars of about the same altitude as the variable should be selected. Binoculars bring many more variables into range, though of course most variables are telescopic objects. Novæ are estimated in the same way as for ordinary variables.

102

TABLE 50. DATA FOR BRIGHT NOVÆ

Year A.D.	Nova	Greatest Mag.	Approx. Long.	Galactic Lat.	Position 1950·0 R.A.	Dec.
1572	Cassiopeiæ (B)	>1	120°	−2°	00 h 22 m	+63° 53′
1600	Cygni No. 1 (P)	3·5	76	+1	20 16	+37 52
1604	Ophiuchi No. 1	>1	5	+7	17 28	−21 27
1670	Vulpeculæ (11)	3	63	+1	19 46	+27 11
1848	Ophiuchi No. 2	5·5	8	+18	16 57	−12 48
1860	Scorpii (T)	7	353	+20	16 14	−22 31
1866	Coronæ (T)	2	42	+48	15 57	+26 04
1876	Cygni No. 2 (Q)	3	90	−8	21 40	+42 34
1885	Andromedæ (S)	7	121	−22	00 40	+40 59
1887	Persei No. 1 (V)	9·2	132	−5	01 58	+56 29
1891	Aurigæ (T)	4·5	177	−2	05 29	+30 25
1893	Normæ (R)	7	327	+5	15 26	−50 25
1895	Carinæ (RS)	8	291	−1	11 06	−61 40
1895	Centauri (Z)	7	315	+30	13 37	−31 23
1898	Sagittarii No. 1	4·7	23	−8	18 59	−13 14
1899	Sagittarii No. 3	8·5	9	−5	18 17	−25 13
1899	Aquilæ No. 1	7	36	−6	19 18	−00 14
1901	Persei No. 2 (GK)	0·0	141	−10	03 26	+43 24
1903	Geminorum No. 1	5·1	185	+12	06 41	+30 00
1905	Aquilæ No. 2	9	31	−4	19 00	−04 31
1910	Sagittarii No. 2	7·5	3	−2	17 57	−27 33
1910	Lacertæ No. 1	5·0	103	−5	22 33	+52 22
1910	Aræ	6·0	334	−4	16 37	−52 20
1912	Geminorum No. 2	3·3	184	+15	06 52	+32 12
1913	Sagittæ	7·2	57	−8	20 05	+17 32
1917	Ophiuchi No. 5	6·5	352	+8	16 50	−29 33
1918	Aquilæ No. 3	−0·7	32	+1	18 46	+00 32
1919	Ophiuchi	7·5	38	+13	18 11	+11 35
1919	Lyræ	6·5	59	+12	18 51	+29 09
1920	Cygni No. 3	1·8	87	+12	19 57	+53 29
1925	Pictoris (RR)	1·1	272	−26	06 35	−62 36
1934	Herculis (DQ)	1·3	73	+26	18 07	+45 51
1936	Lacertæ (CP)	2·0	102	−1	22 14	+55 23
1936	Aquilæ	7·0	37	−5	19 15	+01 38
1936	Sagittarii	4·5	358	−7	18 05	−34 21
1936	Aquilæ	5·0	43	−5	19 24	+07 30
1942	Puppis	0·4	253	−1	08 10	−35 13
1946	Coronæ (T)	3·1	(As yr. 1866 above)			
1950	Lacertæ	6·0	105	−5	22 48	+53 02
1960	Herculis	3·0	45	+4	18 55	+13 10
1963	Herculis	3·9	69	+24	18 13	+41 50
1967	Delphini (HR)	3·7	64	−14	20 40	+18 59
1968	Vulpeculæ (LV)	4·9	63	+1	19 46	+27 03
1970	Serpentis	4·4	33	+6	18 28	+02 40

Observing Novæ. Amateurs have had considerable success in discovering novæ; thus G. E. D. Alcock has now found three, including the exceptionally interesting HR Delphini of 1967. Magnitude estimates at an early stage in the outburst are very valuable, and are, of course, made in exactly the same way as with ordinary variable stars.

Estimating Magnitudes: Atmospheric Extinction. For accurate valuation of the magnitudes of bright variable stars, if the comparison stars are not at about the same altitude, allowance must be made for the difference, as atmospheric absorption diminishes the brightness (apart from haze) by approximately the following magnitudes:

Zenith distance:	47°	58°	64°	69°	71°	73°	75°	77°	79°	80°	84°	86°	88°	89°
No. of magnitudes diminished:	$\frac{1}{10}$	$\frac{2}{10}$	$\frac{3}{10}$	$\frac{4}{10}$	$\frac{5}{10}$	$\frac{6}{10}$	$\frac{7}{10}$	$\frac{8}{10}$	$\frac{9}{10}$	1	$1\frac{1}{2}$	2	$2\frac{1}{2}$	3
Altitude above horizon:	43°	32°	26°	21°	19°	17°	15°	13°	11°	10°	6°	4°	2°	1°

INTERSTELLAR MATTER

The space between the stars is not empty, but is filled with tenuous interstellar matter, principally hydrogen gas, together with a small proportion (about 1%) of solid matter known as *interstellar dust*. The mass of interstellar matter makes up about 10%–20% of the mass of our star system, *the Galaxy* (see below). Most of the hydrogen gas is neutral but there are regions, in the neighbourhood of stars, where ionized hydrogen is found, such areas being 'H II regions'. Neutral hydrogen can be detected over large distances due to its radiating at a wavelength of 21 cm (see *Radio Astronomy*). Recent work has shown that molecules exist in interstellar space, and by 1971 more than 20 interstellar molecules had been identified. The mean density of the interstellar matter is of the order 10^{-24} g/cm³, although in practice the matter tends to exist in the form of discrete clouds.

Interstellar dust reveals its presence by the effect it has on starlight. Because of scattering and absorption effects due to the dust particles starlight is attenuated, and the amount of *interstellar extinction* present is inversely proportional to the wavelength of light. Thus short-wave light, i.e. blue light, is attenuated more than longer-wave light, i.e. red light. As a result the light reaching the Earth from a star is reddened—this phenomenon being known as *interstellar reddening*. The interstellar dust particles are thought to consist of graphite or silicate grains, some of which may have coatings of ice. They are thought to have radii of the order of 0·1 microns.

NEBULÆ

Visually, nebulæ are seen as faint luminous, or in some cases dark, patches. There are several types:

Bright Emission Nebulæ. These are gaseous clouds which shine by absorbing light from hot stars embedded in the gas, and re-emitting it as a result of downward atomic transitions. They thus have bright line spectra. A typical example is the Great Nebula in Orion, M42, which is some 44 light-years in diameter.

Bright Reflection Nebulæ are less prominent than emission nebulæ, and are due to light from stars being reflected by interstellar dust grains in the clouds surrounding such stars. Reflection nebulæ thus display star-like spectra. Typical reflection nebulæ can be seen in long-exposure photographs of the Pleiades cluster.

Planetary Nebulæ are small luminous nebulæ, more or less circular in form, called 'planetary' because under low magnification they resemble the disks of planets. They usually contain hot central stars apparently evolving to the white-dwarf stage. The gaseous shell is thought to have been ejected from the central star. (A well known example is the Ring Nebula in Lyra.)

Dark Nebulæ are relatively dense regions of interstellar dust which therefore obscure the light from stars lying behind the clouds. Consequently, they show up as dark patches against the stellar background. A typical example of a dark nebula is the 'Horsehead' Nebula in Orion.

Observing Nebulæ

These faint objects lose least light by atmospheric absorption when near the zenith; hence those near the Galactic Plane are best seen when the Milky Way passes nearly overhead, and those near the Galactic Poles when the Milky Way lies near the horizon.

Nomenclature. The brighter nebulæ are often referred to by their numbers in the catalogue published by Charles Messier in 1771–84, or by their number and classification in the catalogues of Sir William Herschel (1786–1802). These designations are used on the star charts in this Atlas, all other nebulæ (the term here being used in the broad sense and including clusters and galaxies as well as gaseous nebulæ) being identified by their number in the 'N.G.C.' (J. L. E. Dreyer's *New General Catalogue of Nebulae and Clusters*, first published in 1888, and in a revised and supplemented edition in 1953).

GALACTIC STRUCTURE

The Sun is known to be a member of a star system, known as *the Galaxy*, which is estimated to contain 10^{11} stars, together with approximately 10^{10} solar masses in the form of interstellar matter. The Galaxy is a disk-like structure with a central ellipsoidal nucleus, and is seen in cross-section in Fig. 21. The diameter of the disk is about 30,000 parsecs, compared to a maximum thickness of the central nucleus of some 4000 pc. The galactic disk is thin, only some few hundred parsecs thick. Interstellar matter and nebulæ are found within the disk, i.e. they are confined to the plane of the Galaxy, but the entire Galaxy system is surrounded by an approximately spherical halo of globular clusters. Population II (metal deficient) stars are found in the globular clusters and towards the galactic centre. Population I stars, such as the Sun, are found in the disk of the Galaxy.

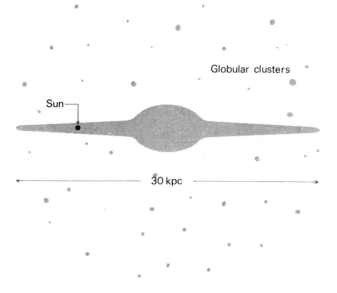

FIGURE 21. Cross-section of the Galaxy

The majority of the stars in the galactic disk are assumed to be revolving around the galactic centre in approximately circular orbits, in such a way that stars closer to the centre complete their orbits in shorter periods than stars further from the nucleus; i.e., the Galaxy does not rotate as a solid body, but exhibits *differential rotation*. The Sun, lying at a distance of 10 kpc from the galactic centre, makes one circuit of the Galaxy in a period of 225 million years.

Because of interstellar extinction, the range at which stars can be observed in the plane of the Galaxy in visible light is restricted to a few kpc, and in particular the centre of the galaxy is not visible optically. However, the 21 cm radiation from clouds of neutral hydrogen is largely unattenuated by the interstellar dust, and so the overall structure of the galaxy has been determined by observations of this radiation. In particular, the galactic centre has been identified with the strong radio source Sagittarius A, this point being in reasonable agreement with the position of the centre of the galaxy determined from the distribution of globular clusters (it was assumed that the centre of the system of globular clusters would coincide with the centre of the Galaxy). The detailed distribution of hydrogen clouds reveals that the galactic disk possesses spiral structure, and most of the Population I stars and the gas in the galactic disk is grouped into spiral arms radiating from the nucleus. In the arms, new stars are still in the process of formation from interstellar clouds.

The Galactic Plane, i.e. the equator of the galaxy, is used as a fundamental reference plane of the system of *Galactic Co-ordinates*. *Galactic longitude* is defined to be 0° in the direction of the galaxy centre, and increases in an anticlockwise direction from this point along the plane of the galaxy from 0° to 360°. *Galactic latitude* is measured perpendicular to this plane, from 0° to +90° north of the plane, and 0° to −90° south of the plane. The equatorial co-ordinates of the galactic centre are R.A. 17 h 42·4 m, Dec. −28° 55′ (Epoch 1950·0), and of the Galactic North Pole, R.A. 12 h 49 m, Dec. +27·4°.

The Milky Way (otherwise **The Galaxy**), composed of thousands of millions of stars, may be seen as a great ring of faint light, extending right round the star sphere and inclined about 61° to the plane of the ecliptic. It is brightest in Cygnus and Aquila (Northern Hemisphere), in Scorpio and Sagittarius (Southern Hemisphere), and faintest in Monoceros.

Between Cygnus and Scorpio the Milky Way forms two narrow parallel bands for some 110°, then it is very much broken up and complex for a considerable distance, but brighter, especially in

TABLE 51. APPROXIMATE GALACTIC LONGITUDE AND LATITUDE OF CERTAIN STARS

Star	Long.	Lat.	Star	Long.	Lat.	Star	Long.	Lat.
α Ophiuchi	35°	+22°	υ Ursæ Maj.	154°	+46°	γ Velorum	263°	− 8°
α Coronæ Bor.	40°	+54°	α Aurigæ (*Capella*)	162°	+ 4°	β Virginis	270°	+61°
α Aquilæ (*Altair*)	47°	− 8°	ψ Ursæ Maj.	165°	+63°	α Volantis	282°	−13°
ζ Herculis	53°	+40°	β Aurigæ	167°	+10°	α Eridani (*Achernar*)	290°	−59°
γ Lyræ	63°	+13°	α Tauri (*Aldebaran*)	182°	−20°	α Crucis	300°	+ 1°
α Lyræ (*Vega*)	67°	+19°	α Geminorum (*Castor*)	187°	+22°	β Centauri	312°	+ 1°
γ Cygni	78°	+ 2°	β Geminorum (*Pollux*)	192°	+23°	α Centauri	316°	0°
α Cygni (*Deneb*)	84°	+ 2°	γ Orionis (*Bellatrix*)	197°	−16°	α Virginis (*Spica*)	317°	+51°
η Draconis	92°	+41°	α Orionis (*Betelgeuse*)	200°	− 9°	α Trianguli Aus.	321°	−15°
η Ursæ Maj.	100°	+66°	β Orionis (*Rigel*)	209°	−25°	ζ Aræ	323°	− 8°
β Ursæ Min.	150°	+55°	α Canis Min. (*Procyon*)	214°	+13°	β Gruis	346°	−58°
ζ Ursæ Maj. (*Mizar*)	112°	+62°	α Leonis (*Regulus*)	227°	+49°	α Gruis	350°	−52°
ε Ursæ Maj.	122°	+61°	α Canis Maj. (*Sirius*)	227°	− 8°	α Scorpii (*Antares*)	352°	+15°
β Ceti	110°	−80°	θ Leonis	237°	+64°	β Scorpii	354°	+23°
α Ursæ Min. (*Polaris*)	123°	+26°	α Hydræ (*Alphard*)	241°	+29°	ε Sagittarii	359°	−10°
γ Cassiopeiæ	123°	− 2°	η Canis Maj.	242°	− 6°	α Boötis (*Arcturus*)	14°	+69°
δ Ursæ Maj.	133°	+59°	β Leonis (*Denebola*)	251°	+71°	α Pisc. A. (*Fomalhaut*)	20°	−65°
α Ursæ Maj. (*Dubhe*)	143°	+50°	α Carinæ (*Canopus*)	261°	−25°	η Serpentis	27°	+ 5°

Sagittarius, where the star clouds are very dense. In Argo, near Canopus, the Milky Way is visually completely divided across for a short distance, but near Canis Major it again becomes a single, but fainter, band which narrows to about 5° in Taurus, and broadens out once more in Perseus and Cassiopeia; its width is very variable, averaging 15° but in places reaching 20° or 30°.

The Coal Sack, a remarkable gap in the Milky Way (starless to the naked eye), close to the foot of Crux, has the appearance of a dark abyss in the surrounding luminescence. This gap, numerous similar but smaller gaps (especially in the Cygnus region) and the Great Rift in Argo are all believed to be due to the presence of dark nebulæ (see page 103), close to the Galactic Plane, intervening between us and the star clouds of the Galaxy beyond.

Observing the Milky Way. The Milky Way circles round the Celestial poles once each sidereal day, its central line passing within 27° of the North Pole, in the W of Cassiopeia, and within 27° of the South Pole, near α Crucis.

In the northern hemisphere, in the latitude of Britain and the U.S.A., it passes through or near the zenith during the hours when R.A. 22 h to 4 h are on the meridian; thereafter it approaches the horizon, until, when R.A. 13 h is on the meridian—and for some time before and after—it lies so close along the northern horizon for most of its visible length that it is hardly observable, after which its altitude begins to increase again. The Cassiopeia–Argo section is visible to its maximum extent when R.A. 8 h is on the meridian, and the Cassiopeia–Scorpus section when R.A. 16 h is on the meridian, but the portions near the horizon are not well seen.

In the southern hemisphere, in the latitude of South Africa and southern Australia, the corresponding phases are: overhead, R.A. 10 h to 16 h on the meridian; on the horizon, R.A. 1 h on the meridian. The Crux–Cygnus and Crux–Perseus sections are visible to their maximum extent when R.A. 20 h and R.A. 4 h, respectively, are on the meridian.

GALAXIES

Our Galaxy is not unique in the universe, and within the range of present-day telescopes lie thousands of millions of such systems beyond our own. The best known example of an external galaxy is the Great Galaxy in Andromeda (M 31), formerly known as the *Andromeda Nebula*; the term 'nebula' is misleading, and is now used only for objects within our own Galaxy. M 31 is visible to the naked eye under good conditions as a faint misty patch of light. The Andromeda galaxy is considerably larger than our own, and also has spiral structure. It is currently estimated to lie at a distance of 2·2 million light years. The first reliable estimate of its distance was made by E. P. Hubble in 1923, using the 100-inch (2·5 m) telescope at Mount Wilson Observatory, California.

Not all galaxies have spiral structure. The four basic types of galaxy observed are as follows:

Elliptical Galaxies. These are highly symmetrical systems, ranging in shape from spherical (E0) to highly flattened systems (E7), which are deficient in interstellar matter. The most massive ellipticals are considerably more massive than our Galaxy.

Normal Spiral Galaxies. Like our own, these galaxies have spiral arms consisting of stars, gas and dust, emerging from a central nucleus. They are classified Sa, Sb, Sc, according to the degree of tightness of the winding of the spiral arms. Spirals with tightly wound-up arms are Sa, those with loose, open arms, Sc.

Barred Spiral Galaxies. These are similar to the ordinary spirals, except that the spiral arms emanate from the ends of a luminous bar of material which straddles the nucleus. They are classified, like the spirals, from SBa to SBc. No satisfactory dynamical explanation of the bar phenomenon exists.

Irregular Galaxies. These galaxies possess no ordered structure, and frequently have low masses compared to our Galaxy. They are classified I or Irr.

The Magellanic Clouds

The Magellanic Clouds, or Nubecula Major (the 'Greater Little Cloud') and Nubecula Minor (the 'Lesser Little Cloud'), which are visible in the southern hemisphere as extensive nebulous naked-eye objects, are the nearest neighbours of our own Galaxy. They are, in fact, dwarf irregular galaxies—satellites of our own galactic system—lying at distances of the order of 50 kpc. Their positions are: Large Magellanic Cloud, R.A. 5 h 30 m, Dec. − 70°; Small Magellanic Cloud, R.A. 0 h 50 m, Dec. − 73°.

Clusters of Galaxies

A large proportion of galaxies occur in clusters, which are groups of galaxies containing between a few and a few thousand members. Our own Galaxy is a member of a cluster of some two dozen members, known as the *Local Group*. Most of the members are dwarf elliptical or irregular galaxies, but there are at

TABLE 52. CLUSTERS OF GALAXIES

Cluster	Galactic Long.	Lat.	Angular Diameter	Number of Galaxies	Distance (Mpc)	Radial Velocity (km/s)
Local group				24	0·4	
Virgo	284°	+74°	12°	2500	11	+1150
Pegasus I	86°	−48°	1°	100	40	3800
Pisces	128°	−29°	10°	100	40	5000
Cancer	202°	+29°	3°	150	50	4800
Perseus	150°	−4°	4°	500	58	5400
Coma	80°	+88°	6°	1000	68	6700
Ursa Maj. III	152°	+64°	0°·7	90	80	
Hercules	31°	+44°			105	10,300
Pegasus II	84°	−47°				12,800
Cluster A	144°	−78°	0°·9	400	150	15,800
Centaurus	313°	+31°	2°	300	150	
Ursa Maj. I	140°	+58°	0°·7	300	160	15,400
Leo	232°	+53°	0°·6	300	175	19,500
Gemini	182°	+19°	0°·5	200	175	23,300
Corona Bor.	41°	+56°	0°·5	400	190	21,600
Cluster B	345°	−55°	0°·6	300	200	
Boötes	50°	+67°	0°·3	150	380	39,400
Ursa Maj. II	149°	+54°	0°·2	200	380	41,000
Hydra II	226°	+30°				60,600

least three spirals—our Galaxy, M 31 and M 33. Infra-red observations reported in 1971 have shown the existence of two further galaxies within the Local Group, lying close to the plane of our Galaxy so that their radiation is excessively reddened. One of these objects (Maffei 1) is thought to be a giant elliptical galaxy, the other, Maffei 2, seems to be a spiral of lower mass. It is still uncertain whether or not these objects are permanent members of the Local Group. Details of the principal clusters of galaxies are given in Table 52.

The Recession of the Galaxies

All the galaxies outside the Local Group show strong red shifts in their spectra which indicate that the galaxies are receding from us. Furthermore, the velocity of recession is proportional to the distance of the galaxies, and so a galaxy at twice the distance of another will be receding at twice the velocity of the first. This relationship was established by Hubble in the 1920s, and became known as *Hubble's Law*. The constant relating the velocity of recession to the distance is *Hubble's Constant, H*. Currently accepted values of *H* range from 100 km/s/Mpc to 50 km/s/Mpc. If Hubble's Law holds true at very large distances, then it implies that there is an ultimate distance limit beyond which galaxies will not be visible, i.e. where the velocity of recession approaches the velocity of light. Current values of *H* suggest that the limit of the observable universe lies at a range of the order of 10^{10} light years.

The most distant objects presently detectable are thought to be the strong *radio galaxies* (galaxies emitting a large proportion of their energy at radio wavelengths) and *quasars* (Quasi-stellar Radio Sources—very compact objects which appear to be radiating more energy than conventional galaxies, and which show enormous red shifts).

The recession of the galaxies is interpreted as a general expansion of the universe, and leads to several theories of the origin and evolution of the universe, in particular the following:

(1) **The Steady-State Theory.** It is assumed that new matter is formed in the space between the receding galaxies, so that the average density of galaxies remains the same and the universe is infinite in space and time.

(2) **The Evolutionary, 'Big Bang', Theory.** It is suggested that at a time in the past (determined by Hubble's Constant) all the matter of the universe was concentrated at a point. The matter was then explosively ejected in all directions, so that the present expansion of the universe is the remnant of this original 'Big Bang'. On this hypothesis, the universe has a finite size and age.

(3) **The Oscillating Universe.** A variation on (2), this theory suggests that the expansion will eventually cease and a contraction phase commence. It is feasible that this process could be repeated cyclically, so that the universe continually oscillates in radius.

V. TELESCOPES AND ACCESSORIES

ASTRONOMICAL TELESCOPES

These are of two kinds—*refracting* and *reflecting*. Both types have their advantages. Their 'power' is rated, in both cases, by the *aperture*—i.e. the *clear* diameter of the large lens in a refracting telescope, and of the main mirror in a reflector. The larger the aperture, the greater the 'light-gathering power' of the telescope, and hence the greater its power to render visible faint objects. As this power theoretically increases in proportion to the *square* of the diameter, a telescope of 7·5 cm (3 in.) aperture is twice as powerful as one of 5 cm (2 in.), while a 10 cm (4 in.) has nearly twice the power of a 7·5 cm (3 in.), or four times that of a 5 cm (2 in.)—the actual ratios are 4, 9, 16. In refractors, however, the theoretical power falls off rapidly with increasing diameter, as the increasing thickness of the object glass absorbs more and more light, although up to about 25 cm (10 in.) aperture refractors are rather more powerful than reflectors of equal size. For astronomical purposes, an aperture of 7·5–10 cm (3–4 in.) is about the smallest that will permit the satisfaction of undertaking regular and varied observational work, although pleasing views of many objects may be obtained with smaller telescopes of good quality.

TABLE 53. POWER AND RESOLUTION OF TELESCOPES OF VARIOUS APERTURES

Clear aperture of object glass	(cm)	2·5	3·75	5·0	6·25	7·5	8·75	10·0	11·25	12·5	15·0	20·0	25·0	30·0
	(in.)	1	1½	2	2½	3	3½	4	4½	5	6	8	10	12
Faintest star shown (approx.)	(mag.)	9·0	9·9	10·5	11·0	11·4	11·7	12·0	12·3	12·5	12·9	13·5	14·0	14·4
Closest star divided (approx.)	(″)	4·56	3·04	2·28	1·82	1·52	1·30	1·14	1·01	0·91	0·76	0·57	0·46	0·38

The Refractor

This essentially consists of two convex lenses—(i) a large one of considerable focal length, known as the *object glass*, which forms at its focus an image of the distant star or other object, and (ii) a small lens of much shorter focal length; this is called the *eyepiece*, and is used to magnify the image formed by the object glass.

The Object Glass (O.G., or 'objective') is the most important part of the refractor, whose excellence depends upon the accuracy of the curves of the component lenses of the O.G., their high polish, and their transparency. In all astronomical telescopes worthy of the name, the object glass is *achromatic*; that is to say, it is composed of two (sometimes three or more) lenses of equal diameter, but made of glasses of different density. These are so proportioned as to form an image almost free from *chromatic aberration*—the false colours which are inevitably present when a bright object is viewed through an object glass composed of a single lens. A good object glass must be treated with scrupulous care.

The Reflector

In this form of telescope a large, concave mirror with a parabolic curve takes the place of the object glass of the refractor. The objective mirror is held in a cell at the lower end of the telescope tube. The light rays from the object pass down the tube and are reflected towards the focus of the main, or primary, mirror. They are intercepted:

(i) in the *Newtonian* reflector, inside the prime focus by a small, elliptical, optically flat mirror inclined at 45° to the optical axis of the main mirror [or, less satisfactorily, by a right-angled, totally reflecting prism], which reflects them at right angles, through the side of the telescope to the eyepiece;

(ii) in the *Cassegrain* reflector, inside the prime focus by a small, convex mirror of hyperboloidal curve, which reflects them back through a small hole at the centre of the primary mirror behind which a camera or eyepiece is located; or

(iii) in the *Gregorian* reflector, outside the prime focus, where a small convex mirror of ellipsoidal form reflects the rays through a small hole in the main mirror towards a focus at the open end similar to that in the Cassegrain form. The mirrors for a Gregorian telescope are difficult to manufacture, and it is longer than the Cassegrain, and therefore more difficult to handle, and is subject to greater aberrations. For these reasons, the Gregorian—although the first form of reflector to be invented, and of which numerous examples were constructed in the seventeenth century—was never very successful for astronomical purposes and need not be considered further here. The invention of the Newtonian form, by Sir Isaac Newton in about 1668, marked a great step forward in observational astronomy; the form is widely used for large observatory instruments, and is also most popular with amateurs, owing to its simple construction and the convenience of the off-axis observing position—especially important in instruments of small aperture. The Cassegrain form is very important for large instruments, where observing can be carried out on the main optical axis, the observer being carried in a 'cage' at the Cassegrain focus. It is also used in more modest aperture instruments for photography at the Cassegrain focus, or visually by combining the Cassegrain form with a Newtonian flat to bring the light rays to an eyepiece at the side of the tube.

Both the Newtonian and Cassegrain forms give an inverted image, but this is of little consequence in astronomical work. The Cassegrain reflector gives a greater focal length and therefore a larger primary image than a Newtonian of the same aperture and tube length, but its field of view is smaller and the image fainter.

Telescope Mirrors are usually made of glass, on which a film of silver is often deposited chemically; this is very easily tarnished, and vaporized aluminium is now usually used, which is about as efficient as fresh silver, lasts for years with little deterioration, and reflects the ultra-violet rays and blue end of the spectrum better—of great advantage photographically—but the red and infra-red rays less efficiently. Stainless steel mirrors last well, but only give 65 per cent efficiency, compared with the 90 per cent average of fresh silver.

The life of an aluminium-coated mirror can now be extended by the deposition of a protective 'over-coat'—usually of silicon dioxide. Rhodium has also been used for the reflecting surface, especially for telescopes intended to be used in corrosive atmospheres, e.g. close to the sea.

Eyepieces

These are used to magnify the image formed by the object glass or the large mirror. For very high powers, and in special cases, a single lens is sometimes used in order to minimize loss of light, but generally an eyepiece consists of two lenses—a *field lens*, furthest from the eye, and an *eye lens*, nearest the eye. These are mounted in a short tube which screws or 'push-fits' into the focusing tube of the telescope.

Inverted Image. All astronomical eyepieces show the object inverted (unless used with Gregorian reflectors), but this is of no disadvantage in practice. To make the object appear right way up requires additional lenses, or prisms, which absorb light, making the image fainter with no compensating gain.

Positive and Negative Eyepieces. Eyepieces are of two types: (a) *positive*, in which the image-plane is outside the eyepiece—between it and the object-glass or mirror—so that it can be used with a micrometer; (b) *negative*, which cannot be employed with a micrometer, as the image-plane lies inside the eyepiece.

Types of Eyepiece. Among many varieties of eyepiece are the following:

Huyghenian eyepiece (negative). The most common form, two plano-convex lenses having their flat surfaces towards the eye. Note that, though negative, fine cross-wires can be inserted on its diaphragm, at the focus of the eye lens, for use in a 'finder', or for 'guiding' in celestial photography.

Ramsden eyepiece (positive). Two plano-convex lenses with their plane faces outward. Field of view 'flatter' than that of the Huyghenian, i.e., not so blurred round the edges when the centre is sharply focused. Performs well on planets.

Tolles Solid Ocular (negative) is practically a Huyghenian eyepiece made out of a single glass cylinder, the foci of its curved ends falling inside it. Transmits more light than the Huyghenian, and gives very good definition when well made.

Orthoscopic eyepiece (positive) contains a triple field lens and a simple eye lens. It yields a flat field free from distortion, and is specially recommended for medium and high powers. ('Orthoscopic' means 'giving a correct image'.)

Kellner eyepiece (positive). A convex or plano-convex field lens with a much smaller over-corrected plano-convex achromatic eye lens. Field very large, colourless, and 'orthoscopic'; low powers are suitable for comets and extended objects.

Monocentric eyepiece (positive). A triple cemented lens, particularly recommended for the critical study of lunar and planetary detail, as it gives exquisite definition, and freedom from 'ghosts': its small field is its weak point.

Barlow Lens. A concave or concave-meniscus lens of about 5–7 cm negative focal length, mounted in a short tube—made a sliding fit—inside the eyepiece draw-tube, and placed between the objective and eyepiece, 10–12 cm from the eyepiece.

It increases considerably the focal length of the object glass or mirror, giving an image of double the size, more or less, according to its distance from the eyepiece. This valuable device, at the cost of a slight loss of light, and a tendency to form 'ghosts', gives a flatter field and an increase of the powers of all eyepieces used, thus doubling the set at small expense.

The Magnifying Power of a telescope depends entirely upon the ratio of the focal length (f_0) of the object glass to that of the eyepiece (f_e), the formula being $f_0 \div f_e$; thus, with an object glass of 75 cm focal length, and an eyepiece having a focal length of 1 cm, the magnifying power will be 75 diameters, or 'power 75' as it is termed. Note that, as the power is increased: (*a*) the image gets fainter, and the area included less; (*b*) stars pass more quickly across the field; and (*c*) the atmospheric disturbances are also magnified, as well as any vibrations of the stand or ground. It is advisable to have at least three eyepieces of different power:

(i) One of low power with a large field (i.e., showing a considerable area of the sky), for viewing comets, large and scattered clusters, extended nebulæ, etc. A power of ×3 to ×4 per cm of aperture will be found appropriate; thus for a 7·5 cm telescope a suitable power will be ×25 to ×30, for a 10 cm aperture ×30 to ×40, etc.

(ii) One of moderate power, say ×10 to ×12 per cm of aperture (×75 to ×100 for a 7·5 cm aperture, ×100 to ×120 for a 10 cm, etc.).

(iii) One of high power—say ×20 to ×25 per cm of aperture (e.g. ×150 to ×185 for a 7·5 cm aperture, ×200 to ×250 for a 10 cm).

When really experienced, the observer may occasionally use eyepieces of even higher power—the extreme limit of useful power is about ×40 per cm of aperture—but such powers are useful only for certain tasks (e.g. separating close double stars), and for use with telescopes having optics of the highest standard. Nights when the atmospheric conditions are sufficiently steady to permit the use of such high powers are extremely rare.

Accessories

There are many possible accessories that can be used with a good astronomical telescope of moderate aperture. Most of them are for use in specialized fields of observation, however, and even for less sophisticated work every observer will have his own favourite accessories. This section will therefore deal briefly with only a few of the most common items.

Stands. Much depends upon the rigidity of the telescope stand, and good observations must not be expected from the open window of an ordinary room, as the vibration of the floor and the mixed currents of air, will cause the image of the observed object to be very unsteady and poorly defined.

The Altazimuth Stand. For small telescopes, the ordinary garden tripod stand, with altazimuth head giving freedom of movement in azimuth and altitude, will be found quite convenient. A useful alternative to the folding tripod is an iron or steel pipe of about 10 cm diameter, partly sunk into the ground and rammed full of clay to deaden vibration; this will provide a good support for a telescope of moderate size.

The Equatorial Stand provides enormous advantages, but is rather expensive. It has one of the axes which carry the telescope directed towards the celestial pole (being adjustable for latitude). The result is that a star may be followed by a single circular movement of the telescope, instead of the instrument having to be moved both in altitude and azimuth. A make-shift is to screw to the stand top a wooden block cut off at an angle, as shown in Fig. 22 (*A*), and which has a V-groove, with sides at an angle of 60°,

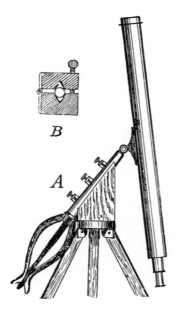

FIGURE 22. A simple equatorial stand

cut along the inclined face, for receiving the pillar. The claw legs of the stand, folded up, will act as a counterpoise, and two or three screw clamps will keep the pillar firm. A piece of hard wood (not shown in the illustration), also V-grooved, should be interposed between the point of the screws and the pillar, to prevent damage when tightening up the screws. A somewhat simpler construction is to hinge this upper block at one side to the lower block, and pass the screws through both blocks at the other side, as shown in the illustration at (*B*).

The angle of the sloping top, from the vertical, must be the latitude of the observer subtracted from 90°. Thus for latitude 52° it will be 90° − 52° = 38°.

Finders. A finder is a small telescope fixed by supports to the body of the larger instrument. When high powers are used, this adjunct is a necessity, and in all cases it adds much to the comfort of observing. The finder may be roughly adjusted by day on a distant steeple or some other definite object. To improve the adjustment, bring the polar star into the centre of the field of a low-power eyepiece on the large telescope; then alter the direction of the finder, by means of the adjusting screws, until the star image is in the centre of the field of the telescope, and also bisected by the cross wires of the finder at the same moment. Now replace the low-power eyepiece by one of high power, and perfect the adjustments in the same way. For small telescopes, up to 7·5 cm, 'sights' similar to those on rifles will be found of some service.

It is usual for all telescopes to be fitted with a small finder giving a wide field and very low magnification—often × 1 or × 2—to enable the observer to relate the finder field to the naked-eye view. Larger instruments may also have a higher-power finder for fine setting, once the desired object has been located.

Guiding Telescopes. Larger instruments used for photographic work are provided with a fairly high-power finder, accurately adjusted so that a guide star can be located in the cross-wires of the finder and the slow motion controls manipulated to keep it there, thus ensuring that the main instrument is kept accurately trained on the object being photographed throughout the exposure, which may be anything from a few seconds for a bright object to several hours for a faint, diffuse nebula or faint star-field.

112

Star Diagonal. An L-shaped tube containing a right-angled totally-reflecting prism. One end of the fitting screws into the focusing-tube of the telescope, while the other end is threaded to receive an ordinary eyepiece. Its use prevents awkward positions of the body when viewing objects at high altitudes, but results in some loss of light and definition.

Solar Diagonal. This device is frequently offered for sale by telescope dealers, and older telescopes were often provided with one as a standard accessory. It consists of a star diagonal in which the prism is replaced by an unsilvered flat inclined at 45°, which reflects only a small portion of the Sun's radiation into the eyepiece, allowing the rest to pass straight through. A better version utilizes a specially designed thin prism (the *Herschel wedge*, designed by Sir John Herschel) instead of the flat. A solar diagonal is usually used with one or more of a graded series of dark filters. It is intended for use by the specialist solar observer of great experience, and perfect safety cannot be guaranteed with any such gadget. The amateur observer is therefore strongly recommended *to have nothing whatever to do with any accessory intended for direct observation of the Sun, however safe the manufacturer may claim it to be.*

Dew-cap. To guard against the deposition of dew on the object glass of a refractor, the O.G. should be fitted with a dew-cap. If this is not the case, one can be made from a tube of tin, cardboard, or some such material, 20 to 30 cm long, and of such diameter as to fit closely onto the O.G. end of the telescope tube. The inside surface of the dew-cap should be covered with black velvet, or painted with non-reflective matt black paint.

Berthon's Dynamometer (usually so named, although more properly termed a *dynameter*). This is a little gauge used for measuring the diameters of small objects. It is a most useful aid to the astronomer, as by placing it against the eyepiece of his telescope it can be used to measure the diameter of the emergent pencil of light, thus permitting the magnifying power of the objective/eyepiece combination to be accurately determined (Fig. 23). The disk of light should be observed from a distance of about 25 cm (10 in.) when the dynameter is being used.

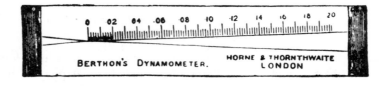

FIGURE 23

It has two flat metal sides, the internal straight edges of which meet towards the end, and are inclined to each other at a small angle. One of the edges is graduated from 0 to $\frac{2}{10}$ of an inch. The figures on the scale denote the width of the gap between the two straight edges. To measure the diameter of any small object by means of this little appliance, it is only necessary to see at what part of the scale the object *just* fills the space between the internal edges of the gauge, and then take the reading from the scale. The scale is divided into 20 long divisions of ·01 or 1/100th of an inch. These are subdivided into five parts, each equal to ·002 or 1/500th of an inch. The first two long divisions are again divided into parts equal to ·001 or 1/1000th of an inch.

Secondhand metal Berthon's Dynamometers can sometimes be located; the manufacture of a perfectly adequate one in card is detailed by A. C. Curtis in *J.B.A.A.*, vol. **81**, p. 24, 1970.

TESTS AND ADJUSTMENTS OF THE TELESCOPE

Tests

The actual performance of a telescope on a celestial object is the only really satisfactory test. Seen through a telescope bearing its highest power, a fixed star of the second magnitude should appear as a minute, well-defined, circular disk of light, almost a point, and surrounded by one or two thin, concentric, bright rings. There should be no false rays of light, and the rest of the field should be uniformly dark. The telescope should not, however, be condemned too hastily, as an inferior eyepiece, or the state of the atmosphere, may be responsible for apparent defects. A close double star with very unequal components forms a most severe test. A telescope of the finest quality should separate a double, consisting of two 6th magnitude stars, whose distance from centre to centre in seconds of arc is equal to 4·56 divided by the aperture expressed in inches (*see* Table 53).

To find the Focal Length. (*a*) *of an object glass or mirror.* Remove the eyepiece and stretch a piece of semi-transparent paper over the end of the draw-tube. Point the telescope at the Moon, and focus its image on the paper screen; the measured distance between the back of the object glass and the screen—in Newtonians, between the centres of the surfaces of the large mirror and flat, and thence to the screen—is, for practical purposes, the focal length required.

(*b*) *of an Huyghenian eyepiece.* The normal separation, *d*, of the field and eye lenses is half the sum of their focal lengths, i.e. $d = (f_1 + f_2)/2$; when this is the case the focal length of an equivalent single lens, F, can be found by dividing twice the product of the focal lengths of the component lenses by the sum of their focal lengths, i.e.

$$F = \frac{2(f_1 \times f_2)}{f_1 + f_2}.$$

Sometimes, however, the spacing departs from this ideal, in which case the required focal length can be found from

$$F = \frac{f_1 \times f_2}{f_1 + f_2 - d}.$$

To find the Power of an Eyepiece. Make a scale with plainly-marked equal divisions. Set this up at a considerable distance away, and holding both eyes open, view the scale through the telescope with one eye and directly with the other. The number of divisions on the scale, covered by the magnified image of one of them, is equal to the magnifying power of the eyepiece used. For low powers, a distant brick wall will serve as a scale.

Another method: Focus the telescope on a star. Next morning, without altering the focus, point the telescope to the bright sky. When the eye is placed about 25 cm behind the eyepiece, there will be seen a small, clearly defined disk of light. Measure the diameter of this disk by means of a Berthon Dynamometer (see p. 112) placed against the eyepiece—a pocket lens, of low power, may be used as an aid in doing this. The magnifying power of the eyepiece is found by dividing the clear diameter of the object glass by the measured diameter of the bright image.

To find the Diameter of the Field of an eyepiece, observe how long a star situated near the equator (for instance, δ Orionis, or ζ Virginis) takes to pass centrally across the field from one side to the other. This time, expressed in minutes and seconds and multiplied by 15, will give the diameter of the field in minutes and seconds of arc.

Adjustments

Setting up a Portable Instrument. This seldom presents any problem. Some heavier instruments are only semi-portable and may require assistance in setting up. There are no special requirements when setting up altazimuth-mounted instruments, other than a suitable area of level ground. Many portable and semi-portable instruments are equatorially mounted, however, and these must be set up with care to obtain the best results. The minimum requirements are that the polar axis is aligned north–south (use a pocket compass and allow for the current magnetic variation to find true north, or set on *Polaris*), and that it is inclined to the horizontal by an angle equal to the latitude.

Setting up a Permanent Equatorial. Again the first requirement is for accurate setting of the equatorial head in altitude and azimuth; larger instruments usually have some provision for fine adjustment, but it is still essential to set up the mounting with great care.

The local meridian must first be ascertained, roughly in the first instance with the aid of a magnetic compass (allow for magnetic variation). A more accurate determination must then be made by observations of *Polaris* when close to its upper or lower transit. (Upper transit of *Polaris* occurs when the Local Sidereal Time is equal to its R.A., about 2 h 09 m,* and lower transit twelve hours later.) Two plumb-lines should be used, one being suspended at each end of the approximate meridian line. *Polaris* should then be sighted across both plumb-lines, and one of them moved until they are exactly aligned on the star. Another check on the meridian line is to observe the direction of the shadow of the plumb-lines at local noon (noon G.M.T. corrected for longitude difference from Greenwich and the equation of time for the date).

* In 1977.

The telescope mounting should then be erected on the defined meridian line with its polar axis exactly parallel to it, and inclined to the horizontal by an angle exactly equal to the latitude of the site (measured by protractor or specially made template), using the adjusting screws for fine adjustment of both these alignments where they are provided in the mounting. (Where adjustments are provided, they should of course be set in the middle of their run before erection.)

Adjusting an Equatorial Head. To be properly adjusted an equatorial head must be set so that (i) the polar and declination axes are exactly perpendicular; (ii) the optical axis is perpendicular to the declination axis; (iii) the polar axis is exactly parallel to the Earth's axis of rotation, and if setting circles are fitted they must also be set to read true R.A./Hour Angle and Declination. Of these, (i) should be correct and unchanging if the head has been properly manufactured; (ii) is a matter for adjustment where necessary by a skilled optician; (iii) is roughly achieved during setting-up (see above), and must be improved by a process of repeated observation and adjustment, as follows.

The adjustments are carried out in the sequence (1) zero setting of declination circle pointer; (2) final setting of polar axis in altitude; (3) final setting of polar axis in azimuth; (4) zero setting of hour circle pointer.

(1) *Setting Declination Circle.* Choose a bright star fairly close to the meridian. Position telescope on east side of its mounting. Set telescope on star and read declination circle. Move instrument to west side of mounting, set on star again, read declination circle. Set pointer to mean of the two readings. Repeat; the reading should then be the same in both positions of the instrument. As a check repeat using a star of quite different Declination.

(2) *Altitude Setting of Polar Axis.* If the instrument has setting circles, choose a star close to the zenith, set declination circle to its Declination and clamp. Adjust elevation of polar axis until star can be centred in field by sweeping in R.A. only. Repeat with telescope on other side of its mounting and readjust if necessary. Repeat the operation with a different star.

If the telescope has no circles, the following method can be used, but only when the Local Sidereal Time is close to 8 h 09 m or 20 h 09 m:

Using a plumb-line, set the declination axis in vertical plane through the polar axis, and clamp the polar axis; then adjust elevation of polar axis until *Polaris* can be centred in field by sweeping in declination only.

(3) *Azimuth Setting of the Polar Axis.* Choose a star 40° to 50° above the eastern horizon. Set declination circle to Declination of star and clamp. Rotate polar axis in azimuth until star can be centred in the field by sweeping in R.A. alone. Repeat using a star 40° to 50° above the western horizon.

If the telescope has no circles, use the following procedure at L.S.T. 02 h 09 m or 14 h 09 m: Set declination axis horizontal with the aid of a spirit level and clamp the polar axis. Adjust the azimuth of the equatorial head until *Polaris* can be centred in the field by sweeping in declination only; the axis will then be about 1′ east of the correct position if the adjustment is being made at L.S.T. 02 h 09 m, or 1′ west of correct position if L.S.T. is 14 h 09 m.

(4) *Setting the Hour Circle.* Set declination axis horizontal using spirit level and clamp polar axis. Set hour circle pointer to read zero. For greater precision, calculate the time of transit of a particular star across the local meridian. Fit an eyepiece of fairly high power with cross-wires, and observe the star a little before the calculated time of transit. Set the star exactly at the centre of the field, and clamp both axes. Keep the star centred using the R.A. slow motion, and stop at the instant calculated for meridian transit; set hour circle pointer to read zero and the R.A. pointer, if any, to the R.A. of the star.

Adjusting the Optics. The correct positioning and alignment of the optical components of a telescope are the prime requirements for it to function satisfactorily; in particular each component should be centred on, and squared on to, the optical axis. The process of achieving this is termed *collimation* of the instrument.

Refractors should require little adjustment as they will have been properly adjusted by the manufacturer and should not be disturbed by anyone other than an expert optician.

Cassegrain reflectors are collimated by ensuring that the axis of the primary mirror passes through the centre of the secondary mirror, and that the eyepiece and the secondary mirror lie on the same axis.

When adjusting the Cassegrain reflector it is helpful to use a high-power eyepiece with the lenses removed. Make the adjustment in daylight, with the instrument pointed towards the sky so that the primary mirror is illuminated. Look into the eyepiece aperture and the primary mirror will be seen reflected in the secondary. Centre the image of the primary by adjusting the position of the secondary. The small dark silhouette of the secondary should be seen centred in the image of the primary. If it is off-centre, tilt the secondary mirror until it is centred.

Newtonian Reflectors are collimated when the axes of the primary mirror and the eyepiece intersect at the centre of the reflecting surface of the flat, and are each inclined to the normal to that surface by the same angle.

Adjustment of a Newtonian reflector should be carried out in daylight, and will be easier if an assistant is available. Remove the eyepiece and look into the empty draw-tube. The flat should be moved until it appears approximately central in the draw-tube when viewed from a distance of 1 to 2 feet (30 to 60 cm). It should be rotated about the axis of the telescope until it is directing the light from the main mirror along the axis of the draw-tube (i.e. when its outline appears circular). Remove the lenses from a high-power eyepiece and fit it into the draw-tube. (It is best to use an old unwanted eyepiece for this purpose; if this is not possible, it may be advisable to have the eyepiece dismantled and reassembled by an experienced person.) Look through the eyepiece aperture and further adjust the orientation of the flat until the bright reflection of the primary is concentric with the edge of the flat. Finally, adjust the tilt of the primary mirror until the dark silhouette of the flat appears central in the bright image of the primary mirror. *The dark spot is always most distant from the adjusting screw that must be turned inwards.* Thus, in Figure 24(a) the screw nearest to the position marked by the arrow must be turned inwards to bring the dark spot to the centre. The same result could be achieved by turning the other two screws equally outwards. The circular outline of the flat itself should not be exactly concentric with the mirror edge and draw-tube, but slightly displaced toward the upper end of the main tube, as shown in Figure 24(b) where all is

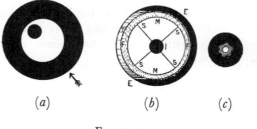

(a)   (b)   (c)

FIGURE 24

in perfect adjustment. The outer circle EE represents the far end of the draw-tube, T part of the tube which holds the flat, FF the flat itself, MM the bright image of the main mirror, I the dark image of the flat and S the images of a four-legged 'spider' supporting the flat mount.

Figure 24(c) shows the appearance of a fairly bright star in a good telescope, when the air is steady and the instrument correctly adjusted and carefully focused—a bright round spot of light surrounded by two or three concentric rings of light. It is impossible to portray the extreme delicacy of these diffraction rings as they appear on the best observing nights.

CARE AND MAINTENANCE OF THE TELESCOPE

General. Before removing a portable telescope indoors after the night's work, cover the object glass or mirror with the cover provided for the purpose. Never take the instrument from the cold outer air into a warm room, or the object glass will become dewed. If this should happen, the object glass must not be left in that state; but should be placed in a warm room, at a safe distance from a fire, until the moisture has vanished. Any stains left on the glass must be removed by gentle polishing. Never wipe an object glass when it is damp.

Cleaning Lenses. When it becomes necessary to clean any of the telescope or eyepiece lenses, any dust on the surface should first of all be removed using a soft lens brush. The lens should then be wiped very gently using a clean piece of fine wash-leather or a clean, lint-free soft cloth.

If the lens is really stained or dirty, a lint-free cotton swab soaked in pure alcohol should be used. Wipe in one direction only, never with a 'to-and-fro' motion, and use a clean area of the swab for every wipe. Each wipe should end with a lifting motion, and cleaning should be from the centre of the lens outwards. A circular motion will be found the most satisfactory, each wipe forming part of a spiral path.

When not in use, all brushes and materials employed for lens-cleaning should be carefully protected from dust by keeping them in clean stoppered bottles or air-tight cases.

Refracting Telescope. A good object glass is so delicately figured that it should be cleaned as rarely and carefully as possible, for fear of affecting the accuracy of its form. The lenses should never be taken out of their cell by an inexperienced person.

The object glass should be held in its cell with slight 'play'; if screwed up tightly it causes strains in the glass which mar perfect definition.

Reflecting Telescope. A silvered mirror requires to be kept with very special care, as the silver is exceedingly liable to tarnish—especially in or near large towns—from the sulphurous fumes in the air. An aluminized mirror will last much longer, but the slow formation of aluminium oxide will give the surface a milky appearance and slightly impair performance after a while.

Easing Stiff Draw-tubes. If used without attention for a long period, draw-tubes and rack-focusing mounts may become very stiff. Unless they have been deformed by accident or misuse, the cause will be found to be that old lubricant and dust have combined to form a thin layer of 'goo' which binds the moving parts together. The parts should be removed from the instrument and carefully separated; the sliding surfaces should then be twice cleaned (more if badly contaminated) with a clean, fluffless cloth dipped in clean paraffin or petrol. When thoroughly clean and dry they should be re-lubricated with white petroleum jelly (*not* oil which will creep into parts of the instrument that should be oil- and grease-free, such as the optical surfaces). The parts can then be reassembled and refitted to the telescope.

It may also be necessary to adjust the rack-focusing mount after cleaning in this way. The pinion shaft will be retained by a small plate fastened with four small screws: these should be adjusted so that the plate presses evenly along the shaft, and so as to permit just the right degree of freedom of movement. The mount should be just tight enough to prevent the heaviest eyepiece (with Barlow lens if used) from slowly racking out when in a near-vertical position.

APPENDIX: USEFUL ADDRESSES

Royal Astronomical Society, Burlington House, Piccadilly, London W1V oNL, U.K.

British Astronomical Association, Burlington House, Piccadilly, London W1V oNL, U.K.

Junior Astronomical Society, 58 Vaughan Gardens, Ilford, Essex, U.K.

Irish Astronomical Society, 1 Garville Road, Dublin 6, Eire, *or* c/o The Planetarium, Armagh, Northern Ireland.

British Astronomical Association (New South Wales Branch), 33 Cotswold Road, Strathfield, N.S.W. 2135, Australia.

Royal Astronomical Society of Canada, 252 College Street, Toronto 2-B, Canada.

Royal Astronomical Society of New Zealand, P.O. Box 3181, Wellington C1, New Zealand.

South African Astronomical Society, c/o The Royal Observatory, Observatory, Cape Province, South Africa.

American Astronomical Society, 335 East 45th Street, New York, N.Y. 10017, U.S.A.

Astronomical Society of the Pacific, c/o California Academy of Sciences, Golden Gate Park, San Francisco 18, California 94118, U.S.A.

Association of Lunar and Planetary Observers, c/o The Observatory, New Mexico State University, Las Cruces, New Mexico 88001, U.S.A.

American Association of Variable Star Observers, 187 Concord Avenue, Cambridge, Massachusetts 02138, U.S.A.

Société Astronomique de France, Hôtel des Sociétés Savantes, 28 rue Serpente, Paris 6e, France.

Koninklijk Sterrenkundig Genootschap van Antwerpen, Leeuw van Vlaanderenstraat 1, B. 2000 Antwerp, Belgium.

Vereinigung der Sternfreunde e.V., 8 München 90, Theodolindenstrasse 6, West Germany.

Schweizerische Astronomische Gesellschaft, Schaffhausen, Vordergasse 57, Switzerland.

Svenska Astronomiska Sällskapet, Stockholm Observatorium, Saltsjöbaden, Sweden.

Meteor reports to International Centre for Meteor Observations, c/o Dr K. B. Hindley, Department of Organic Chemistry, University of Leeds, Leeds LS2 9JT, U.K.

Reports of bright fireballs and meteorites to Mr H. G. Miles, 21 Babbacombe Road, Styvechale, Coventry CV3 5PE, U.K.

Reports of Aurorae to Mr James Paton, Mornington House, Abernethy, Perthshire, Scotland, U.K.

International Astronomical Union, c/o Space Research Laboratory, The Astronomical Institute, 21 Beneluxlaan, Utrecht, The Netherlands.

International Union of Amateur Astronomers, 93 Currie Street, Hamilton, Ontario L8T 3N1, Canada.

VI. STAR CHARTS

ABBREVIATIONS AND EXPLANATIONS

Small Crosses (+) indicate the points of intersection of lines of intermediate 20 minutes of R.A. and 5° of Declination.

Marginal Divisions in R.A. denote 5 minutes of sidereal time, and in Declination 1 degree of arc.

Identification of Stars

Greek or Roman letter. The Bayer Letter (see p. 88).
Number only. The Flamsteed Number (see p. 88).
Number underlined, e.g. 56. The hour number in Piazzi's catalogue.
R or Ru. In the case of E–B̄ red stars the letter R is not added as the letters E–B are a sufficient indication of the colour.
v denotes variability. A variable star which reaches 6th magnitude or less at maximum is denoted by a small circle (∘) only.

Identification of Nebulæ

Number only. The N.G.C. number (see pp. 39, 103).
Number with superscript M, e.g. 33^M. The number in Messier's catalogue (see p. 103).
Number with superscript number, e.g. 37^4. The number and classification in Sir William Herschel's catalogue (see pp. 39, 103). Thus $37^4 = $ H IV 37. The classes are:

I Bright nebulæ.	V Very large nebulæ.
II Faint nebulæ.	VI Very compressed and rich clusters of stars.
III Very faint nebulæ.	VII Compressed clusters of small and large stars.
IV Planetary nebulæ.	VIII Coarsely scattered clusters of stars.

Abbreviations of the Names of Observers, generally followed by the current number from their catalogues

A	Aitken, R. G.	L	Lacaille, N. L. de.
Ar	Argelander, F. W. A.	Ll	Lalande, J. J. de.
A C	Clark, Alvan.	Lv	Leavenworth, F. P.
Bar	Barnard, E. E.	M	Messier, C.
Brs	Brisbane, T.	Mel	Melbourne Obs.
Cor	Cordoba Obs.	R	Russell, H. C.
Cp	Cape Obs.	Rmk	Rümker, C. L. C.
Es	Espin, T. E. H.	S	South, J.
E–B	Espin–Birmingham.	Sa	Santiago Obs.
H	Herschel, Sir William.	Slr	Sellors.
h	Herschel, Sir John.	U. A.	Uranometria Argentina.
Hh	J. Herschel's catalogue of W. Herschel's double stars.	Wnc	Winnecke.
He	Howe, H. A.	β	Burnham, S. W.
Hn	Holden, E. S.	Δ	Dunlop, J.
Ho	Hough, G. W.	λ	Lowell Obs., See.
Hrg	Hargreaves, J.	ΟΣ	Struve, Otto.
Hu	Hussey, W. J.	ΟΣΣ	Pulkova Catalogue, Part II.
I	Innes, R. T. A.	Σ	Struve, F. G. W.
Jc	Jacob, W. S.	σ	Pulkova Obs. Appendix, Vol. III.

Interesting Objects, Maps 1 & 2

(Circumpolar, North); Dec. 60°N – 90°N

Double Stars

	1950·0 R.A.		Dec.		Mags	P.A.	Dist.	Notes
	h	m	°	'		°	"	
YZ Cassiopeiæ	00	42·3	+74	43	var., 9·7	160	36·1	Optical. Primary is of Algol type: 5·6–6·0, 4·5 days.
γ Cassiopeiæ	00	53·7	+60	27	2v., 11·0	248	2·1	Relatively fixed.
ψ Cassiopeiæ	01	22·4	+67	52	5·0, 9·8	112	25·2	B is double: 254°, 3".0.
α Ursæ Minoris (*Polaris*)	01	48·8	+89	02	2·0, 9·0	217	18·3	Optical pair.
48 Cassiopeiæ	01	57·8	+70	40	4·8, 6·5			Binary, 63·3 years. Distance below 1".
ι Cassiopeiæ	02	24·9	+67	11	4·7, 7·0, 7·1	240 116	2·3 8·2	Triple star. Little change. Fine object in 10cm.
OΣ 67 Camelopardalis	03	52·9	+60	58	5·2, 8·5	042	1·6	Yellowish, greenish.
19 Camelopardalis	05	32·4	+64	07	6·0, 10·5	047	1·3	Relatively fixed.
Σ 1193 Ursæ Majoris	08	15·2	+72	34	6·2, 9·9	087	43·1	Relatively fixed.
σ² Ursæ Majoris	09	06·0	+67	20	4·9, 8·5	024	2·2	Binary. P.A. decreasing; opening.
23 Ursæ Majoris	09	27·6	+63	17	3·7, 9·3	271	22·8	Slow binary. Little change.
Σ 1694 Camelopardalis	12	48·6	+83	41	5·3, 5·8	325	21·5	Yellowish, bluish. Fixed.
Σ 1882 Draconis	14	42·8	+61	19	6·8, 8·3	000	11·6	Little change.
π¹ Ursæ Minoris	15	32·0	+80	37	6·5, 7·2	081	31·0	Slow binary, but little change.
π² Ursæ Minoris	15	42·3	+80	08	7·4, 8·1	035	0·6	Close, difficult binary.
η Draconis	16	23·3	+61	38	2·9, 8·8	142	6·1	Easy test for 7·5cm. Slow binary.
20 Draconis	16	56·2	+65	07	7·1, 7·3	071	1·0	Slow binary.
26 Draconis	17	34·5	+61	55	5·4, 8·5			Binary, 111 years. Distance over 1".
ψ Draconis	17	42·8	+72	11	4·9, 6·1	016	30·3	Fixed. Yellowish, bluish.
40/41 Draconis	18	03·9	+80	00	5·8, 6·2	232	19·4	Slow binary, but little change.
Σ 2573 Draconis	19	39·4	+60	23	6·2, 8·4	027	18·4	Little change.
ε Draconis	19	48·4	+70	08	4·0, 7·1	012	3·3	Slow binary, but little change.
Σ 2640 Draconis	20	04·1	+63	45	6·2, 9·7	018	5·5	P.A. decreasing slowly.
κ Cephei	20	10·6	+77	34	4·4, 8·2	122	7·4	Very slow binary. Little change.
β Cephei	21	28·0	+70	20	3·3, 8·0	250	13·7	Fixed. A is a spectroscopic binary.
ξ Cephei	22	02·3	+64	23	4·6, 6·6	280	7·2	Very slow binary; little change.
Σ 2883 Cephei	22	09·5	+69	53	5·5, 8·6	254	14·7	Relatively fixed.
Σ 2893 Cephei	22	12·0	+73	04	6·1, 8·4	348	29·1	Relatively fixed.
π Cephei	23	06·3	+75	07	4·7, 6·7	300	0·7	Binary.
ο Cephei	23	16·6	+67	50	5·0, 7·3	208	2·7	Binary. Test for 5cm.
6 Cassiopeiæ	23	46·4	+61	56	5·7, 8·2	189	1·8	Binary.

Variable Stars

	1950·0 R.A.		Dec.		Range of mags	Period	Sp type	Notes
	h	m	°	'		d		
U Cephei	00	57·7	+81	36	6·6– 9·8	2·5	B + G	Algol type
S Cassiopeiæ	01	16·0	+72	21	7·9–15·2	611·5	S	Mira type
RZ Cassiopeiæ	02	44·3	+69	26	6·4– 7·8	1·2	A	Algol type
SU Cassiopeiæ	02	47·5	+68	41	5·9– 6·3	1·9	F	Cepheid
U Camelopardalis	03	37·5	+62	29	7·7– 8·7	400	N	Semi-regular
SS Cephei	03	41·5	+80	10	6·7– 7·8	90	M	Semi-regular
T Camelopardalis	04	35·2	+66	03	7·3–14·2	374·0	S	Mira type
X Camelopardalis	04	39·2	+75	00	7·4–13·7	143·4	M	Mira type

Interesting Objects, Maps 1 & 2

(Circumpolar, North); Dec. 60°N – 90°N

Variable Stars (contd)

	1950·0 R.A.		Dec.		Range of mags	Period	Sp. type	Notes
	h	m	°	′		d		
VZ Camelopardalis	07	20·7	+82	31	4·8– 5·2	24	M	Semi-regular
R Ursæ Majoris	10	41·1	+69	02	6·7–13·4	301·7	M	Mira type
VY Ursæ Majoris	10	41·6	+67	40	6·0– 6·6	—	N	Irregular
RY Ursæ Majoris	12	18·1	+61	36	7·0– 8·0	311·2	M	Semi-regular
S Ursæ Majoris	12	41·8	+61	22	7·4–12·3	226·1	S	Mira type
RY Draconis	12	54·5	+66	16	5·6– 8·0	172·5	Np	Semi-regular
V Ursæ Minoris	13	37·8	+74	34	7·4– 8·8	72·0	M	Semi-regular
U Ursæ Minoris	14	16·2	+67	01	7·4–12·7	326·5	M	Mira type
R Camelopardalis	14	21·3	+84	04	7·9–14·4	269·7	S	Mira type
TW Draconis	15	33·1	+64	04	7·7–10·0	2·8	A + K	Algol type
VW Draconis	17	15·9	+60	43	6·0– 6·5	—	G9	Irregular
UX Draconis	19	23·4	+76	28	6·2– 6·9	168	N	Semi-regular
T Cephei	21	08·9	+68	17	5·4–11·0	389·3	M	Mira type
S Cephei	21	35·9	+78	24	7·4–12·9	487·5	N	Mira type
VV Cephei	21	55·2	+63	23	6·7– 7·5	7430	M + B	Eclipsing
AR Cephei	22	52·6	+84	47	7·1– 7·8	116	M	Semi-regular
V Cephei	23	54·1	+82	55	6·6	—	A	Suspected variable
WZ Cassiopeiæ	23	58·7	+60	05	6·9– 8·5	186·0	N	Semi-regular

Nebulæ and Clusters

		1950·0 R.A.		Dec.		Notes
		h	m	°	′	
NGC 225	H.VIII 78 Cassiopeiæ	00	40·6	+61	31	Fine cluster, somewhat W-shaped.
NGC 581	M 103 Cassiopeiæ	01	29·9	+60	27	Mag. 7·4; galactic cluster which is rather loose but lies in a beautiful field.
NGC 663	H.VI 31 Cassiopeiæ	01	42·5	+61	00	Fine open cluster, visible in finder.
NGC 3031	M 81 Ursæ Majoris	09	51·5	+69	18	Mag. 8; Sb-type spiral; bright, condensed nucleus with rather faint spiral arms.
NGC 3034	M 82 Ursæ Majoris	09	51·9	+69	56	The celebrated irregular galaxy; mag. 8·8. Radio source. In the same low-power field as M 81.
NGC 5322	H.I 256 Ursæ Majoris	13	47·9	+60	25	Bright, roundish nebula, with a brighter central part.
NGC 6543	H.IV 37 Draconis	17	58·6	+66	38	Planetary. Bright oval disk resembling a star out of focus, with a central star of mag. 9·6.
NGC 7654	M 52 Cassiopeiæ	23	22·0	+61	19	Mag. 7·3. Irregular, rather inconspicuous open cluster.

MAP I

EPOCH 1950

For Abbreviations and
Contractions see page 117

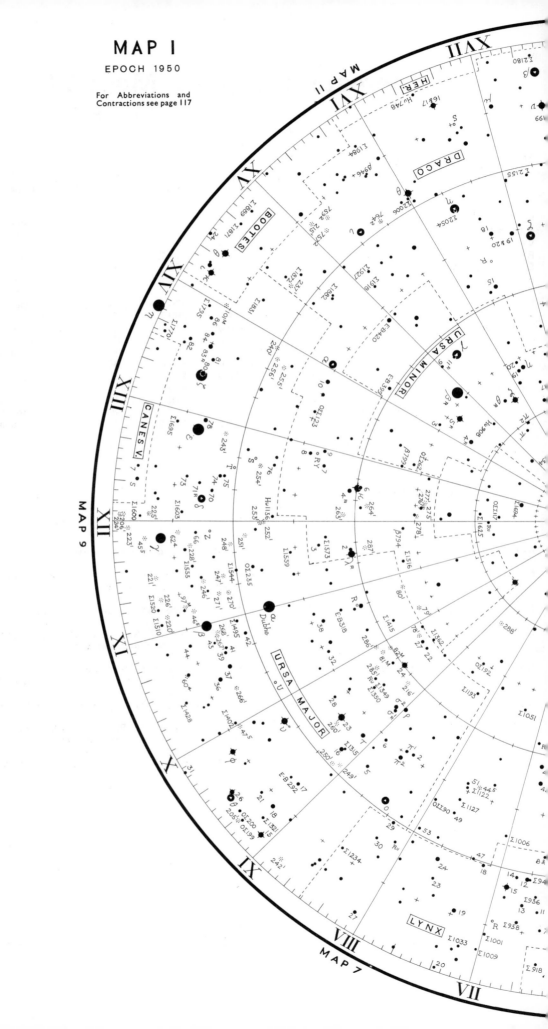

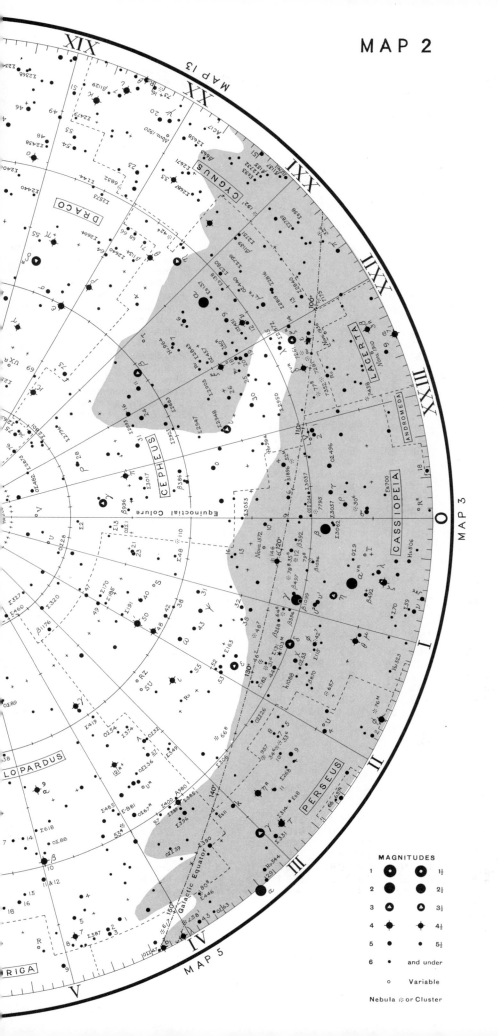

MAP 2

MAGNITUDES

1	⬤	⬤	1½
2	⬤	⬤	2½
3	△	△	3½
4	✦	✦	4½
5	●	•	5½
6	•	and under	
	○	Variable	
Nebula	✳	or Cluster	

Interesting Objects, Maps 3 & 4

R. A. XXII h – II h; Dec. 60°N – 60°S

Double Stars

	1950·0 R.A.		Dec.		Mags	P.A.	Dist.	Notes
	h	m	°	′		°	″	
41 Aquarii	22	11·5	−21	19	5·7, 7·2	116	5·0	Slow binary. Little change.
Σ 2894 Lacertæ	22	16·7	+37	31	6·1, 8·9	193	15·9	Relatively fixed; slow binary.
53 Aquarii	22	23·8	−17	00	5·7, 6·3	313	5·8	P.A. slowly increasing, distance diminishing. Binary.
ζ Aquarii	22	26·3	−00	17	4·4, 4·6	266	2·0	Slow binary. P.A. and distance decreasing. Test for 5cm.
δ Cephei	22	27·3	+58	10	var., 7·5	192	41·0	Common proper motion. Primary yellow, companion bluish.
β Piscis Austrini	22	28·7	−32	36	4·4, 7·9	172	30·4	Fixed. Optical pair.
8 Lacertæ	22	33·6	+39	23	5·8, 6·5	186	22·3	Common proper motion. Distant stars, mags. 10 and 11.
τ¹ Aquarii	22	45·1	−14	19	5·7, 9·6	120	25·6	Optical pair.
ξ Pegasi	22	44·2	+11	55	4·3, 11·7	108	11·9	Slow binary. P.A. decreasing.
γ Piscis Austrini	22	49·8	−33	08	4·5, 8·1	264	4·3	P.A. slowly decreasing. Slow binary.
θ Gruis	23	04·1	−43	47	4·5, 7·0	052	1·4	Slow binary. P.A. increasing.
ψ¹ Aquarii	23	13·3	−09	22	4·5, 9·4	312	49·4	Common proper motion.
94 Aquarii	23	16·5	−13	44	5·3, 7·5	348	13·3	Slow binary. Yellowish, bluish.
θ Phœnicis	23	36·7	−46	55	6·7, 7·4	272	4·2	Slow binary. Little change.
78 Pegasi	23	41·5	+29	05	5·0, 8·1	231	1·0	Binary. P.A. increasing.
107 Aquarii	23	43·4	−18	57	5·7, 7·0	136	6·5	Distance increasing. Slow binary.
σ Cassiopeiæ	23	56·5	+55	29	5·1, 7·2	332	3·1	Very slow binary; little change. Fine field in low power.
κ¹ Sculptoris	00	08·8	−28	16	6·2, 6·3	086	1·4	Slow binary.
35 Piscium	00	12·4	+08	33	5·9, 7·6	148	11·8	Slow binary. Little change.
λ Cassiopeiæ	00	29·0	+54	15	5·5, 5·8	171	0·5	Slow binary.
π Andromedæ	00	34·2	+33	27	4·4, 8·7	174	36·1	Common proper motion. Relatively fixed.
55 Piscium	00	37·3	+21	10	5·6, 8·8	193	6·6	Slow binary. Primary orange, companion bluish.
η Cassiopeiæ	00	46·1	+57	33	3·6, 7·5	293	10·1	Binary; period very long (over 500 years).
65 Piscium	00	47·2	+27	26	6·3, 6·3	296	4·4	Relatively fixed.
ψ¹ Piscium	01	03·0	+21	12	5·5, 5·8	160	30·0	Relatively fixed
β Phœnicis	01	03·9	−46	59	4·1, 4·1	352	1·3	Slow binary. P.A. decreasing.
ζ Piscium	01	11·1	+07	19	5·6, 6·5	063	23·6	Relatively fixed. Common proper motion.
37 Ceti	01	11·9	−08	11	5·2, 7·8	331	49·6	Relatively fixed.
42 Ceti	01	17·2	−00	46	6·4, 7·3	006	1·6	Slow binary. P.A. increasing.
ε Sculptoris	01	43·3	−25	18	5·4, 9·4	048	4·7	Slow binary. Little change.
1 Arietis	01	47·4	+22	02	6·3, 7·4	166	2·8	Slow binary. Test for 5cm.
γ Arietis	01	50·8	+19	03	4·8, 4·8	359	8·2	Beautiful fixed pair; very easy.
λ Arietis	01	55·1	+23	21	4·8, 7·4	046	37·4	Relatively fixed.
α Piscium	01	59·4	+02	31	4·3, 5·2	297	2·1	Test for 5cm. Slow binary; P.A. and distance decreasing.

Variable Stars

	1950·0 R.A.		Dec.		Range of mags	Period	Sp. type	Notes
	h	m	°	′		d		
X Aquarii	22	15·9	−21	09	7·5–14·8	311·3	S	Mira type
S Gruis	22	23·0	−48	41	6·0–15·0	410·0	M	Mira type
S Lacertæ	22	26·8	+40	04	7·6–13·9	240·0	M	Mira type
δ Cephei	22	27·3	+58	10	3·6– 4·3	5·37	G	Cepheid
W Cephei	22	34·5	+58	10	6·9– 8·6	1100?	K	Semi-regular
S Aquarii	22	54·6	−20	37	7·6–15·0	379·1	M	Mira type
β Pegasi	23	01·3	+27	49	2·1– 3·0	~35	M	Semi-regular

Interesting Objects, Maps 3 & 4

R. A. XXII h – II h; Dec. 60°N – 60°S

Variable Stars (contd)

	1950·0 R.A.		Dec.		Range of mags	Period	Sp. type	Notes
	h	m	°	′		d		
R Pegasi	23	04·1	+10	16	7·1–13·8	377·5	M	Mira type
V Cassiopeiæ	23	09·5	+59	25	7·3–12·8	227·9	M	Mira type
W Pegasi	23	17·4	+26	00	7·9–13·0	344·0	M	Mira type
S Pegasi	23	18·0	+08	39	7·4–13·8	318·8	M	Mira type
R Aquarii	23	41·2	−15	34	5·8–11·5	386·9	M + pec.	Mira (neb.)
ρ Cassiopeiæ	23	51·9	+57	13	4·1– 6·2	—	F-K	Type unknown
R Phœnicis	23	53·9	−50	05	7·5–14·4	268·0	M	Mira type
R Cassiopeiæ	23	55·9	+51	07	5·5–13·0	431·2	M	Mira type
W Ceti	23	59·6	−14	58	7·1–14·6	350·9	S	Mira type
S Sculptoris	00	12·9	−32	19	6·1–13·6	366·2	M	Mira type
T Andromedæ	00	19·8	+26	43	7·7–14·3	280·4	M	Mira type
R Andromedæ	00	21·4	+38	18	5·9–14·9	409·2	S	Mira type
S Ceti	00	21·5	−09	36	7·6–14·7	319·8	M	Mira type
α Cassiopeiæ	00	37·7	+56	16	2·1– 2·5?	—	K	Suspected variable
U Cassiopeiæ	00	43·6	+47	58	7·9–15·4	429·3	M	Mira type
ζ Phœnicis	01	06·3	−55	31	3·6– 4·1	1·67	B7	Eclipsing
R Sculptoris	01	24·7	−32	48	5·8– 7·7	363	N	Semi-regular
R Piscium	01	28·1	+02	37	7·1–14·8	344·1	M	Mira type
UV Ceti	01	36·4	−18	13	6·8–12·9	—	dM	Flare star
U Persei	01	56·2	+54	35	7·6–12·3	320·6	M	Mira type

Nebulæ and Clusters

		1950·0 R.A.		Dec.		Notes
		h	m	°	′	
NGC 224	M 31 Andromedæ	00	40·0	+41	00	Great Spiral (type Sb). Mag. 4·8. Distance 2·2 million l.y. Faintly visible with the naked eye.
NGC 221	M 32 Andromedæ	00	40·0	+40	36	Mag. 8·7. Elliptical galaxy (type E2). One of the companions to M 31. The other is NGC 205, also elliptical.
NGC 457	H.VII 42 Cassiopeiæ	01	16·0	+58	03	Open cluster, 18′ diameter, reasonably condensed. Close to φ Cassiopeiæ.
NGC 598	M 33 Trianguli	01	31·0	+30	24	Mag. 67. Sc-type spiral. Faint and ill-defined, best seen with a very low power on a dark, clear night; visible with binoculars. Member of the Local Group (2·35 million l.y.).
NGC 628	M 74 Piscium	01	34·0	+15	32	Mag. 10·2. Sc-type spiral. Faint and elusive.
NGC 650/1	M 76 Persei	01	38·8	+51	19	Mag. 12·2. Planetary nebula of irregular form; central star magnitude 16. M 76 is the faintest object in Messier's catalogue.
NGC 7243	H.VIII 75 Lacertæ	22	13·1	+49	38	Irregular open cluster; beautiful field following.
NGC 7662	H.IV 18 Andromedæ	23	23·4	+42	12	Bright, slightly elliptical planetary nebula, 32″ x 28″. Almost starlike with a low power. Dusky centre visible with 30cm telescope. Nucleus, mag. 14.
NGC 7789	H.VI 30 Cassiopeiæ	23	54·5	+56	26	Cluster of very faint stars between ρ and σ.
NGC 7772	Pegasi	23	49·0	+15	59	V-shaped group of faint stars; not a true cluster.

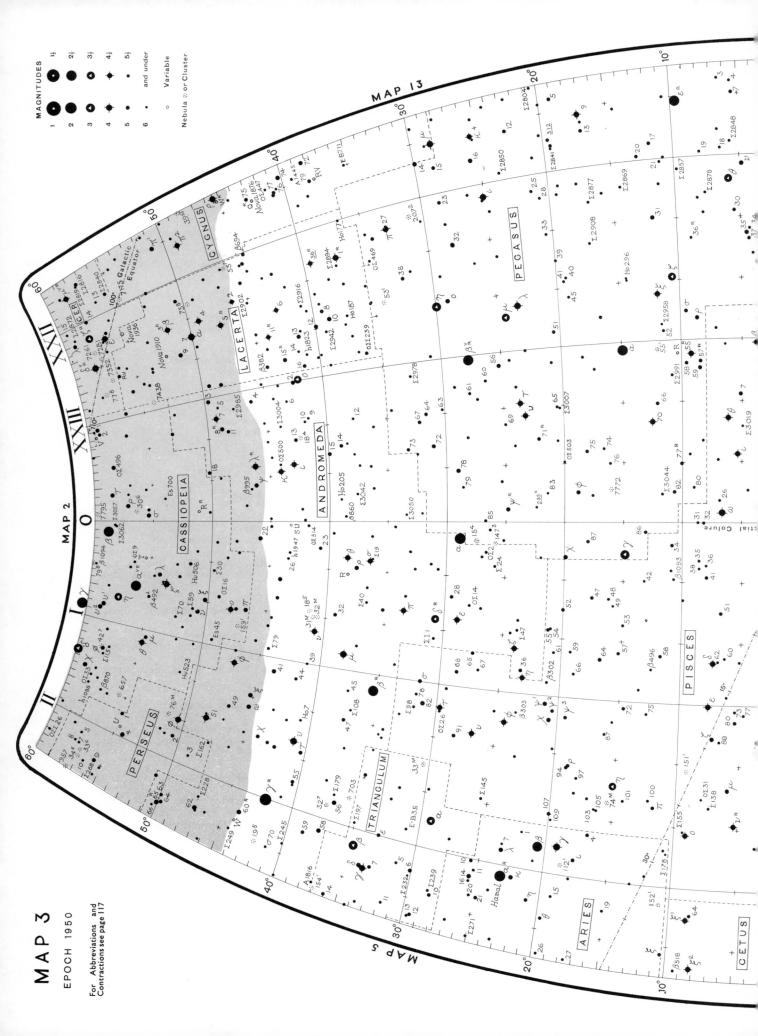

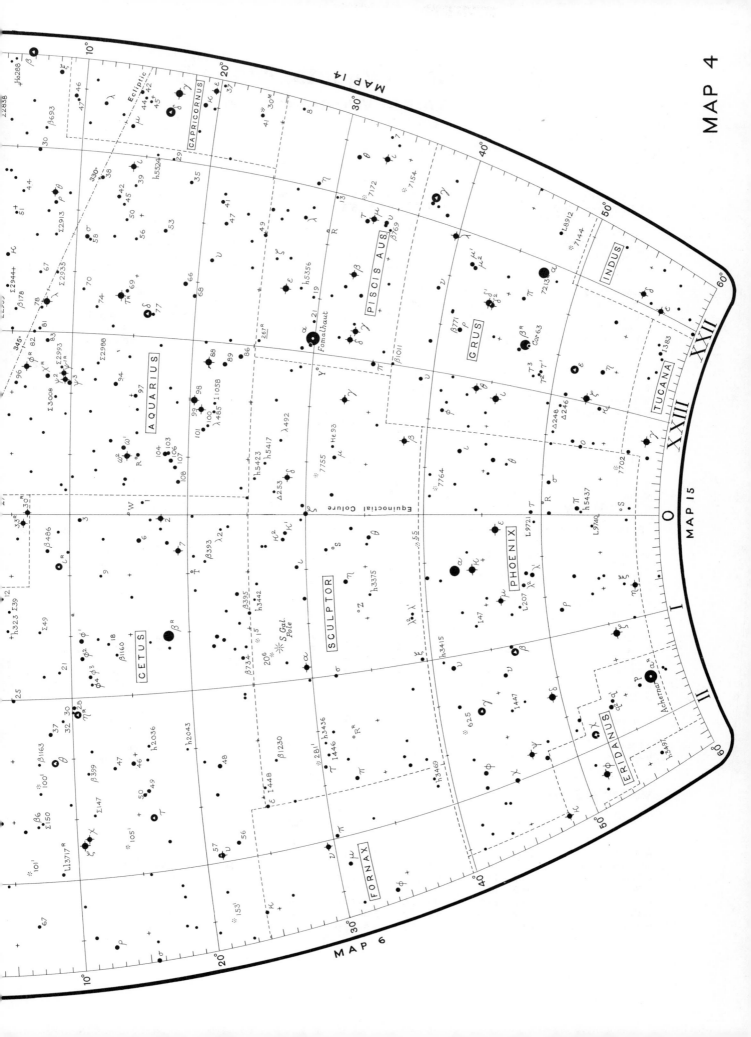

MAP 4

Interesting Objects, Maps 5 & 6

R.A. II h – VI h; Dec. 60°N – 60°S

Double Stars

	1950·0 R.A.		Dec.		Mags		P.A.	Dist.	Notes
	h	m	°	′			°	″	
γ Andromedæ	02	00·8	+42	06	2·3,	5·1	063	10·0	Superb pair; orange, bluish.
γ² Andromedæ	02	00·8	+42	06	5·5,	6·3	—		Companion of γ Andromedæ. Binary, period 61 years. Max. separation 0″·6 (1971).
59 Andromedæ	02	07·8	+38	48	6·1,	6·7	034	16·7	Relatively fixed.
ι Trianguli	02	09·5	+30	04	5·4,	7·0	071	3·6	Slow binary. Yellowish, bluish.
66 Ceti	02	10·2	−02	38	5·7,	7·7	232	16·3	Slow binary. Yellow, blue. Fine pair.
o Ceti (*Mira*)	02	16·8	−03	12	var,	10·0	131	0·8	Slow binary.
ω Fornacis	02	31·6	−28	27	4·9,	8·7	245	10·8	Slow binary.
γ Ceti	02	40·7	+03	02	3·7,	6·4	293	3·0	Slow binary; little change.
η Persei	02	47·0	+55	41	3·9,	8·6	301	28·4	Yellowish, bluish. Relatively fixed.
20 Persei	02	50·5	+38	08	5·3,	9·5	237	14·0	Closely following 16 Per. Test for 7·5cm. Brighter component is very close binary, period 31·6 years.
ε Arietis	02	56·4	+21	08	5·2,	5·5	208	1·5	Test for 7·5cm. Slow binary.
θ Eridani	02	56·3	−40	30	3·4,	4·4	088	8·5	Slow increase of P.A. Fine pair.
ρ² Eridani	03	00·2	−07	53	5·5,	9·6	081	2·2	Relatively fixed.
β Persei (*Algol*)	03	04·9	+40	46	var,	10·5	193	82·1	Optical pair.
ζ Persei	03	51·0	+31	44	2·9,	9·4	208	12·9	Relatively fixed.
ε Persei	03	54·5	+39	52	3·0,	8·1	009	9·0	Relatively fixed.
39 Eridani	04	12·0	−10	23	5·1,	8·9	147	6·4	Slow binary. Little change.
40 Eridani	04	13·0	−07	44	4·5,	9·4	105	82·8	B again double; 9·6, 11·1; 348°; 7″·3.
φ Tauri	04	17·3	+27	14	5·1,	8·7	250	52·1	Optical. Fixed pair.
χ Tauri	04	19·5	+25	31	5·4,	8·2	025	19·9	Relatively fixed.
α Tauri (*Aldebaran*)	04	33·0	+16	25	1·0,	11·0	112	31·4	Distance increasing, P.A. decreasing.
ι Pictoris	04	49·8	−53	33	5·6,	6·4	058	12·0	Relatively fixed. Combined mag. 5·2.
ω Aurigæ	04	55·9	+37	49	5·0,	8·0	355	5·8	Slow binary. P.A. increasing.
γ Cæli	05	02·6	−35	33	4·6,	8·5	311	3·1	Slow binary. Little change.
ρ Orionis	05	10·7	+02	48	4·7,	8·6	063	7·0	Fixed. Other stars in the field.
κ Leporis	05	10·9	−13	00	4·5,	7·5	258	2·6	Relatively fixed. Yellowish, bluish.
β Orionis (*Rigel*)	05	12·1	−08	15	0·2,	7·0	206	9·2	Fixed. Test for 5cm.
η Orionis	05	22·0	−02	26	3·7,	5·1	083	1·5	Test for 10cm. P.A. slowly increasing.
θ Pictoris	05	23·6	−52	22	6·3,	6·8	287	38·2	Optical pair.
β Leporis	05	26·1	−20	48	3·0,	11·0	308	2·6	P.A. increasing. Slow binary.
δ Orionis	05	29·4	−00	20	2·5v,	6·9	000	52·8	Relatively fixed.
λ Orionis	05	32·4	+09	54	3·7,	5·6	042	4·4	Fixed. Very fine region.
θ Orionis	05	32·8	−05	25					The Trapezium in Orion. Two other stars test for 10cm. Fine multiple group.
σ Orionis	05	36·2	−02	38					
ζ Orionis	05	38·2	−01	58	2·0,	4·2	164	2·4	P.A. slowly increasing. Test for 5cm.
γ Leporis	05	42·4	−22	28	3·8,	6·4	351	94·9	Little change.
θ Aurigæ	05	56·3	+37	13	2·7,	7·5	320	3·0	Slow binary. Test for 10cm.

Variable Stars

	1950·0 R.A.		Dec.		Range of mags	Period	Sp. type	Notes
	h	m	°	′		d		
R Arietis	02	13·3	+24	50	7·5–13·7	186·7	M	Mira type
W Andromedæ	02	14·3	+44	04	6·7–14·5	397·0	M	Mira type
o Ceti	02	16·8	−03	12	1·7–10·1	331·6	M	Mira Ceti
S Persei	02	19·3	+56	23	7·9–11·1	?	M	Semi-regular ?
R Ceti	02	23·5	−00	24	7·2–14·0	166·2	M	Mira type
U Ceti	02	31·3	−13	22	6·8–13·4	234·5	M	Mira type
R Trianguli	02	34·0	+34	03	5·4–12·0	266·4	M	Mira type

Interesting Objects, Maps 5 & 6

R.A. II h – VI h; Dec. 60°N – 60°S

Variable Stars (contd)

	R.A.		Dec.		Range of mags	Period	Sp. type	Notes
	1950·0							
	h	m	°	′		d		
T Arietis	02	45·5	+17	18	7·5–11·3	319·6	M	Semi-regular
B Horologii	02	52·3	−50	06	4·7–14·3	402·7	M	Mira type
T Horologii	02	59·5	−50	50	7·2–13·7	217·2	M	Mira type
ρ Persei	03	02·0	+38	39	3·3– 4·2	33–55	M	Semi-regular
β Persei	03	04·9	+40	46	2·2– 3·5	2·87	B8	Algol
U Arietis	03	08·2	+14	36	6·4–15·2	371·4	M	Mira type
T Eridani	03	53·1	−24	11	7·4–13·2	252·0	M	Mira type
λ Tauri	03	57·9	+12	21	3·3– 4·2	3·95	B + A	Algol type
R Cæli	04	38·7	−38	20	6·7–13·7	391·0	M	Mira type
R Pictoris	04	44·8	−49	20	6·7–10·0	171	M	Semi-regular
R Leporis	04	57·3	−14	53	5·9–10·5	432·5	N	Mira type
ε Aurigæ	04	58·4	+43	45	3·3– 4·2	9898·5	F	Eclipsing
ζ Aurigæ	04	59·0	+41	00	4·9– 5·5	972·1	K + B7	Eclipsing
T Leporis	05	02·7	−21	58	7·4–13·5	368·1	M	Mira type
W Orionis	05	02·8	+01	07	5·9– 7·7	212	N	Semi-regular
S Pictoris	05	09·6	−48	34	7·2–14·0	426·7	M	Mira type
AE Aurigæ	05	13·0	+34	15	5·4– 6·1	—	09	Irregular
R Aurigæ	05	13·3	+53	32	6·7–13·7	458·9	M	Mira type
T Columbæ	05	17·5	−33	45	6·6–12·7	225·3	M	Mira type
S Orionis	05	26·5	−04	44	7·5–13·5	416·3	M	Mira type
U Aurigæ	05	38·9	+32	01	7·5–15·5	407·3	M	Mira type
Y Tauri	05	42·7	+20	40	6·8– 9·2	241	N	Semi-regular
α Orionis (*Betelgeuse*)	05	52·5	+07	24	0·2– 1·0	2070 ?	M	Semi-regular
U Orionis	05	52·9	+20	10	5·3–12·6	372·2	M	Mira type
BQ Orionis	05	54·1	+22	50	6·9– 8·9	110	M	Semi-regular

Nebulæ and Clusters

		R.A.		Dec.		Notes
		1950·0				
		h	m	°	′	
NGC 869 884	H.VI 33 Persei H.VI 34 Persei	02 02	17·2 20·4	+56 +56	55 53	The Sword-Handle in Perseus. Two superb clusters, visible with the naked eye; each 45′ diameter. Red star near the centre of 884.
NGC 1039	M 34 Persei	02	38·8	+42	34	Mag. 5·5. Open cluster, just visible with the naked eye A low power is required to cover the large field.
NGC 1068	M 77 Ceti	02	40·1	−00	14	Mag. 8·9. Seyfert galaxy; Sb spiral, near δ. Distance, 52 million l.y.
—	M 45 Tauri (The Pleiades)	03	44	+24		Mag. 1·6; brightest star η Tauri (3·0). Most famous of the open clusters: distance 410 l.y. Near *Merope* in the Pleiades is the faint gaseous nebula NGC 1435.
NGC 1904	M 79 Leporis	05	22·2	−24	34	Mag. 7·9. Small globular; diameter about 3′.
NGC 1912	M 38 Aurigæ	05	25·3	+35	48	Mag. 7·4. Open cluster, cruciform; rich region.
NGC 1952	M 1 Tauri (Crab)	05	31·5	+21	59	Mag. 8·4. Remnant of supernova of 1054; contains a pulsar. Radio and X-ray source.
NGC 1960	M 36 Aurigæ	05	32·0	+34	07	Mag. 6·3. Fairly regular open cluster.
NGC 1976	M 42 Orionis	05	32·5	−05	25	The Great Nebula in Orion, visible to the naked eye as θ Orionis. A greenish, irregular, fan shaped mass, best seen with a low power. With high powers the bright 'Huygenian' region shows a mottled appearance 'like the breaking up of a mackerel sky' (Sir J. Herschel). Includes the Trapezium (see previous page).
NGC 2099	M 37 Aurigæ	05	49·1	+32	32	Mag. 6·2. Fine rich cluster, much more striking than M 36. The brightest star, near the centre, is reddish.

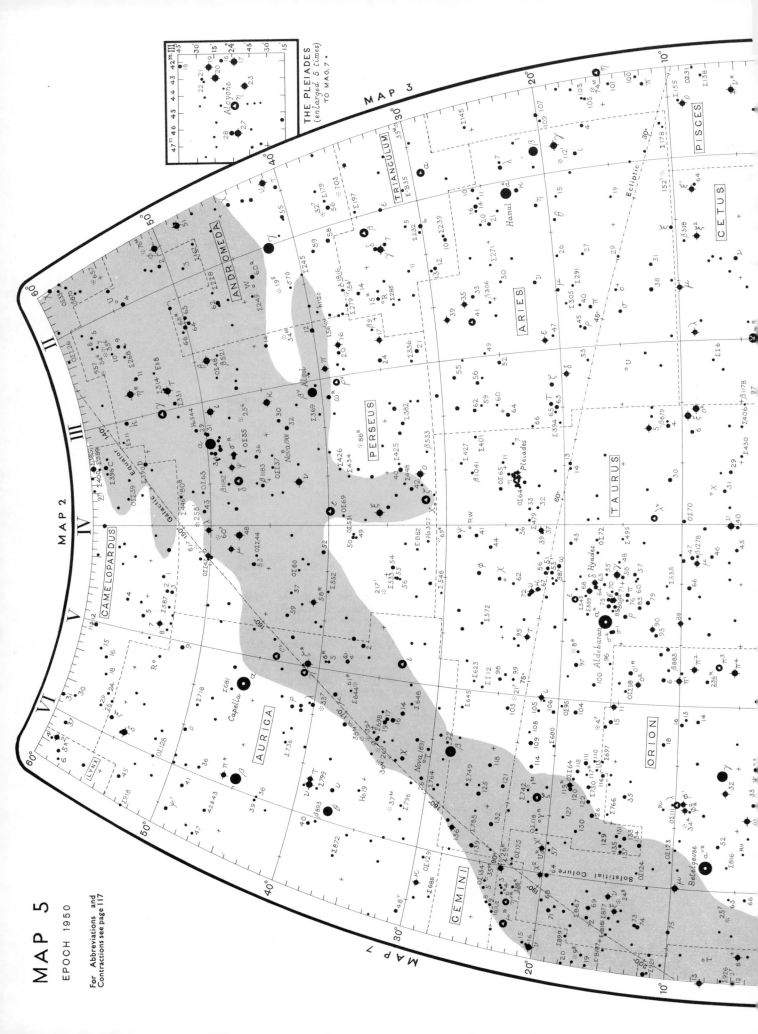

MAP 5

EPOCH 1950

For Abbreviations and
Contractions see page 117

MAP 6

MAP 15

MAGNITUDES

1	1½
2	2½
3	3½
4	4½
5	5½
6	and under
	Variable

Nebula ✳ or Cluster

MONOCEROS
CANIS MAJ.
LEPUS
COLUMBA
PUPPIS
PICTOR
DORADO
CAELUM
RETICULUM
HOROLOGIUM
PHOENIX
FORNAX
CETUS
ERIDANUS

Solstitial Colure

MAP 4
MAP 8

Interesting Objects, Maps 7 & 8

R.A. VI h – X h; Dec. 60°N – 60°S

Double Stars

	R.A. 1950·0		Dec.		Mags	P.A.	Dist.	Notes
	h	m	°	′		°	″	
41 Aurigæ	06	07·8	+48	43	6·1, 6·8	356	7·7	Little change. Very slow binary.
η Geminorum	06	11·9	+22	31	var, 8·8	278	1·3	Slow binary.
μ Geminorum	06	20·0	+22	32	3·0, 9·8	141	122·5	Wide optical pair. Fixed.
ε Monocerotis	06	21·1	+04	37	4·5, 6·5	027	13·2	Fixed. Yellowish, bluish. Fine field with low power.
β Monocerotis	06	26·4	−07	00	4·6, 4·7	132	7·4	Brighter component again double: 5·2, 5·6: 108°: 2″·8. Fine fixed triple.
20 Geminorum	06	29·4	+17	49	6·7, 6·9	211	19·8	Little change. Yellowish, bluish.
μ Pictoris	06	31·2	−58	43	5·8, 9·3	231	2·4	Relatively fixed.
ν¹ Canis Majoris	06	34·2	−18	37	5·8, 7·9	263	17·5	Relatively fixed.
Y Puppis	06	37·3	−48	10	5·0, 8·3	320	12·8	Slow binary.
12 Lyncis	06	41·8	+59	30	4·9, 5·4, 8·5	390, 090	8·5 1·8	Brighter components make a slow binary. Test for 7·5cm.
α Canis Majoris (Sirius)	06	42·9	−16	39	−1·4, 8·7			Binary, 50 years. Widest in 1975 (11″·5).
μ Canis Majoris	06	53·8	−13	59	5·2, 8·5	339	3·0	Fixed. Yellowish, bluish.
ε Canis Majoris	06	56·7	−28	54	1·6, 8·1	160	7·4	Fixed.
λ Geminorum	07	15·2	+16	38	3·7, 10·0	033	10·0	Fixed. Easy test for 7·5cm.
δ Geminorum	07	17·1	+22	05	3·5, 8·1	211	6·8	Optical pair. Test for 5cm.
η Canis Minoris	07	25·3	+07	03	5·3, 11·3	026	4·1	Fixed. Companion faint: test object.
σ Puppis	07	27·6	−43	12	3·3, 8·5	074	22·4	Relatively fixed.
α Geminorum (Castor)	07	31·4	+32	00	2·0, 2·9			Binary, 350 years. Closing; not now very easy with small apertures. Castor C (YY Gem), mag. 9·5, lies at 165°, 73″·4.
n Puppis	07	32·2	−23	22	5·9, 6·0	113	9·4	Slow binary.
κ Puppis	07	36·8	−26	41	4·5, 4·6	318	9·8	Relatively fixed. A again double.
κ Geminorum	07	41·4	+24	31	3·7, 9·5	236	6·8	Very slow binary. Little change.
γ Velorum	08	07·9	−47	12	2·2, 4·8	220	41·0	Relatively fixed.
ζ Cancri	08	09·3	+17	48	5·1, 6·0	089	5·9	ζ¹: 5·7, 6·0: binary, 59·6 years; widest (1″·1) in 1960. ζ²: 6·3, 7·8: binary, 17·6 years; very close (below 0″·2).
h² Puppis	08	12·3	−40	12	4·4, 9·1	341	51·1	Fixed.
φ² Cancri	08	23·8	+27	06	6·3, 6·3	216	5·0	Slow binary. Little change.
ι Cancri	08	43·7	+28	57	4·2, 6·6	307	30·7	Little change. Yellowish, bluish.
ε Hydræ	08	44·1	+06	36	3·5, 6·9	269	2·9	A is a close binary, 15 years.
H Velorum	08	54·8	−52	32	4·9, 7·7	339	2·7	Little change.
ι Ursæ Majoris	08	55·8	+48	14	3·1, 10·8	014	5·0	Test for 10cm. P.A. increasing, distance decreasing.
38 Lyncis	09	15·7	+37	01	4·0, 6·0	231	2·9	Slow binary. P.A. decreasing.
κ Leonis	09	21·7	+26	24	4·6, 9·7	208	2·6	Slow binary.
ω Leonis	09	25·8	+09	17	6·0, 6·7	224	0·2	Close binary, 117 years. Difficult.
ξ¹ Antliæ	09	28·6	−31	40	6·3, 7·2	211	8·2	Little change.
ψ Velorum	09	28·7	−40	15	4·2, 4·7			Binary, 34 years. Distance below 1″.
I Hydræ	09	39·0	−23	22	4·8, 8·1	292	54·4	Optical pair.
φ Ursæ Majoris	09	48·7	+54	18	5·2, 5·3			Binary, 112½ years. Distance below 1″.
γ Sextantis	09	50·0	−07	52	5·8, 6·1			Binary, 78½ years. Distance below 1″.

Variable Stars

	R.A. 1950·0		Dec.		Range of mags	Period	Sp. type	Notes
	h	m	°	′		d		
S Leporis	06	03·7	−24	11	7·0– 8·8	90	M	Semi-regular
η Geminorum	06	11·9	+22	31	3·1– 3·9	233·4	M	Semi-regular
V Monocerotis	06	20·2	+02	10	6·0–13·7	334·7	M	Mira type
T Monocerotis	06	22·5	+07	07	5·8– 6·8	27·0	G	Cepheid

Interesting Objects, Maps 7 & 8
R.A. VI h – X h; Dec. 60°N – 60°S

Variable Stars (contd)

	1950.0 R.A.		Dec.		Range of mags	Period	Sp. type	Notes
	h	m	°	′		d		
W Geminorum	06	32·1	+15	22	6·9– 7·9	7·9	G	Cepheid
UU Aurigæ	06	33·1	+38	29	5·1– 6·8	235	N	Semi-regular
X Geminorum	06	43·9	+30	20	7·6–13·6	263·5	M	Mira type
X Monocerotis	06	54·8	–09	00	6·9–10·0	155·7	M	Semi-regular
R Lyncis	06	57·2	+55	24	7·2–14·0	378·6	S	Mira type
ζ Geminorum	07	01·0	+20	39	3·7– 4·3	10·2	G	Cepheid
R Geminorum	07	04·3	+22	47	6·0–14·0	369·9	S	Mira type
R Canis Minoris	07	06·0	+10	06	7·4–11·6	337·9	S	Mira type
L² Puppis	07	12·0	–44	33	2·6– 6·0	140·8	M	Semi-regular
V Geminorum	07	20·3	+13	12	7·8–14·4	275·4	M	Mira type
Y Lyncis	07	24·6	+46	06	6·9– 7·4	110	M	Semi-regular
U Monocerotis	07	28·4	–09	40	6·0– 8·0	92·3	G	RV Tauri type
S Canis Minoris	07	30·0	+08	26	7·0–13·2	332·2	M	Mira type
Z Puppis	07	30·5	–20	33	7·2–14·6	509·9	M	Mira type
R Cancri	08	13·8	+11	53	6·2–11·8	362·0	M	Mira type
V Cancri	08	18·9	+17	27	7·5–13·9	272·1	S	Mira type
RT Hydræ	08	27·2	–06	09	7·1–10·2	253·2	M	Semi-regular
S Hydræ	08	51·0	+03	16	7·4–13·3	256·7	M	Mira type
X Cancri	08	52·6	+17	25	5·9– 7·3	±170?	N	Semi-regular
T Hydræ	08	53·2	–08	57	7·2–13·2	288·5	M	Mira type
T Cancri	08	53·8	+20	02	7·6–10·5	482·3	N	Semi-regular
T Pyxidis	09	02·6	–32	11	7·0–14·0	—	Pec	Recurrent nova (1920, 1944)
W Cancri	09	06·9	+25	27	7·4–14·4	393·3	M	Mira type
R Leonis Minoris	09	42·6	+34	45	6·3–13·2	372·3	M	Mira type
R Leonis	09	44·9	+11	40	5·4–10·5	312·6	M	Mira type
S Leonis Minoris	09	50·8	+35	10	7·9–14·3	234·1	M	Mira type
SY Ursæ Majoris	09	52·5	+50	03	5·1– 6·0	?	A	Type unknown

Nebulæ and Clusters

		1950·0 R.A.		Dec.		Notes
		h	m	°		
NGC 2168	M 35 Geminorum	06	05·8	+24	21	Mag. 5·3. Fine open cluster, visible with naked eye. The brightest star is of magnitude 9.
NGC 2244	H.VII 2 Monocerotis	06	30·0	+04	54	Open cluster, just visible to the naked eye. Round the star 12 Monocerotis.
NGC 2287	M 41 Canis Majoris	06	44·9	–20	41	Mag. 4·6. Roughly circular; just visible with the naked ,eye. The brightest star, near the centre, is orange.
NGC 2323	M 50 Monocerotis	07	00·6	–08	16	Mag. 6·3. Loose cluster; diameter about 16′.
NGC 2422	M 47 Puppis	07	34·3	–14	22	Mag. 5·2. Loose cluster, just visible with the naked eye.
NGC 2437	M 46 Puppis	07	39·5	–14	42	Open cluster of faint stars, about 30′ in diameter. On its northern edge is the planetary nebula NGC 2438.
NGC 2440	H.IV 64 Puppis	07	39·6	–18	05	Bright planetary, in a rich neighbourhood, best seen with a fairly high power. A 10 mag. reddish star follows.
NGC 2447	M 93 Puppis	07	42·4	–23	45	Mag. 6·0. Loose cluster, fairly bright.
NGC 2506	H.VI 37 Monocerotis	07	57·5	–10	27	Fine cloud of faint stars. Best seen with a low power.
NGC 2548	M 48 Hydræ	08	11·2	–05	38	Open cluster; magnitude 5·5, and just visible with the naked eye, but not too easy to locate.
NGC 2632	M 44 Cancri (Præsepe)	08	37·4	+20	10	A large open cluster almost resolved with the naked eye; best seen with a very low power.
NGC 2682	M 67 Cancri	08	47·8	+12	00	Famous cluster; magnitude 6·1, diameter 27′. Well seen in binoculars or with a low power.

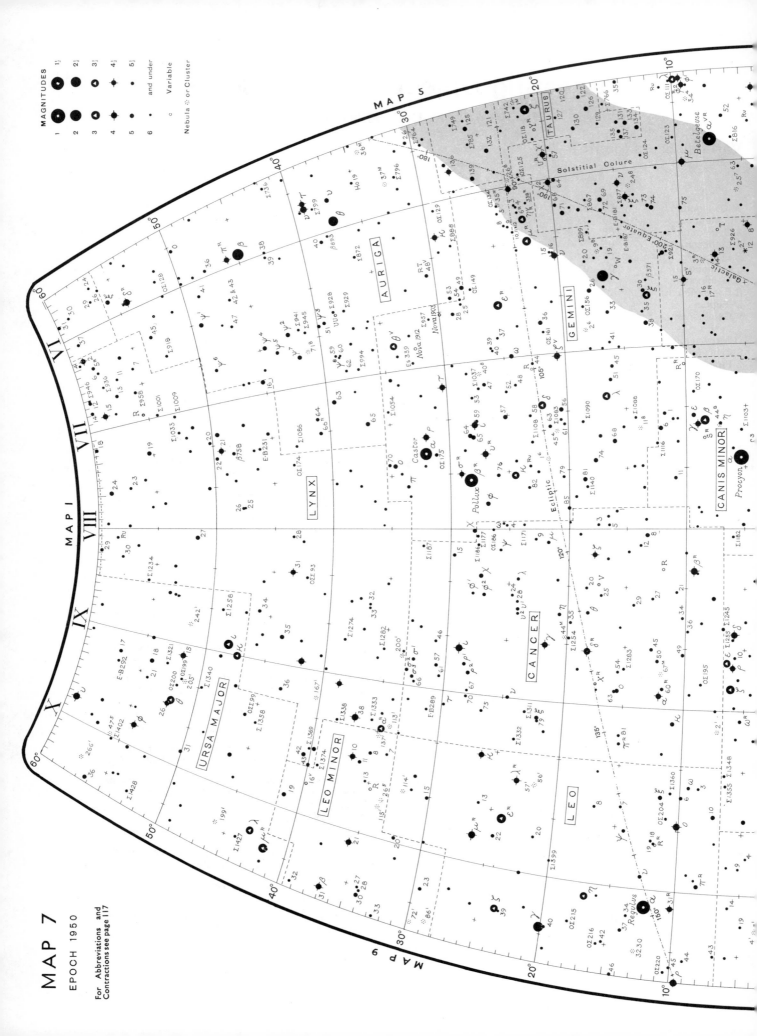

MAP 7

EPOCH 1950

For Abbreviations and
Contractions see page 117

MAGNITUDES

Variable

Nebula or Cluster

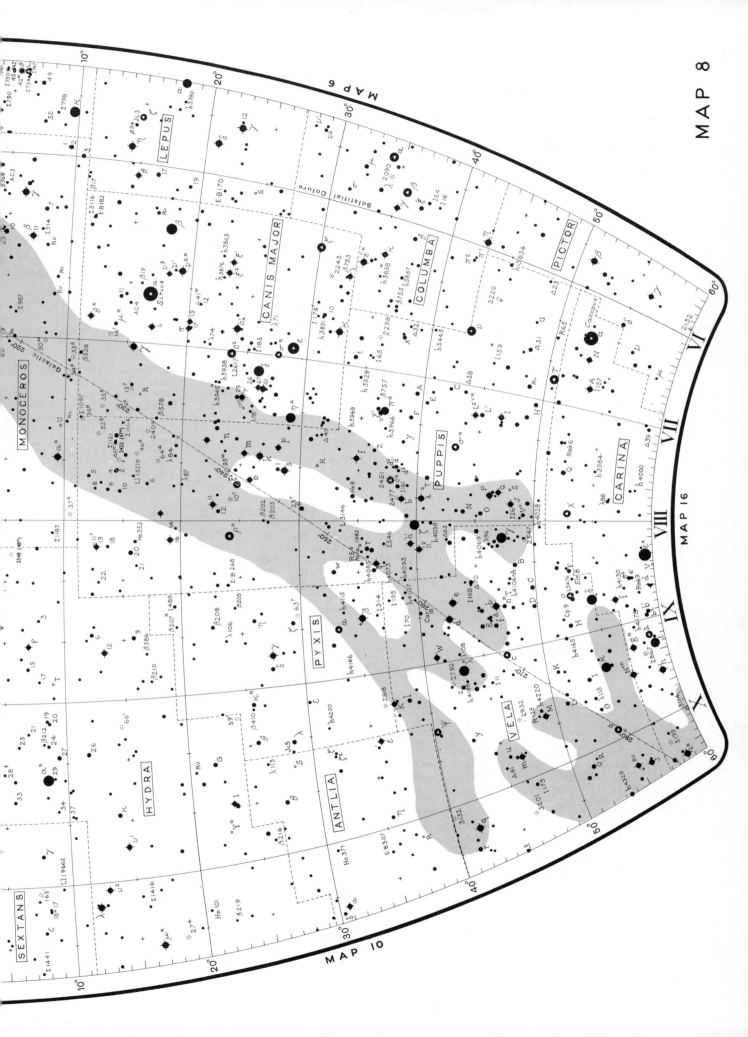

MAP 8

Interesting Objects, Maps 9 & 10

R.A. X h – XIV h; Dec. 60°N – 60°S

Double Stars

	R.A. h	R.A. m	Dec. °	Dec. ′	Mags		P.A. °	Dist. ″	Notes
			1950·0						
α Leonis (*Regulus*)	10	05·7	+12	13	1·3,	7·6	307	176·5	Fixed.
γ Leonis	10	17·2	+20	06	2·6,	3·8	122	4·3	Binary, 407 years. P.A. and distance increasing. Fine pair.
I Velorum	10	19·0	−55	47	4·6,	8·3	102	7·2	Little change. Slow binary.
δ Antliæ	10	27·3	−30	21	5·6,	9·7	226	11·0	Slow binary.
ξ Ursæ Majoris	11	15·5	+31	49	4·4,	4·8			Binary, 60 years. Widest 1980 (2″·9).
ν Ursæ Majoris	11	15·8	+33	22	3·7,	9·7	147	7·2	Relatively fixed.
ι Leonis	11	21·3	+10	48	4·1,	7·0	219	1·0	Slow binary.
γ Crateris	11	22·4	−17	25	4·1,	9·5	097	5·2	Relatively fixed.
57 Ursæ Majoris	11	26·4	+39	37	5·3,	8·5	001	5·5	P.A. slowly decreasing.
88 Leonis	11	29·2	+14	39	6·1,	8·6	326	15·4	Relatively fixed. Yellow, bluish.
β Hydræ	11	50·4	−33	38	4·8,	5·6	001	1·2	P.A. slowly increasing.
2 Comæ	12	01·7	+21	44	6·0,	7·5	239	3·8	Little change.
D Centauri	12	11·4	−45	27	5·6,	6·8	245	2·9	Slow binary. Little change.
δ Corvi	12	27·3	−16	14	3·1,	8·4	212	24·2	Fixed. A is yellowish.
γ Crucis	12	28·4	−56	50	1·6,	6·7	031	110·6	Wide optical pair.
24 Comæ	12	32·6	+18	39	5·2,	6·7	271	20·3	Little change. Yellow, bluish.
γ Centauri	12	38·7	−48	41	3·1,	3·2			Binary, 80 years. Combined magnitude 2·4.
γ Virginis	12	39·1	−01	11	3·6,	3·6			Binary, 180 years. Closing: though still (1972) an easy pair at 5″. By the year 2016 it will be very difficult.
α Canum Venaticorum (*Cor Caroli*)	12	53·7	+38	35	2·9,	5·4	228	19·7	Little change.
θ Virginis	13	07·4	−05	16	4·4,	8·6	345	7·2	Fixed. Test for 7·5cm. 10 mag. star at 71″.
ζ Ursæ Maj. (*Mizar*)	13	21·9	+55	11	2·4,	3·9	150	14·5	Naked-eye pair with *Alcor*.
Q Centauri	13	38·5	−54	18	5·6,	7·1	164	5·3	Slow binary. Very little change.
84 Virginis	13	40·5	+03	47	5·7,	8·6	230	3·3	Slow binary. Test for 7·5cm.
τ Boötis	13	44·9	+17	42	4·5,	10·6	007	5·7	Optical pair.
k Centauri	13	48·9	−32	45	4·7,	6·2	110	7·6	Little change.
h Centauri	13	50·3	−31	41	4·8,	8·5	186	15·1	Relatively fixed.
τ Virginis	13	59·1	+01	47	4·3,	9·5	290	80·1	Optical pair.

Variable Stars

	R.A. h	R.A. m	Dec. °	Dec. ′	Range of mags	Period d	Sp. type	Notes
			1950·0					
U Hydræ	10	35·1	−13	07	4·8– 5·8	—	N	Irregular
η Carinæ	10	43·1	−59	25	−0·8– 7·9	—	Pec.	Irregular
V Hydræ	10	49·2	−20	59	6·0–12·5	533·0	N	Mira type
U Carinæ	10	55·8	−59	28	6·4– 8·4	38·8	G	Cepheid
ST Ursæ Majoris	11	25·1	+45	28	6·4– 7·5	81	M	Semi-regular
X Centauri	11	46·7	−41	28	7·0–13·9	314·6	M	Mira type
Z Ursæ Majoris	11	53·9	+58	09	6·6– 9·1	198	M	Semi-regular
X Virginis	11	59·4	+09	22	7·3–11·2	?	Fp	Type unknown
R Comæ	12	01·7	+19	04	7·3–14·6	362·2	M	Mira type
R Corvi	12	17·0	−18	59	6·7–14·4	316·7	M	Mira type
U Centauri	12	30·7	−54	23	7·2–14·0	220·2	M	Mira type
T Ursæ Majoris	12	34·1	+59	46	6·6–13·4	256·9	M	Mira type
R Virginis	12	36·0	+07	16	6·2–12·1	145·6	M	Mira type
Y Canum Venaticorum	12	42·8	+45	43	5·2– 6·6	158·0	N	Semi-regular
U Virginis	12	48·6	+05	50	7·5–13·5	206·8	M	Mira type
S Crucis	12	51·4	−58	10	6·6– 7·7	4·7	G	Cepheid
R Hydræ	13	27·0	−23	01	4·0–10·0	386·2	M	Mira type
S Virginis	13	30·4	−06	56	6·3–13·2	378·0	M	Mira type
RV Centauri	13	34·3	−56	13	7·0–10·8	446·0	N	Mira type
T Centauri	13	38·9	−33	21	5·5– 9·0	90·6	M	Semi-regular
W Hydræ	13	46·2	−28	07	7·5–11·4	382·2	M	Semi-regular
R Canum Venaticorum	13	46·8	+39	47	7·3–12·9	328·1	M	Mira type

Interesting Objects, Maps 9 & 10

R.A. X h – XI h; Dec. 60°N – 60°S

Nebulæ and Clusters

		1950·0 R.A.		Dec.		Notes
		h	m	°	′	
NGC 3242	H.IV 27 Hydræ	10	22·3	−18	23	Planetary, 40″ x 35″, with brighter inner ring.
NGC 3368	M 96 Leonis	10	44·1	+12	05	Sa-type spiral. Close to M 95, and somewhat brighter (magnitude 9).
NGC 3532	Δ 323 Carinæ	11	04·3	−58	24	Open cluster; stars from magnitudes 8 to 12.
NGC 3587	M 97 Ursæ Majoris	11	11·8	+55	17	The Owl Nebula; a large, faint, planetary of magnitude 12. Hard to find with telescopes smaller than 15cm. Central star is mag. 14.
NGC 3372	Δ 309 Carinæ	10	43·0	−59	25	The Keyhole Nebula, round η Carinæ. Gaseous.
NGC 3623	M 65 Leonis	11	16·3	+13	22	Mag. 9·5. Sa-type spiral.
NGC 3627	M 66 Leonis	11	17·6	+13	16	Mag. 8·8. Sb-type spiral, near M 65 and rather brighter.
NGC 4258	H.V.43 Canum Venaticorum	12	16·5	+47	34	Large, pear-shaped object; spiral galaxy with two main arms and many condensations.
NGC 4374	M 84 Virginis	12	22·5	+13	10	Mag. 9·3. SO-type galaxy.
NGC 4382	M 85 Virginis	12	22·9	+18	28	Mag. 9·3. SO-type galaxy; small and condensed.
NGC 4406	M 86 Virginis	12	23·7	+13	13	Mag. 9·7. E3-type galaxy; same low-power field as M 84.
NGC 4472	M 49 Virginis	12	27·2	+08	16	E1-type galaxy; one of the brighter members of the Virgo Cluster (mag. 8·6) and easy to find.
NGC 4486	M 87 Virginis	12	28·3	+12	40	Giant elliptical EO-type galaxy; magnitude 9·2. The famous radio source. Well-marked nucleus.
NGC 4501	M 88 Comæ	12	29·5	+14	42	Sc-type galaxy. Easy to find; there is a close pair of stars near its edge.
NGC 4552	M 89 Virginis	12	33·1	+12	50	EO-type galaxy, magnitude 9·5.
NGC 4565	H.V 24 Comæ	12	33·9	+26	16	Elongated spiral galaxy, 15′ x 1′, with bright centre and dark longitudinal central streak.
NGC 4569	M 90 Virginis	12	34·3	+13	26	Sb-type galaxy, mag. 10·0. In low-power field with, and slightly fainter than, M 89.
NGC 4579	M 58 Virginis	12	35·0	+12	05	SBc-type barred spiral; easily found, and the brightest Messier object in the Virgo Cluster.
NGC 4590	M 68 Hydræ	12	36·8	−26	29	Globular cluster; mag. 8·2. Fairly easy to resolve.
NGC 4594	M 104 Virginis	12	37·4	−11	21	'Sombrero Hat' Sb-type galaxy. Mag. 8·7. Easy to locate; beautiful field. Stands high powers well.
NGC 4621	M 59 Virginis	12	39·5	+11	55	E5-type galaxy; mag. 9·3.
NGC 4649	M 60 Virginis	12	41·1	+11	49	E2-type galaxy; mag. 9·2. A giant system. In the same low-power field as M 59.
NGC 4736	M 94 Canum Venat.	12	48·5	+41	24	Sb-type galaxy, mag. 7·9. Bright, sharp nucleus.
NGC 4826	M 64 Comæ	12	54·3	+21	57	'Black-eye' Galaxy; type Sb, mag. 6·6. Bright, but the structure needs a telescope of over 20cm.
NGC 5024	M 53 Comæ	13	10·5	+18	26	Globular cluster; mag. 7·6. Not large, but a splendid object.
NGC 5055	M 63 Canum Venat.	13	13·6	+42	18	Sb-type spiral; mag. 10·1. Bright nucleus.
NGC 5139	ω Centauri	13	23·7	−47	03	Naked-eye globular cluster, 30′ in diameter. Thousands of 12–15 magnitude stars.
NGC 5194/5	M 51 Canum Ven.	13	27·8	+47	27	'Whirlpool' Galaxy; mag. 8; near η Ursæ Majoris. A 30cm will show the indications of spirality.
NGC 5272	M 3 Canum Venat.	13	39·9	+28	38	A beautiful bright, condensed globular; mag. 6·4. Most of it can be resolved with a 15cm with high power, and the outer parts can be resolved with a 10cm.

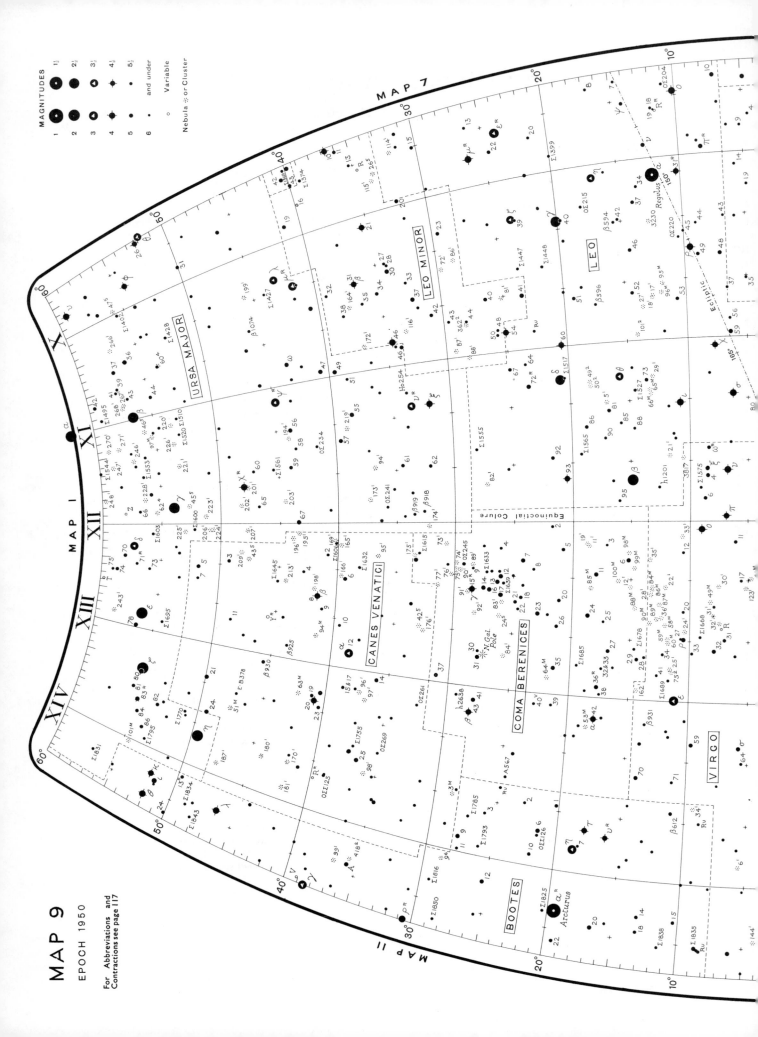

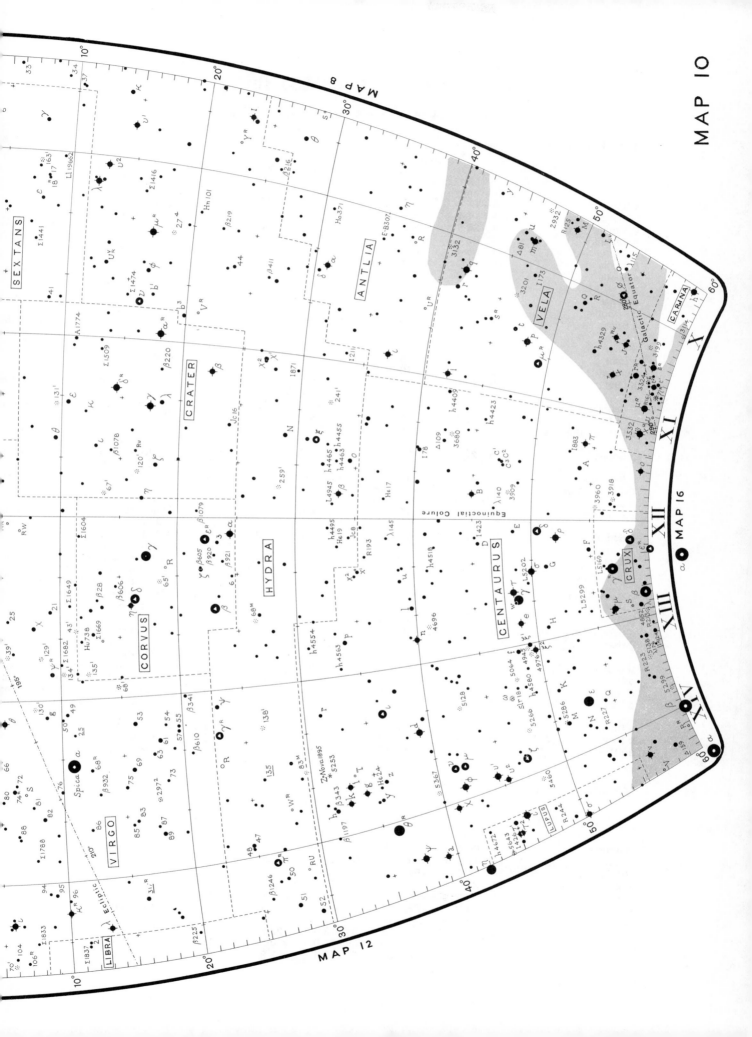

MAP 10

Interesting Objects, Maps 11 & 12

R.A. XIV h −XVIII h; Dec. 60°N − 60°S

Double Stars

	R.A. (1950·0)		Dec.		Mags	P.A.	Dist.	Notes
	h	m	°	′		°	″	
κ Boötis	14	11·7	+52	01	4·6, 6·6	236	13·2	Little change.
ι Boötis	14	14·4	+51	36	4·8, 8·3	033	38·4	Relatively fixed.
φ Virginis	14	25·6	−02	00	5·0, 9·2	110	4·7	Little change. Test for 7·5cm.
η Centauri	14	32·3	−41	56	2·6, 13·5	270	5·6	Optical. Companion very faint.
π Boötis	14	38·4	+16	38	4·9, 5·8	108	5·6	P.A. slowly increasing.
ζ Boötis	14	38·8	+13	57	4·6, 4·6	313	1·2	Binary; 130 years.
ε Boötis	14	42·8	+27	17	2·7, 5·1	338	2·9	P.A. increasing. Yellowish, bluish. Test for 5cm.
μ Libræ	14	46·6	−13	57	5·8, 6·7	355	1·7	Easy test for 7·5cm. Slow binary.
39 Boötis	14	48·0	+48	56	6·1, 6·6	045	3·1	Little change.
ξ Boötis	14	49·1	+19	18	4·8, 6·9	350	6·7	Binary, 152 years. Closest in 1982 (7″·2).
π Lupi	15	01·7	−46	51	4·7, 4·8	076	1·7	P.A. decreasing.
κ Lupi	15	08·5	−48	33	4·1, 6·0	144	27·0	Fixed.
ι Libræ	15	09·4	−19	36	4·7, 9·7	111	58·6	Fixed.
μ Lupi	15	15·0	−47	42	5·0, 5·2	146	1·4	P.A. decreasing. 7·2 mag. star at 24″ n.f.
5 Serpentis	15	16·8	+01	57	5·2, 10·0	037	11·0	Little change. Near nebula M5.
γ Circini	15	19·4	−59	09	5·2, 5·3	051	1·3	Slow binary.
η Coronæ Borealis	15	21·1	+30	28	5·7, 6·0			Binary, 42 years. 1″·1 in 1950; now closing.
μ Boötis	15	22·6	+37	33	4·5, 6·7	171	108·8	Relatively fixed. μ² is double: 7·2, 7·8: 025°: 2″·0.
δ Serpentis	15	32·4	+10	42	4·2, 5·2	179	3·9	Binary. P.A. decreasing; opening.
ζ Coronæ Borealis	15	37·5	+36	48	5·1, 6·0	305	6·3	Little change.
η Lupi	15	56·8	−38	15	3·6, 7·7	021	15·2	Slow binary.
ξ Scorpii	16	01·6	−11	14	4·9, 4·9			Binary, 45·7 years. Distance below 2″ (1971).
β Scorpii	16	02·5	−19	40	2·9, 5·1	023	13·7	A has a companion, mag. 9·7, at 0″·8, P.A. 105.
ν Scorpii	16	09·1	−19	20	4·3, 6·5	337	41·4	Both components are close doubles. A: 4·4, 6·4: 002°: 1″·0. B: 6·8, 7·8: 050°: 2″·1.
σ Coronæ Borealis	16	12·8	+33	59	5·7, 6·7	229	6·2	Slow binary; opening, P.A. increasing.
ρ Ophiuchi	16	22·6	−23	20	5·2, 5·9	347	3·5	Slow binary.
α Scorpii (Antares)	16	26·3	−26	19	1·2, 6·5	274	2·9	Red, green. Relatively fixed.
ζ Herculis	16	39·4	+31	42	3·1, 5·6			Binary, 34 years. Widest in 1988 (1″·6).
μ Draconis	17	04·3	+54	32	5·8, 5·8	081	2·2	Slow binary. Gradually opening.
α Herculis	17	12·4	+14	27	var, 5·4	109	4·6	Little change. Reddish, greenish.
δ Herculis	17	13·0	+24	54	3·2, 8·8	216	10·0	Optical pair. Distance decreasing.
ρ Herculis	17	22·0	+37	11	4·5, 5·5	317	4·0	P.A. slowly increasing. Slow binary.
ν Draconis	17	31·2	+55	13	4·9, 5·0	312	62·0	Physical pair. Very wide and easy.
μ Herculis	17	44·5	+27	45	3·5, 9·9	247	33·5	Slow binary.
90 Herculis	17	51·7	+40	01	5·1, 8·5	123	1·7	Yellowish, bluish.

Variable Stars

	R.A. (1950·0)		Dec.		Range of mags	Period	Sp. type	Notes
	h	m	°	′		d		
θ Apodis	14	00·4	−76	33	6·4− 8·6	119	M	Semi-regular
R Centauri	14	12·9	−59	41	5·4−11·8	546·6	M	Mira type
RR Centauri	14	13·4	−57	37	7·5− 8·0	0·6	F	W UMa type
V Boötis	14	27·7	+39	05	7·0−11·3	258·2	M	Semi-regular
R Boötis	14	35·0	+26	57	6·7−12·8	223·3	M	Mira type
δ Libræ	14	58·3	−08	19	4·8− 6·1	2·3	A	Algol type
U Coronæ Borealis	15	16·1	+31	50	7·0− 8·3	3·5	A	Algol type
S Libræ	15	18·5	−20	13	8·0−13·0	192·6	M	Mira type
S Coronæ Borealis	15	19·4	+31	33	6·6−14·0	360·7	M	Mira type
T Normæ	15	40·2	−54	50	6·2−13·4	292·9	M	Mira type

Interesting Objects, Maps 11 & 12
R.A. XIV h – XVIII h; Dec. 60°N – 60°S

Variable Stars (contd)

	R.A. 1950.0		Dec.		Range of mags	Period	Sp. type	Notes
	h	m	°	′		d		
R Coronæ Borealis	15	46·5	+28	19	5·8–15	—	Gp	R CrB type
V Coronæ Borealis	15	47·7	+39	43	6·9–12·2	357·8	N	Mira type
R Serpentis	15	48·4	+15	17	5·7–14·4	356·8	M	Mira type
T Coronæ Borealis	15	57·4	+26	04	2·0–10·8	—	Q + M	Recurrent nova (1866, 1946)
U Serpentis	16	04·9	+10	04	7·8–14·0	238·2	M	Mira type
W Coronæ Borealis	16	13·6	+37	54	7·8–14·3	238·2	M	Mira type
U Herculis	16	23·6	+19	00	7·0–13·4	406·0	M	Mira type
V Ophiuchi	16	23·9	−12	19	7·3–11·0	298·0	N	Mira type
g Herculis	16	27·0	+41	59	4·6– 6·0	70	M	Semi-regular
R Aræ	16	35·6	−56	54	5·9– 6·9	4·4	B9	Algol type
S Herculis	16	49·6	+15	01	7·0–13·8	307·4	M	Mira type
SS Scorpii	16	52·0	−32	33	7·5– 9·5	—	K	Irregular
α Herculis	17	12·4	+14	27	3·0– 4·0	?	M	Semi-regular
U Ophiuchi	17	14·0	+01	16	5·8– 6·5	1·7	B	Algol type
u Herculis	17	15·5	+33	09	4·6– 5·3	2·1	B	β Lyr type
Z Ophiuchi	17	17·0	+01	34	7·6–13·2	348·5	M	Mira type
RS Herculis	17	19·6	+22	58	7·4–12·9	219·5	M	Mira type
RW Aræ	17	30·5	−57	07	8·7–12·1	4·4	A	Algol type
RS Ophiuchi	17	47·5	−06	42	5·2–12·2	—	Op	Recurrent nova (1898, 1933, 1958)
T Draconis	17	55·7	+58	14	7·2–13·5	421·7	N	Mira type
UW Draconis	17	56·5	+54	50	7·0– 8·0	?	K	Irregular?

Nebulæ and Clusters

		R.A. 1950·0		Dec.		Notes
		h	m	°	′	
NGC 5457	M 101 Ursæ Majoris	14	01·1	+54	35	Sc-type spiral galaxy; mag. 9·6. Face-on. Rather diffuse and dim.
NGC 5904	M 5 Serpentis	15	16·0	+02	16	Fine globular, 15′ in diameter, made up of stars of mag. 11 to 15; condensed centre. Easy to find, as the integrated magnitude is 6·2.
NGC 6067	Δ 360 Normæ	16	09·4	−54	05	Rich cluster, 20′ in diameter, composed of stars of mags 10 to 15.
NGC 6093	M 80 Scorpii	16	14·1	−22	52	Bright, condensed globular; mag. 7·7, between *Antares* and β Scorpii.
NGC 6121	M 4 Scorpii	16	20·6	−26	24	Mag. 6·4; near *Antares*. Globular cluster, easy to resolve.
NGC 6205	M 13 Herculis	16	39·9	+36	33	Great globular cluster; contains thousands of stars, and resolvable with a 15cm telescope. Just visible to the naked eye; mag. 5·7.
NGC 6210	Σ 5N Herculis	16	42·4	+25	34	Small, bright planetary, 8″ in diameter and surrounded by a faint glow. *s.p.* 51 Herculis.
NGC 6218	M 12 Ophiuchi	16	44·6	−01	52	Globular, mag. 6·6; less condensed than most globulars, and therefore easy to resolve.
NGC 6254	M 10 Ophiuchi	16	54·5	−04	02	Mag. 6·7; globular, about equal in brightness to its neighbour M 12.
NGC 6266	M 62 Ophiuchi	16	58·1	−30	03	Mag. 6·6. Small, bright globular, less symmetrical than most.
NGC 6273	M 19 Ophiuchi	16	59·5	−26	11	Globular, mag. 6·6; somewhat elliptical.
NGC 6341	M 92 Herculis	17	15·6	+43	12	Mag. 6·1. Large, fine globular, about 8′ in diameter, resembling M 13 but smaller and less striking.
NGC 6333	M 9 Ophiuchi	17	16·2	−18	28	Mag. 7·3. Small but distinctive globular.
NGC 6402	M 14 Ophiuchi	17	35·0	−03	13	Mag. 8. Globular, not too easy to resolve.
NGC 6405	M 6 Scorpii	17	36·8	−32	11	Mag. 5·3. A beautiful open cluster, 'like a butterfly with wings'.
NGC 6475	M 7 Scorpii	17	50·6	−34	48	Mag. 4. A brilliant open cluster of bright stars, visible with the naked eye. Best seen with very low powers.
NGC 6494	M 23 Sagittarii	17	54·0	−19	01	Mag. 6·9. Fine open cluster.
NGC 6514	M 20 Sagittarii	17	58·9	−23	02	Mag. 9. The Trifid Nebula (gaseous). Details require a fairly large aperture telescope.

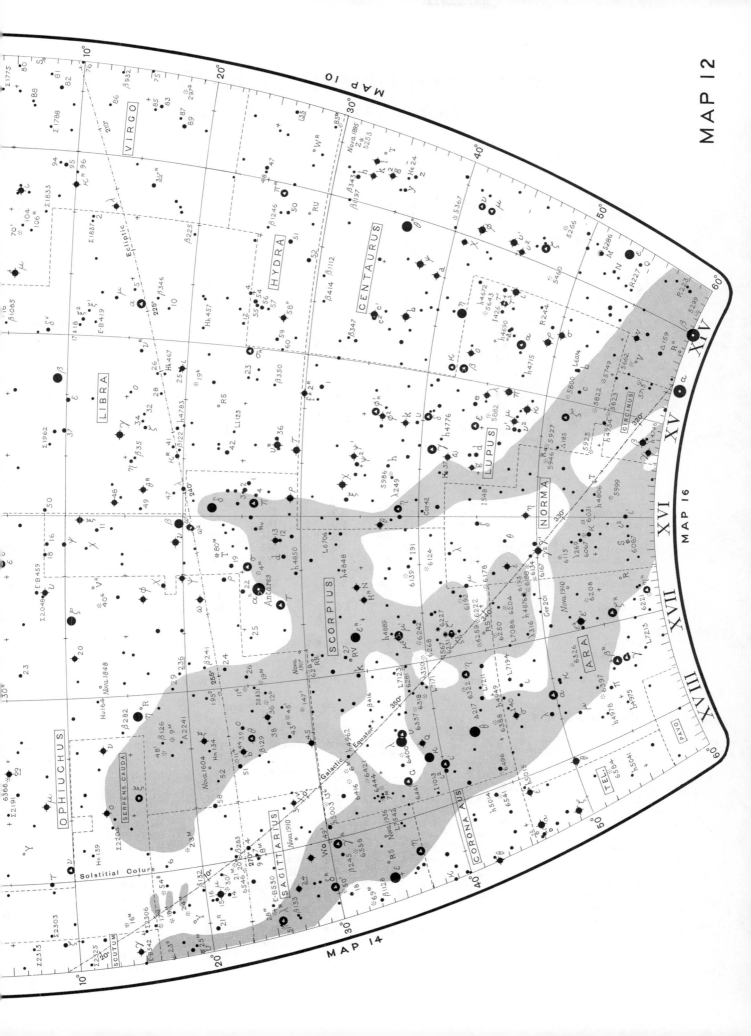

MAP 12

Interesting Objects Maps 13 & 14,
R.A. XVIII h – XXII h; Dec. 60°N – 60°S

Double Stars

	1950·0 R.A.		Dec.		Mags		P.A.	Dist.	Notes
	h	m	°	′			°	″	
τ Ophiuchi	18	00·4	−08	11	5·3,	6·0	270	2·0	Binary.
70 Ophiuchi	18	02·9	+02	31	4·3,	6·0			Binary, 88 years. Widest in 1933 (6″·7).
κ Coronæ Australis	18	29·9	−38	46	5·9,	6·5	359	21·6	Little change.
ε Lyræ	18	42·7	+39	37	4·7,	4·5	172	207·8	Naked-eye pair. Both double. ε¹: 5·1, 6·0: 002°: 2″·8. ε²: 5·1, 5·4: 101°: 2″·3.
ζ Lyræ	18	43·0	+37	32	4·3	5·9	150	43·7	Fixed. Very easy pair.
β Lyræ	18	48·2	+33	18	var,	7·8	149	46·6	Fixed.
θ Serpentis	18	53·8	+04	08	4·5,	4·5	103	22·6	Little change. Fine, easy pair.
γ Coronæ Australis	19	03·0	−37	08	5·0,	5·1	054	2·7	Binary pair.
η Lyræ	19	12·1	+39	04	4·5,	8·7	082	28·2	Fixed. Fine low-power field.
β Cygni	19	28·7	+27	52	3·2,	5·4	055	34·6	Fixed. Glorious pair: yellow, greenish.
δ Cygni	19	43·4	+45	00	3·0,	6·5	246	2·1	Binary: 321 years. Test for 10cm.
π Aquilæ	19	46·3	+11	41	6·2,	6·8	111	1·5	Little change. Test for 7·5cm.
ψ Cygni	19	54·3	+52	18	4·9,	7·4	180	3·1	P.A. decreasing; closing slowly.
θ Sagittæ	20	07·7	+20	46	6·3,	8·7	328	11·6	Slow binary.
α Capricorni	20	14·9	−12	40	3·7,	4·5	291	376	Both double. α¹: 4·5, 9·0: 221°: 45″·5. Optical. α²: 3·7, 10·6: 158°: 7″·1. Binary. Fainter component of α² again double: 11·2, 11·5: 238°: 1″·2, binary.
γ Cygni	20	20·4	+40	06	2·3,	9·6	196	141·7	Optical pair.
κ² Sagittarii	20	20·5	−42	35	5·9,	7·3	229	0·9	Closing. P.A. increasing slowly.
ρ Capricorni	20	26·0	−17	59	5·0,	10·0	161	0·9	Closing. P.A. decreasing.
49 Cygni	20	39·0	+32	08	5·9,	8·6	046	2·8	Yellowish, bluish.
52 Cygni	20	43·6	+30	32	4·3,	9·6	065	6·4	Slow binary. In nebula NGC 6960.
γ Delphini	20	44·3	+15	57	4·5,	5·5	269	10·4	Fixed. Yellow, greenish. Combined magnitude 4·1.
ε Equulei	20	56·6	+04	06	5·7,	7·0	322	0·9	Triple. A + B form a close binary, 101 years.
					7·1		072	10·9	
61 Cygni	21	04·7	+38	30	5·5,	6·3	140	27·0	Opening. P.A. increasing.
τ Cygni	21	12·8	+37	50	3·9,	6·3			Binary, 49·8 years. Distance 1″ (1971).
μ Cygni	21	41·9	+28	31	4·7,	6·1	277	1·6	Binary.
κ Pegasi	21	42·4	+25	25	5·0,	5·1			Very close binary: 11·4 years. 10·8 mag. star at 296°, 12″·9.
η Piscis Austrinus	21	58·0	−28	42	5·8,	6·8	119	1·6	Binary.

Variable Stars

	1950·0 R.A.		Dec.		Range of mags	Period	Sp. type	Notes
	h	m	°	′		d		
T Herculis	18	07·2	+31	01	7·1–13·6	165·0	M	Mira type
W Lyræ	18	13·2	+36	39	7·5–13·0	196·4	M	Mira type
U Sagittarii	18	28·9	−19	10	7·0– 8·2	6·7	G	Cepheid
T Lyræ	18	30·7	+36	58	7·8– 9·6	—	R	Irregular
X Ophiuchi	18	36·0	+08	47	5·9– 9·2	334·2	M	Mira type
R Scuti	18	44·8	−05	46	5·7– 8·6	~144	G-K	RV Tau type
β Lyræ	18	48·2	+33	18	3·4– 4·1	12·9	Bp	β Lyr type
R Lyræ	18	53·8	+43	53	4·0– 5·0	47?	M	Semi-regular
V Aquilæ	19	01·7	−05	46	6·7– 8·2	353	N	Semi-regular
R Aquilæ	19	04·0	+08	09	5·7–12·0	300·3	M	Mira type
RY Sagittarii	19	13·3	−33	37	6·5–14·0	—	G	R CrB type
R Sagittarii	19	13·8	−19	24	6·7–12·8	268·6	M	Mira type
U Sagittæ	19	16·6	+19	31	6·4– 9·0	3·4	B + G	Algol type
Z Vulpeculæ	18	19·6	+25	29	7·0– 8·6	2·5	B + A	Algol type
CH Cygni	19	23·2	+50	09	6·6– 7·8	97	M	Semi-regular
RR Lyræ	19	23·9	+42	41	7·0– 8·0	0·6	A-F	RR Lyr type
U Aquilæ	19	26·7	−07	09	6·8– 8·0	7·0	G	Cepheid

Interesting Objects Maps 13 & 14,

R.A. XVIII h – XXII h; Dec. 60°N – 60°S

Variable Stars (contd)

	1950.0 R.A.		Dec.		Range of mags	Period	Sp. type	Notes
	h	m	°	′		d		
R Cygni	19	35·5	+50	05	6·5–14·2	426·3	S	Mira type
RT Cygni	19	42·2	+48	39	6·4–12·7	190·4	M	Mira type
χ Cygni	19	48·6	+32	47	3·3–14·2	406·9	S	Mira type
η Aquilæ	19	49·9	+00	53	3·7– 4·7	7·2	G	Cepheid
S Pavonis	19	51·0	−59	20	6·6–10·4	387·0	M	Semi-regular
Z Cygni	20	00·0	+49	54	7·6–14·7	263·8	M	Mira type
RR Telescopii	20	00·3	−55	52	6·5–16·5	—	Fp	Nova-like
R Delphini	20	12·5	+08	56	7·6–13·7	284·5	M	Mira type
P Cygni	20	15·9	+37	53	3– 6	—	Bp	Nova, 1600
U Cygni	20	18·1	+47	44	6·7–11·4	464·7	N	Mira type
T Microscopii	20	24·9	−28	26	7·7– 9·6	347	M	Semi-regular
EU Delphini	20	35·6	+18	06	6·0– 6·9	60	M	Semi-regular
V Cygni	20	39·7	+47	58	7·7–13·9	421·3	N	Mira type
U Delphini	20	43·2	+17	54	5·6– 7·5	—	M	Irregular
T Aquarii	20	47·3	−05	20	7·2–14·2	202·1	M	Mira type
R Vulpeculæ	21	02·2	+23	37	7·4–13·4	136·8	M	Mira type
W Cygni	21	34·1	+45	09	5·0– 7·6	130?	M	Semi-regular
μ Cephei	21	42·0	+58	33	3·6– 5·1	—	M	Irregular
R Gruis	21	45·3	−47	09	7·4–14·9	332·5	M	Mira type

Nebulæ and Clusters

		1950·0 R.A.		Dec.		Notes
		h	m	°	′	
NGC 6523/30	M 8 Sagittarii	18	00·1	−24	23	Lagoon Nebula (6523) and open cluster (6530). Mag. 6. Visible with the naked eye; a most interesting object.
NGC 6531	M 21 Sagittarii	18	01·7	−22	30	Open cluster, mag. 6·5; in the same low-power field with M 20. Small and fairly compact.
NGC 6572	Σ 6 Ophiuchi	18	10·2	+06	50	Small, bright, elliptical planetary, 7″ in diameter, said to be bluish in colour.
NGC 6603	M 24 Sagittarii	18	15·5	−18	26	M 24 itself is really a detached part of the Milky Way; in it is a true, faint cluster, NGC 6603.
NGC 6611	M 16 Serpentis	18	16·0	−13	48	Gaseous nebula and associated open cluster. Easy to find, as its magnitude is above 7.
NGC 6618	M 17 Sagittarii	18	17·9	−16	12	Omega Nebula; mag. 7. Diffuse nebula; the bright 'bar' is its most conspicuous feature.
NGC 6637	M 69 Sagittarii	18	28·1	−32	23	Small, fairly bright globular; mag. 9.
IC 4725	M 25 Sagittarii	18	28·8	−19	17	Open, rather loose cluster; mag. 6·5.
NGC 6656	M 22 Sagittarii	18	33·3	−23	58	Mag. 5·9; a large, bright globular, about 15′ in diameter. It contains some reddish stars.
NGC 6705	M 11 Scuti	18	48·4	−06	20	The 'Wild Duck'; mag. 6·3. Grand, fan-shaped cluster with a bright star at its apex. Just visible to the naked eye under good conditions.
NGC 6720	M 57 Lyræ	18	51·7	+32	58	The Ring Nebula. Oval planetary, 80″ x 60″; mag. 9, and easy to find. The central star is a difficult object of about mag. 15.
NGC 6715	M 54 Sagittarii	18	52·0	−30	32	Small, bright globular; mag. 7·3.
NGC 6779	M 56 Lyræ	19	14·6	+30	05	Small globular, mag. 8·2; rich region.
NGC 6809	M 55 Sagittarii	19	36·9	−31	03	Globular, mag. 7·6; easy to resolve, as it is less concentrated than most globulars.
NGC 6838	M 71 Sagittæ	19	51·5	+18	39	Cluster, mag. 9; easy to find; usually classed as a rather condensed galactic cluster.
NGC 6853	M 27 Vulpeculæ	19	57·4	+22	35	The Dumb-bell Nebula; a planetary, mag. 7·6. Fine object, lying in a rich region.
NGC 6864	M 75 Sagittarii	20	03·2	−22	04	Globular; mag. 8. Small and condensed.
NGC 7009	H.IV 1 Aquarii	21	01·4	−11	34	The 'Saturn Nebula'; a bright, bluish planetary, 25″ x 17″. The thin rays or ansæ are visible only with large telescopes.
NGC 7078	M 15 Pegasi	21	27·6	+11	57	6th-magnitude globular; very condensed centre. One of the finest of all globulars.
NGC 7092	M 39 Cygni	21	30·4	+48	13	Large open cluster; magnitude 5·2.
NGC 7089	M 2 Aquarii	21	30·9	−01	03	Mag. 6·3. Globular, about 7″ in diameter. A fine object in large telescopes.
NGC 7099	M 30 Capricorni	21	37·5	−23	25	Globular, mag. 8·4; small, with condensed centre.

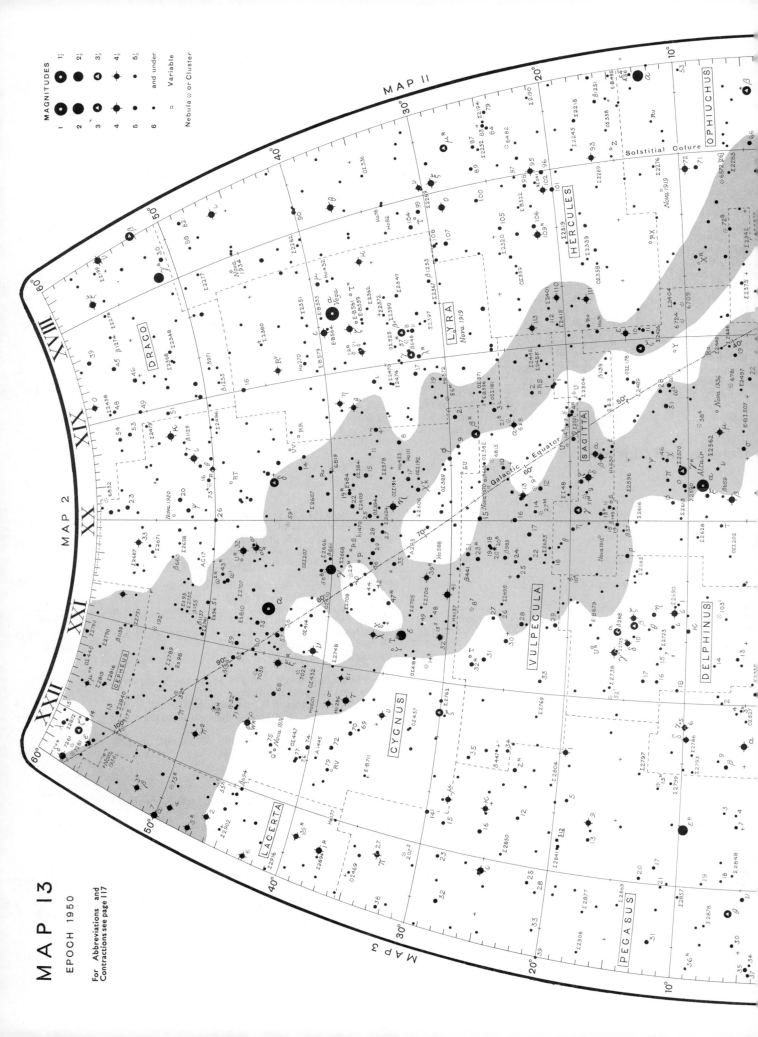

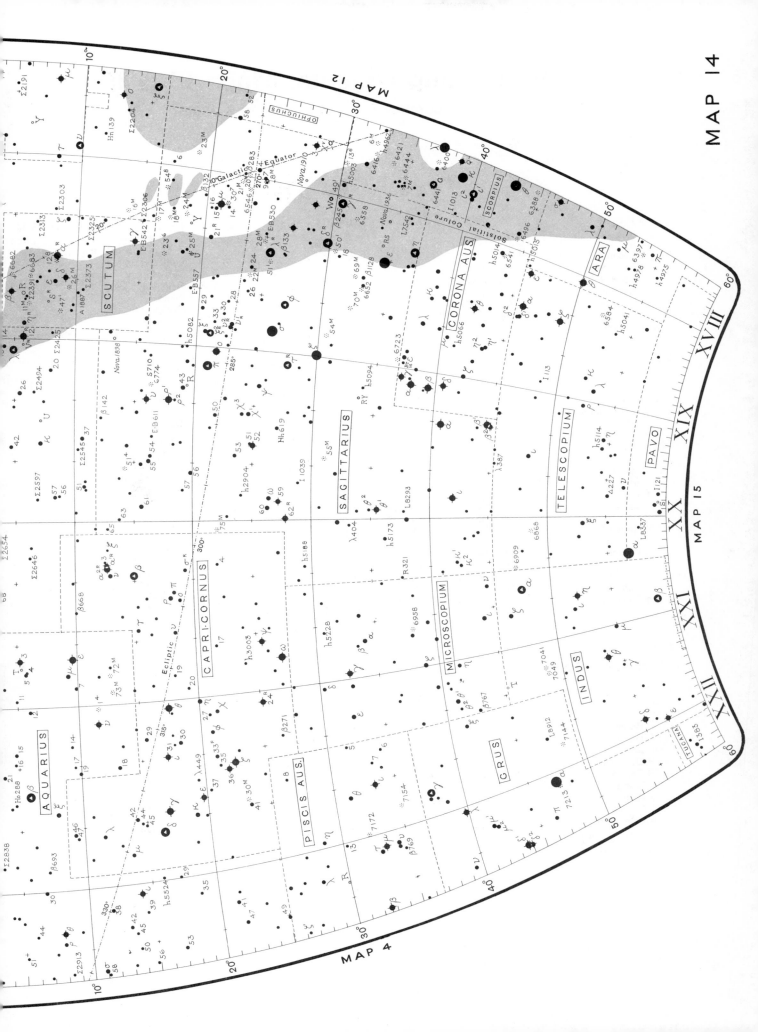

MAP 14

MAP 15

Interesting Objects, Maps 15 & 16

(Circumpolar, South); Dec. 60°S – 90°S

Double Stars

	R.A. (1950·0) h m	Dec. ° ′	Mags	P.A. °	Dist. ″	Notes
β Tucanæ	00 29·3	−63 14	4·5, 4·5	170	27·1	Fixed. Both components double: β¹: 4·5, 14·0: 149°: 2″·2. Fixeb. β²: 4·9, 5·7: binary, 43·1 years.
λ Tucanæ	00 53·1	−59 48	5·3, 7·3	080	20·8	Optical pair.
κ Tucanæ	01 14·1	−69 08	5·1, 7·3	341	5·7	Slow binary.
h 3568 Hydri	03 09·2	−79 11	5·7, 7·8	224	15·4	Relatively fixed.
θ Reticuli	04 17·1	−63 23	6·2, 8·3	004	3·9	Fixed.
h 3670 Reticuli	04 33·0	−62 56	5·9, 8·4	099	32·0	Optical pair.
15 Pictoris	06 37·5	−61 29	6·4, 8·4	269	2·9	Fixed.
γ Volantis	07 09·1	−70 25	3·9, 5·8	299	13·8	Physical pair, but little change.
ε Volantis	08 07·8	−68 28	4·5, 8·0	022	6·1	Fixed. A is a spectroscopic binary.
C Carinæ	08 14·5	−62 46	5·3, 8·5	063	3·8	Fixed.
h 4128 Carinæ	08 38·2	−60 08	6·9, 7·6	213	1·6	Slowly closing; P.A. decreasing.
θ Volantis	08 38·9	−70 13	5·3, 9·8	108	45·0	Optical pair.
υ Carinæ	09 45·9	−64 50	3·1, 6·0	126	4·6	Relatively fixed.
h 4306 Carinæ	10 17·5	−64 25	7·0, 7·0	134	2·1	Relatively fixed.
h 4432 Muscæ	11 21·2	−64 41	5·7, 6·8	299	2·5	P.A. increasing slowly. Binary.
ε Chamæleontis	11 57·1	−77 57	5·5, 6·3	183	1·1	P.A. increasing slowly. Binary.
α Crucis (Acrux)	12 23·8	−62 49	1·6, 2·1	114	4·7	Little change. Very easy. Test for 2·5cm.
ι Crucis	12 42·7	−60 42	4·7, 7·8	027	26·4	Optical pair. P.A. decreasing.
β Muscæ	12 43·2	−67 50	3·9, 4·2	007	1·6	Binary.
θ Muscæ	13 04·9	−65 02	5·6, 7·2	186	5·7	Relatively fixed.
J Centauri	13 19·4	−60 44	4·6, 6·5	343	60·5	Fixed. Wide, easy pair.
β Centauri	14 00·3	−60 08	0·9, 9·0	255	1·4	Relatively fixed.
α Centauri	14 36·2	−60 38	0·0, 1·7			Superb binary: 80 years. Very wide and easy.
α Circini	14 38·4	−64 46	3·4, 8·8	235	15·8	P.A. slowly decreasing.
ι Trianguli Australis	16 23·3	−63 57	5·3, 9·7	061	19·7	Optical pair.
ξ Pavonis	18 18·6	−61 31	4·2, 8·6	151	3·3	Little change.
λ Octantis	21 43·5	−82 57	5·5, 7·6	069	3·1	P.A. decreasing. Slow binary.
δ Tucanæ	22 23·8	−65 13	4·8, 9·3	283	6·8	Relatively fixed.

Variable Stars

	R.A. (1950·0) h m	Dec. ° ′	Range of mags	Period d	Sp. type	Notes
R Reticuli	04 33·0	−63 08	6·8–14·0	278·3	M	Mira type
R Doradûs	04 36·2	−62 11	5·7– 6·8	338	M	Semi-regular
β Doradûs	05 33·2	−62 31	4·5– 5·7	9·8	G	Cepheid
R Octantis	05 41·1	−86 26	6·4–13·2	450·1	M	Mira type
R Carinæ	09 31·0	−62 34	3·9–10·0	380·6	M	Mira type
l Carinæ	09 43·9	−62 17	3·6– 5·0	35·5	G	Cepheid
S Carinæ	10 07·8	−61 18	4·5– 9·9	149·5	M	Mira type
T Carinæ	10 53·3	−60 15	7	—	K	Suspected variable
RS Centauri	11 18·3	−61 36	7·8–13·9	164·4	M	Mira type

Interesting Objects, Maps 15 & 16

(Circumpolar, South); Dec. 60°S – 90°S

Variable Stars (contd)

	1950.0 R.A.		Dec.		Range of mags	Period	Sp. type	Notes
	h	m	°	′		d		
T Crucis	12	18·6	−62	00	7·0– 7·7	6·7	G	Cepheid
R Crucis	12	20·9	−61	21	6·9– 8·0	5·8	G	Cepheid
R Muscæ	12	39·0	−69	08	6·3– 7·3	7·5	G	Cepheid
θ Apodis	14	00·4	−76	33	5·1– 6·6	—	M	Irregular ?
S Trianguli Australis	15	56·7	−63	38	6·4– 7·6	6·3	G	Cepheid
U Trianguli Australis	16	02·9	−62	47	7·9– 8·7	2·6	G	Cepheid
S Octantis	17	46·0	−85	48	7·4–14·0	258·8	M	Mira type
R Pavonis	18	08·1	−63	38	7·5–13·8	230·3	M	Mira type
κ Pavonis	18	51·8	−67	18	4·0– 5·5	9·1	G	W Virginis type
T Pavonis	19	45·1	−71	54	7·0–14·0	244·1	M	Mira type
Y Pavonis	21	19·8	−69	57	5·7– 8·5	233·0	N	Semi-regular

Nebulæ and Clusters

		1950·0 R.A.		Dec.		Notes
		h	m	°	′	
NGC 104	47 Tucanæ	00	21·9	−72	22	Mag. 5; easily visible to the naked eye. A glorious globular of stars from mag. 12 to 14 and below; centre condensed.
NGC 362	Δ 62 Tucanæ	01	00·7	−71	06	Globular, 10′ in diameter, of stars of mags. 13 to 14, with a central blaze of closely-packed stars. It is just visible to the naked eye (mag. 6).
NGC 2070	Δ 142 Doradûs	05	39·1	−69	09	The Looped Nebula round 30 Doradûs. A large, bright nebula, extremely complex in structure. It is visible to the naked eye in the Large Magellanic Cloud.
NGC 2808	Δ 265 Carinæ	09	11·0	−64	39	Large, rich globular of 13th to 15th mag. stars 'like the finest dust'; diameter 5′. The centre is a blaze of loosely-packed stars.
NGC 3766	Δ 289 Centauri	11	33·9	−61	20	Fine cluster; contains at least 200 stars of mags 8 to 13. Visible with binoculars.
NGC 4755	Δ 301 Crucis	12	50·7	−60	05	κ Crucis: the 'Jewel Box'. A beautiful, brilliant cluster of over 100 stars of various colours.
NGC 6025	Δ 304 Trianguli Australis	15	59·4	−60	21	A bright open cluster of stars from mag. 7 downward.
NGC 6752	Δ 295 Pavonis	19	06·4	−60	04	Large, bright globular; diameter 18′; stars from mags 11 to 16.

MAP 15

EPOCH 1950

For Abbreviations and
Contractions see page 117

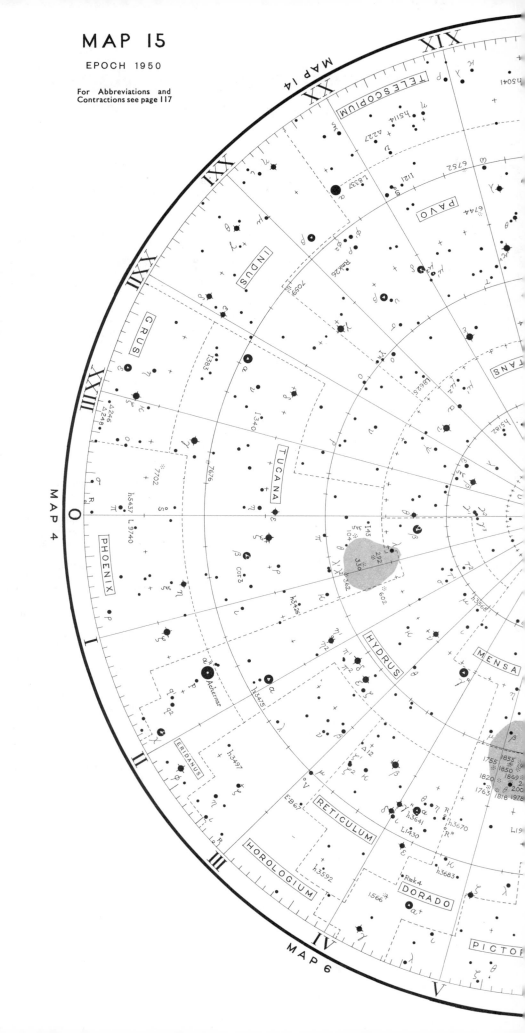

MAP 16

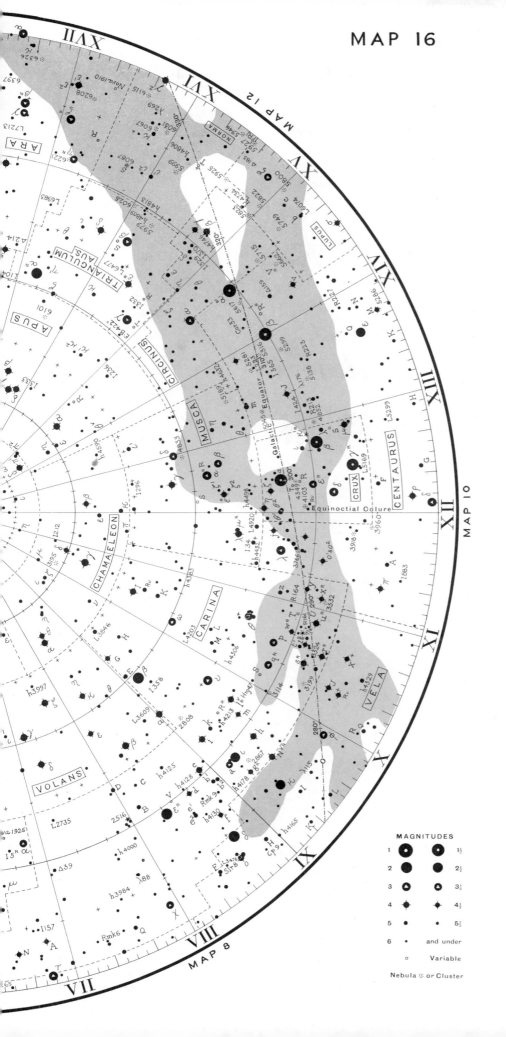

MAGNITUDES

1	●	●	1½
2	●	●	2½
3	◉	▲	3½
4	✦	✦	4½
5	•	•	5½
6	·	and under	

○ Variable

✳ Nebula or Cluster

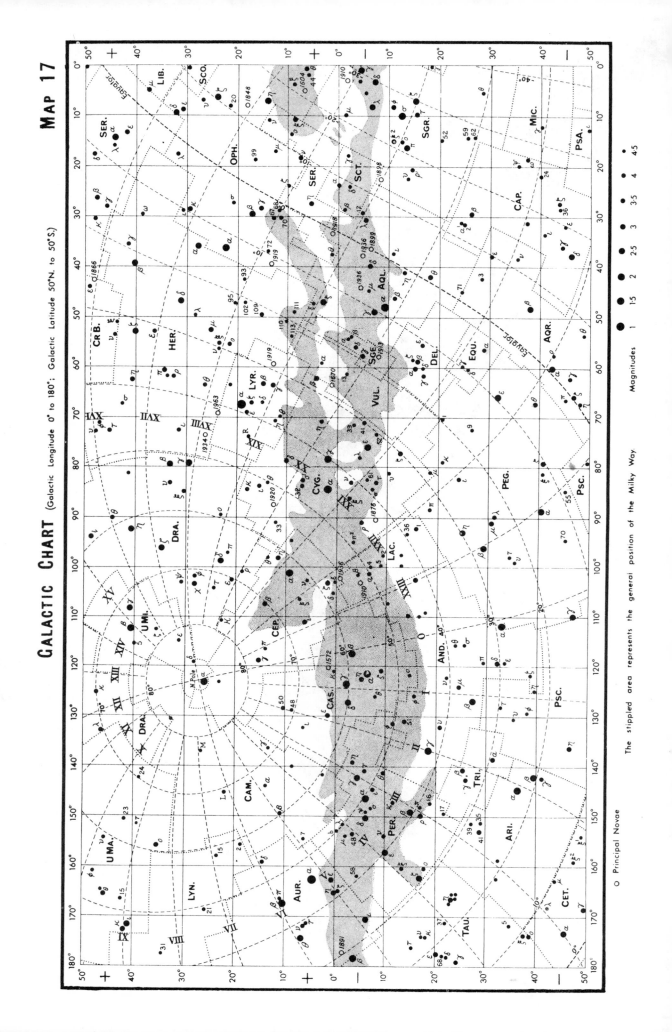

MAP 17

GALACTIC CHART (Galactic Longitude 0° to 180°; Galactic Latitude 50°N. to 50°S.)

O Principal Novae

Magnitudes

The stippled area represents the general position of the Milky Way.

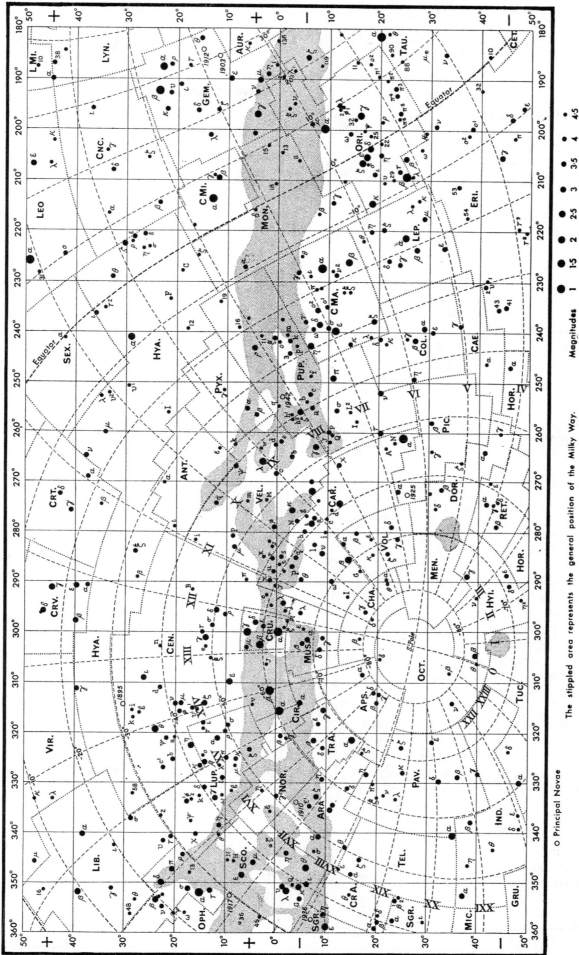

GALACTIC CHART (Galactic Longitude 180° to 360°; Galactic Latitude 50°N. to 50°S.)

MAP 18

The stippled area represents the general position of the Milky Way.

O Principal Novae

Magnitudes

INDEX TO THE CONSTELLATIONS

With the number of the Map in which each is shown, and the approximate date of culmination of
a point on its central hour of Right Ascension at 9 p.m. and midnight

For each HOUR earlier or later than 9 p.m. or midnight:
earlier—add 15 days to dates given in table;
later—subtract 15 days from dates given.

For each WEEK earlier or later than dates below:
earlier—add 28 minutes to 9 p.m. or midnight;
later—subtract 28 minutes from 9 p.m. or midnight.

Constellation	Map	Approximate date of Culmination at 9 p.m.	at midnight	Constellation	Map	Approximate date of Culmination at 9 p.m.	at midnight
ANDROMEDA	3	Nov. 23	Oct. 9	INDUS	14, 15	Sept. 26	Aug. 12
ANTLIA	8, 10	Apr. 10	Feb. 24	LACERTA	3	Oct. 12	Aug. 28
APUS	16	July 5	May 21	LEO	7, 9	Apr. 15	Mar. 1
AQUARIUS	4, 14	Oct. 9	Aug. 25	LEO MINOR	9	Apr. 9	Feb. 23
AQUILA	13, 14	Aug. 30	July 16	LEPUS	6	Jan. 28	Dec. 14
ARA	12, 16	July 25	June 10	LIBRA	12	June 23	May 9
ARGO (see CARINA, VELA and PUPPIS)	8, 10, 16	—	—	LUPUS	12	June 23	May 9
				LYNX	1, 7	Mar. 5	Jan. 19
ARIES	5	Dec. 14	Oct. 30	LYRA	13	Aug. 18	July 4
AURIGA	5, 7	Feb. 4	Dec. 21	MENSA	15, 16	Jan. 28	Dec. 14
BOÖTES	11	June 16	May 2	MICROSCOPIUM	14	Sept. 18	Aug. 4
CAELUM	6	Jan. 15	Dec. 1	MONOCEROS	7, 8	Feb. 19	Jan. 5
CAMELOPARDUS	1, 2	Feb. 6	Dec. 23	MUSCA	16	May 14	Mar. 30
CANCER	7	Mar. 16	Jan. 30	NORMA	12	July 3	May 19
CANES VENATICI	9	May 22	Apr. 7	OCTANS	15, 16	Circumpolar	
CANIS MAJOR	8	Feb. 16	Jan. 2	OPHIUCHUS	11, 12	July 26	June 11
CANIS MINOR	7	Feb. 28	Jan. 14	ORION	5, 6	Jan. 27	Dec. 13
CAPRICORNUS	14	Sept. 22	Aug. 8	PAVO	15	Aug. 29	July 15
CARINA	8, 16	Mar. 17	Jan. 31	PEGASUS	3	Oct. 16	Sept. 1
CASSIOPEIA	2, 3	Nov. 23	Oct. 9	PERSEUS	5	Dec. 22	Nov. 7
CENTAURUS	10, 16	May 14	Mar. 30	PHOENIX	4	Nov. 18	Oct. 4
CEPHEUS	2	Nov. 13	Sept. 29	PICTOR	6, 16	Jan. 30	Dec. 16
CETUS	4, 5	Nov. 29	Oct. 15	PISCES	3	Nov. 11	Sept. 27
CHAMAELEON	16	Apr. 15	Mar. 1	PISCIS AUSTRINUS	4	Oct. 9	Aug. 25
CIRCINUS	16	June 14	Apr. 30	PUPPIS	8	Feb. 22	Jan. 8
COLUMBA	6	Feb. 1	Dec. 18	PYXIS	8	Mar. 21	Feb. 4
COMA BERENICES	9	May 17	Apr. 2	RETICULUM	15	Jan. 3	Nov. 19
CORONA AUSTRALIS	14	Aug. 14	June 30	SAGITTA	13	Aug. 30	July 16
CORONA BOREALIS	11	July 3	May 19	SAGITTARIUS	14	Aug. 21	July 7
CORVUS	10	May 12	Mar. 28	SCORPIUS	12	July 18	June 3
CRATER	10	Apr. 26	Mar. 12	SCULPTOR	4	Nov. 10	Sept. 26
CRUX	16	May 12	Mar. 28	SCUTUM	14	Aug. 15	July 1
CYGNUS	13	Sept. 13	July 30	SERPENS	11	July 21	June 6
DELPHINUS	13	Sept. 14	July 31	SEXTANS	9, 10	Apr. 8	Feb. 22
DORADO	15, 16	Jan. 31	Dec. 17	TAURUS	5	Jan. 14	Nov. 30
DRACO	1, 2	July 8	May 24	TELESCOPIUM	14	Aug. 24	July 10
EQUULEUS	13	Sept. 22	Aug. 8	TRIANGULUM	3	Dec. 7	Oct. 23
ERIDANUS	6	Dec. 25	Nov. 10	TRIANGULUM AUSTRALE	16	July 7	May 23
FORNAX	6	Dec. 17	Nov. 2	TUCANA	15	Nov. 1	Sept. 17
GEMINI	7	Feb. 19	Jan. 5	URSA MAJOR	1, 9	Apr. 25	Mar. 11
GRUS	4	Oct. 12	Aug. 28	URSA MINOR	1	June 27	May 13
HERCULES	11	July 28	June 13	VELA	8, 10	Mar. 30	Feb. 13
HOROLOGIUM	6, 15	Dec. 25	Nov. 10	VIRGO	9, 10	May 26	Apr. 11
HYDRA	8, 10	Apr. 29	Mar. 15	VOLANS	16	Mar. 4	Jan. 18
HYDRUS	15	Dec. 10	Oct. 26	VULPECULA	13	Sept. 8	July 25

SOUTHERN INDEX MAP

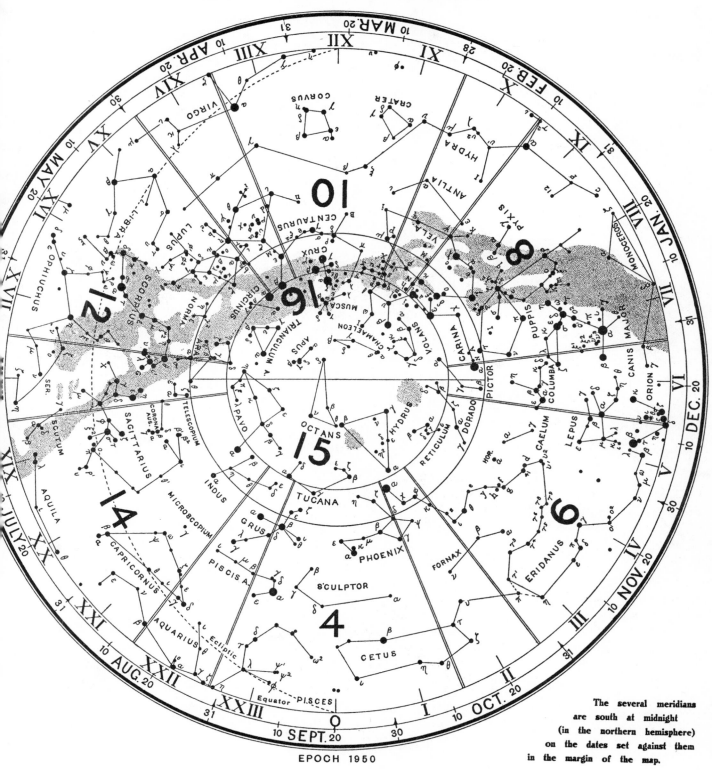

The several meridians
are south at midnight
(in the northern hemisphere)
on the dates set against them
in the margin of the map.

EPOCH 1950